Chaos Is Not God's Will:
The Origin of International Development

Beth Snodderly

WILLIAM CAREY
INTERNATIONAL UNIVERSITY PRESS

Beth Snodderly
Chaos is not God's Will: The Origin of International Development
William Carey International University Press

1539 E. Howard Street, Pasadena, California 91104

E-mail: wciupress@wciu.edu

www.wciupress.org

ISBN: 9780865850309

Library of Congress Control Number: 2014935362

Contents

Chapter One

Introducing International Development
as Cosmic Battle

Images of Light and Dark

In beginning, God created the heavens and the earth.
As for the earth,
> *it was destroyed and desolate* (tohu wabohu),
> *with darkness on the face of the deep,*
> *but the Spirit of God stirring over the face of the waters.*
Then God said, "Let there be light," and there was light!
And God saw that the light was good (tob).
> *So God slashed a separation between the light and the darkness.*
(Gen. 1:1-4, author's translation)

Even in darkness light dawns for the upright,
 for those who are gracious and compassionate and righteous.
(Ps. 112:4)

The people that walked in darkness have seen a great light: they that dwell in
the land of the shadow of death, upon them hath the light shined.
(Isa. 9:2)

Anyone who claims to be in the light but hates a brother or sister is still in the
 darkness.
Anyone who loves their brother and sister lives in the light, and there is nothing
 in them to make them stumble.
(1 John 2:9, 10)

General Overview

Darkness followed by light is part of a pattern found in the opening
verses of Genesis.[1] This pattern, which consists of a general statement

---

[1] Umberto Cassuto, rabbi and biblical scholar, sees Genesis 1:1 as a majestic
summary of the rest of the chapter. How God created the heavens and the earth "will be
related in detail further on, following the principle that one should 'first state the general
proposition and then specify the particulars.'" (Umberto Cassuto, *A Commentary on the*

1

followed by the particulars (such as the moon, stars, and sun), will also serve as a pattern for this book. This opening chapter will give a general overview of the origin of the need for international development, symbolized by the disturbing images in Genesis 1:2. Subsequent chapters will go into detail, following the exegetical guidelines that will be described in chapter two, to justify the interpretations proposed for the first verses of Genesis 1. Each chapter in this book will follow a three-part format. Those who wish to avoid technical exegetical detail may still profitably explore the first two sections of each chapter:

1) Persuasive images from Scripture. "Physical imagery indicated by words induces emotional responses that move people toward understanding and action."[2]

2) A general overview, or big picture, of the topic of the chapter.

3) Particular details that build a case for the main theme of this book: chaos is not God's will.

In a cosmic battle for the rulership of this planet, God is deliberately overcoming evil with good until, in the end, Jesus will reign in his Kingdom of *shalom*. But until God ushers in that final perfect new heaven and new earth, there is a need for believers to engage intentionally in international development efforts to demonstrate God's will for people, for societies, and for God's originally good creation. Jesus' followers serve as God's display window,[3] showing what Jesus' reign is meant to look like. As pastor-theologian, Gregory Boyd, says,

> As Christ gave his all for us, so we are called and empowered to give our all for others. As we abide in Christ and participate in the love of the self-sacrificial God, our lives are to manifest the self-sacrificial love of God to others.[4]

Love eliminates chaos, which is not God's will. We see this in the opening verses of Genesis and in the First Epistle of John, where those causing confusion are ultimately labeled as "children of the devil" (1 John 3:10). We see examples of this theme throughout Israel's history, in the messages of the prophets, in Jesus' demonstrations of authority

---

Book of Genesis. Part One: From Adam to Noah. [Jerusalem: The Magnes Press, 1945], 20.)

[2] Roy R. Jeal, "Blending Two Arts: Rhetorical Words, Rhetorical Pictures, and Social Formation in the Letter to Philemon," *Sino-Christian Studies* 5 (June 2008): 9.

[3] Ed Stetzer, *Subversive Kingdom: Living as Agents of Gospel Transformation* (Nashville: B&H, 2012), 189.

[4] Gregory Boyd, "Living In, and Looking Like, Christ," in *Servant God: The Cosmic Conflict Over God's Trustworthiness* (Loma Linda: Loma Linda University Press, 2013), 407.

over the powers of darkness, in the Epistles where we find principles for living loving, godly, and non-chaotic lives, and finally in the Book of Revelation where, in the end, Jesus victoriously reigns over all. The images in the first few verses of Genesis set the tone and theme for the entire Bible as we see the Spirit of God hovering over the feared unknown of the darkness and deep, ready to stir it to life-giving status. Similarly, in the Gospel of John we see the tradition of an angel stirring up the waters of Bethesda, making them life-producing and healing. These images illustrate the origin of international development: setting right what is not right, something destroyed and desolate, something that is not compatible with life—*tohu wabohu*. "Creation ... constituted bringing order to the cosmos from an originally nonfunctional condition."[5] There is a need in all societies for restoring order and relationships to reflect God's will for this world, overcoming evil with good.

Particular Examples of the Cosmic Battle

Genesis 1: Physical Chaos

Tohu wabohu (Gen. 1:2) describes the disastrous result, at some point following God's original good creation, when a created being used the gift of free will to rebel against God's will.[6] Intelligent evil was (and still is) at work, distorting God's original good purposes. The author of Genesis shows in the rest of the first chapter how God goes about restoring his intentions for the earth, which are the exact opposite of the chaotic conditions. The author does this by emphasizing a definite pattern in the creation story, showing that God has evil under control and patiently counter-acts and replaces it with acts of creativity, including the creation of humans to join God in fighting back against forces that oppose God.

---

[5] John H. Walton, *The Lost World of Genesis One: Ancient Cosmology and the Origins Debate* (Downers Grove: InterVarsity Academic, 2009), 35.

[6] Justification for these and subsequent claims will be explained in detail in later chapters. The condition of the earth prior to creation is described in Genesis 1:2 as "*tohu wabohu*," which can be translated "destroyed and desolate," or "topsy turvey," or, traditionally, "formless and void." In each of the other 18 occurrences of the word "*tohu*," the broad context is judgment for rebellion against God. It seems logical that the first occurrence of the term would also have been in the context of judgment, setting the tone for the remaining usages of the term in the Hebrew Bible.

As a description of the consequences of opposition to God's ways, the figure of speech, *tohu wabohu*, also contains within itself the solution to addressing the root problem behind the chaos and desolation. Believers have the privilege of allowing God's Spirit to work through them to demonstrate God's glory, by bringing order out of chaos, and by overcoming evil with good (Hebrew, *tob*, a word play with the similar-sounding *tohu*)[7]. The rest of the Bible explains how to overcome and/or avoid *tohu* at various levels (physical, personal, family, social, political) or it shows what happens when *tohu* is not overcome. (The observable chaotic result can then be called *tohu wabohu*.) In Genesis 1, physical chaos is being overcome by God's good creation. A later chapter in this book will explore this figure of speech in great detail.

Isaiah 32 and 34: Societal Chaos

In addition to physical chaos, there is a need for chaos to be overcome within societies. In Isaiah 32 societal chaos is being overcome by the intervention of God's Spirit. In this chapter we see a metaphorical image of the consequences for societies whose people practice ungodliness, who use wicked schemes to leave the hungry empty, and who destroy the poor with their lies: "The fortress will be abandoned, the noisy city deserted; citadel and watchtower will become a wasteland forever" (Isa. 32:14). Destruction and desolation are inherent in a person or society rebelling against God. Evil choices are the evidence of a mind in opposition to God, and that mind or society can be characterized by the physical metaphor of *tohu wabohu*—destroyed and desolate. It is destroyed because it isn't working the way God made it to work—it is twisted, turned to wrong purposes, therefore purposeless from God's perspective. It is desolate because the Spirit has withdrawn from that life or society. Ezekiel's vision of the Spirit in the wheels leaving the temple and the land (Ezek. 10:15-19) serves as a visual metaphor of what happens when a person's mind or a society is twisted and turned to wrong purposes. Evil choices result in the Spirit leaving ("My Spirit will not contend with humans forever" [Gen. 6:3]), and the withdrawal of the Spirit of God leaves behind a desolate person or society that will self-destruct without the intervention of the Spirit. "God will stretch out over Edom the measuring line of chaos (*tohu*) and the plumb line of desolation (*bohu*)" (Isa. 34:11). When the people of God, in whom the Spirit of God dwells, are absent, the Spirit of God is

---

[7] John H. Sailhamer, *Genesis Unbound: a Provocative New Look at the Creation Account* (Sisters, OR: Multnomah Books, 1996), 63.

also absent, resulting in desert-like conditions in the physical, social, and spiritual realms. (The chapter in this book on the Hebrew term *tohu wabohu* will demonstrate this in detail.)

But when Spirit-filled people of God bring the light of Christ into a society and enough people respond to the outpouring of the Spirit, then we see real development in that society:

> [Destruction and desolation] ... till the Spirit is poured on us from on high, and the desert becomes a fertile field, and the fertile field seems like a forest. The Lord's justice will dwell in the desert, his righteousness live in the fertile field. The fruit of righteousness will be peace; its effect will be quietness and confidence forever. My people will live in peaceful dwelling places, in secure homes, in undisturbed places of rest (Isa. 32:15-18).

Isaiah is describing *shalom*: the goal of international development.[8]

These verses give an attractive description of the results of the Spirit's outpouring: flourishing, peace, and safety. What might Isaiah have had in mind that would bring about the outpouring of the Spirit on a chaotic and desolate society? In the first verses of the chapter, the prophet seems to be saying that leaders' deliberate choices to follow God's ways, the opposite of the ungodly ways being practiced, will bring the presence of the Spirit. The description at the beginning of Isaiah 32, of a group of rulers collaborating to do what is right, harmonizes with Jesus' saying, "where two or three gather in my name, there am I with them" [through the Spirit] (Matt. 18:20). "See, a king will reign in righteousness and rulers will rule with justice. Each one will be like a shelter from the wind and a refuge from the storm, like streams of water in the desert.... No longer will the fool be called noble nor the scoundrel be highly respected ..." (Isa. 32:1, 2, 5).

Isaiah 45 and Jeremiah 4: Spiritual Chaos

In a later chapter, Isaiah hints that the means of the Spirit's outpouring is through seeking God and turning to him: "I have not said to Jacob's descendants, 'Seek me in vain'" (Isa. 45:19). On the contrary, some of Jacob's descendants did seek God and their purpose in history is specified a few verses later: "Turn to me and be saved, all you ends of

---

[8] Beth Snodderly, *The Goal of International Development: God's Will On Earth as It Is in Heaven.* (Pasadena: WCIU Press, 2009), 157.

the earth; … Before me every knee will bow; by me every tongue will swear" (Isa. 45:22, 23).

The prophet Jeremiah held out a similar plea to rebellious Israel to return to God. But God's people foolishly refused to know and obey God. Their moral values were completely reversed: "They are skilled in doing evil; they know not how to do good" (Jer. 4:22). As a result of their disobedience and the resulting absence of God's Spirit, the land became empty, shaken, ruined, shattered. "I looked at the earth, and it was formless and empty (*tohu wabohu*); and at the heavens, and their light was gone" (Jer. 4:23). Creation is being undone in a sense. The earth will mourn and the heavens will be dark because of this judgment on God's people.

Summary of the Cosmic Battle Theme in Scripture

And Jeremiah brings us right back to Genesis 1:2 where all that can be seen is chaotic and desolate (*tohu wabohu*), but with the Spirit of God hovering over the darkness and the deep, waiting to stir non-productive places back to life.

This is the cosmic battle theme throughout Scripture. The whole theme of Scripture is to fight back against the opposition to God's intentions. This is the biblical worldview demonstrated throughout Israel's history, in the prophets' interpretation of that history, in Jesus' activity and words, and in descriptions of living in the Kingdom found in the Epistles, including a central emphasis in First John on the cosmic battle between the Son of God and the evil one. Where God's rule is not yet acknowledged, confusion and chaos (*tohu*) reign, with visible evidence of conditions contrary to God's will such as disease, violence, and injustice for the poor. Believers need to intentionally participate, with the help of God's Spirit, in continuing the mission of the Son of God to destroy the works of God's adversary, the devil (see 1 John 3:8). Philip Jenkins summarizes this mission in his book, *The New Faces of Christianity*: "In his acts of healing, Jesus was not just curing individuals, but trampling diabolical forces underfoot, and the signs and wonders represented visible and material tokens of Christ's victory over very real forces of evil."[9]

Overcoming *tohu,* the opposite of God's will, is central to the mission of the body of Christ, the Church. Holistic international development engages opposition to God's purposes at all levels of

---

[9] Philip Jenkins, *The New Faces of Christianity: Believing the Bible in the Global South* (New York: Oxford University Press, USA, 2008), 99.

existence: personal, spiritual, societal, physical, and across cultures. Chaos—wherever it is found—is not God's will. Medical missionary Robert Hughes, in Shillong, India from 1939–69, wrote in his journal, "This kingdom of disease, death, ignorance, prejudice, fear, malnutrition, and abject poverty [is] most surely a kingdom which ought to be overthrown by the kingdom of our God."[10] Demonstration of God's love, God's will, and God's glory is the responsibility of the body of Christ, so that all peoples can come to know and obey him.

---

[10] D. Ben Rees, *Vehicles of Grace and Hope: Welsh Missionaries in India 1800– 1970* (Pasadena: William Carey Library, 2003).

Chapter Two

Constructing a Case with an Exegetical / Socio-Rhetorical Approach

Images of Cosmic Development

Where were you when I laid the earth's foundation? ...
Who marked off its dimensions? ...
Who stretched a measuring line across it?
On what were its footings set,
  or who laid its cornerstone—
while the morning stars sang together
  and all the angels shouted for joy?
(Job 38:4-7)

When he marked out the foundations of the earth,
  then I [wisdom] was beside him as a master craftsman.
(Proverbs 8:29, 30a, NET Bible).

Who has measured the waters in the hollow of his hand,
  or with the breadth of his hand marked off the heavens? ...
Do you not know?
  Have you not heard?
Has it not been told you from the beginning?
  Have you not understood since the earth was founded?
He sits enthroned above the circle of the earth,
  and its people are like grasshoppers.
He stretches out the heavens like a canopy,
  and spreads them out like a tent to live in.
(Isaiah 40:12, 21, 22)

Dear children, do not let anyone lead you astray.
        The one who does what is right is righteous, just as he is righteous.
        The one who does what is sinful is of the devil, because the devil has
        been sinning from the beginning.
The reason the Son of God appeared was to destroy the devil's work.
        If anyone has material possessions and sees a brother or sister in need
        but has no pity on them, how can the love of God be in that person?
(1 John 3:7, 8, 17)

General Overview

Quilting and knitting afghans are regular pass-times of many women in rural East Tennessee, where I served as a pastor's wife for 18 years. County Fairs and Country magazines regularly feature prize-winning squares and finished quilts. One blue-ribbon knitted square particularly stands out in my memory. It was very simple—not much to look at as an individual square. The design consisted of a number of diagonal rows of complementary colors. The genius of the prize-winning square was revealed in the finished product. When each square was stitched in place at a particular angle in relationship to surrounding squares, a geometric pattern emerged that could not have been envisioned from seeing one square alone.

In a similar way, this book will construct or stitch together a "fabric of discourse"[11] from a number of separate studies and approaches to make a case for the biblical theme of the cosmic battle, chaos at all levels of existence, and the resulting need for international development to demonstrate that chaos is not God's will. The pieces to be stitched together in this book include studies from both a traditional exegetical approach and the newer methods of socio-rhetorical analysis developed by New Testament scholar, Vernon Robbins, and his cohorts.

Socio-rhetorical analysis draws temporary boundaries around a text for the purpose of close examination from one point of view.[12] In this case we are starting with the first few verses of Genesis and going on to draw from other parts of the Bible, especially the First Epistle of John, to gain a comprehensive biblical understanding of God's battle to overcome chaos and evil. The approach in this book will be to synthesize traditional exegetical principles with the "textures" of socio-rhetorical analysis. Historical and literary context and detailed Hebrew word studies each find a place within one of these "textures" of socio-rhetorical analysis: inner texture, inter-texture and its subdivisions, ideological texture, and theological texture. As an aspect of ideological texture, dialog with other interpreters will be interspersed, sometimes agreeing, sometimes not.

---

[11] As in the title of the book by L. Gregory Bloomquist, Duane F. Watson, and David B. Gowler, eds., *Fabrics of Discourse: Essays in Honor of Vernon K. Robbins* (Harrisburg, PA: Bloomsbury T&T Clark, 2003).

[12] Vernon K. Robbins, *The Tapestry of Early Christian Discourse: Rhetoric, Society, and Ideology* (London: Routledge, 1996), 20.

Socio-rhetorical analysis is an approach "which is simultaneously new and old."[13] Continuity of the relatively new methodology of socio-rhetorical analysis with traditional exegetical methods can be demonstrated through the following categories that we will use to thoroughly investigate selected texts from Genesis 1, the First Epistle of John, and other relevant passages in our exploration of the cosmic battle theme in Scripture.

Inner Texture: This texture consists of approaches to interpreting Scripture that have traditionally been known as exegesis. Content of a passage, structure, literary style, and literary devices at work in the text are examples of exegetical methods that fall into the category of "inner texture."

Inter-Texture:
a. *Scribal inter-texture* looks at written texts from other parts of Scripture or relevant extra-biblical literature for illumination of the meaning of the text under investigation. Extensive word studies in upcoming chapters of this book, from the first two verses of Genesis, are examples of scribal inter-texture. Comparisons of the text of First John with the Gospel of John, with writings from the Early Church father, Ignatius, and with the inter-testamental *Testaments of the Twelve Patriarchs*, are additional examples of this texture that will contribute to the construction of the case for the biblical picture of the cosmic battle.

b. *Historical inter-texture* explores the historical background of the author, audience, and text at the time it was written. We will take into consideration the circumstances of the people of Israel and their neighbors at the time the book of Genesis was being written.

c. *Cultural inter-texture* involves "insider" knowledge of values, scripts, myths, or codes.[14] We will use this texture to examine possible echoes in 1 John 2:13, 14 of the ancient well-known myths of Heracles, in speaking of the young men who were strong and had overcome the evil one.

Ideological Texture: The point of view of the author and interpreters of the text and how they see themselves interacting and changing as a result of the text are features of ideological texture. When scholars approach the text with clearly stated presuppositions, as are doing in this

---

[13] Vernon K. Robbins, "Picking Up the Fragments: From Crossan's Analysis to Rhetorical Analysis," *Foundations & Facets Forum* 1 (1986): 32.

[14] Robbins, *Tapestry*, 58.

chapter and particularly in chapter 3, they are engaging in ideological criticism.

Theological Texture: This texture addresses "the relation of humans to the divine":[15] what is said about God, holy people, holy living, sacred things, and the opposite of each of these. The conclusions reached through exploration of each of the other textures (constructing squares of the quilt fabric) and the overall conclusions will demonstrate theological texture.

Summary: The socio-rhetorical approach presupposes that what is discovered within one bounded area will be put in dialog with discoveries in other bounded areas. This process can be compared to piecing together patterned squares, which have been knitted, crocheted, or hand-sewn separately. Only when the squares are placed in right relation to each other does the overall design emerge. Similarly, when the results of a variety of approaches to studying a text are compared and related, a more complete and aesthetically pleasing interpretation of the text emerges. The chapters of this book will each produce one or more "squares" of a larger "quilt," with the intention of integrating the insights gained to produce a more complete understanding of the overall cosmic battle theme of Scripture and its application for international development today.

Particulars: Principles of Biblical Exegesis

Keeping the socio-rhetorical textures in mind, we will need to integrate the following exegetical and hermeneutical concerns in our study of the cosmic battle theme:

1) Find out what the text in Genesis 1:1-4 (and other texts) meant to the original audience.

2) Learn to hear that same meaning within new contexts, of our own day and in other cultures (hermeneutics).

3) Ask the right questions of the text.

4) Investigate the historical, literary, and biblical contexts.

Before reviewing implications of these four concerns for the two main texts under investigation (Genesis 1 and the First Epistle of John), we will look at two presuppositions related to the way we are engaging in the interpretation of Scripture: the nature of the inspiration of

---

[15] Robbins, *Tapestry*, 4.

Scripture and the assumption that deeper layers of meaning will be uncovered as we engage in the hermeneutical process.

The Hermeneutical Spiral

The first detail to keep in mind in this exegetical, socio-rhetorical analysis is that we will be engaging in a hermeneutical spiral. Some elements will come up again and again, with deeper explanations (or a "thicker texture") each time. In following the processes described generally above and in more detail to follow, the student of Scripture will be increasing in understanding of the text. Dutch biblical scholar, J.P. Fokkelman, describes a hermeneutic circle that starts with an assumption or intuitive judgment.[16] His own initial assumption, that the stories of Genesis have the status of a literary work of art, had to be validated by the results of his interpretive work. With the results of an investigation of an initial assumption, a fresh hypothesis can be made and the hermeneutic circle continues. Reformed evangelical professor of Old Testament, Bruce Waltke, and Arminian evangelical theologian, Grant Osborne, each use the term "hermeneutical spiral,"[17] which acknowledges that there is a goal in the exegetical process of achieving ever-increasing understanding of specific portions of Scripture. Waltke uses this term to describe the dialog the interpreter has with the text. "One approaches the text with ideas about its techniques and principles, which the text then proves or disproves."[18] The third chapter of this book explains the intuitive assumptions with which this study started and represents the ideological texture of the socio-rhetorical approach.

Inspiration of Scripture

An ideological assumption to mention at this point is the nature and manner of the inspiration and revelation of the Bible. The significance of what Genesis 1 and First John other parts of the Bible have to say about our questions about chaos, cosmic battle, the role of people in joining the Son of God to defeat the works of the devil, and the need for international development, implies an acknowledgment that God was

---

[16] J. P. Fokkelman, *Narrative Art in Genesis: Specimens of Stylistic and Structural Analysis* (Amsterdam: Van Gorcum, Assen, 1975), 7.

[17] See Bruce K. Waltke with Cathi J. Fredricks, *Genesis: a Commentary* (Grand Rapids: Zondervan, 2001), 33; and Grant Osborne, *The Hermeneutical Spiral: A Comprehensive Introduction to Biblical Interpretation* (Downers Grove: InterVarsity, 2006).

[18] Waltke, *Genesis*, 33.

involved in a process of revealing himself and his plans to the writers and editors of Scripture.

Catholic theologian, Henricus Renckens, comments:

> When it became God's purpose to reveal himself to Israel, he found it already equipped, so to speak, with a whole world of ideas about all kinds of things, and in revealing the crucial saving events of the past to this people, he had to reckon with a whole set of particular human ideas about the past which they already possessed. ... God has grafted his revelation on to Israel's already existing human knowledge.[19]

In regard to what the biblical authors were able to know and write about, Alexander Heidel gives this translation of Franz Pieper of Concordia Theological Seminary: "As the Holy Ghost employed the style which he found in the individual writers, thus he also utilized the historical knowledge which the writers already possessed."[20] In the process of inspiration, including meditation by the writer of Scripture on actual historical events, God conveyed truths that are timeless and wider than what the author was able to fully understand. American Methodist theologian, Edwin Lewis, points out the need to find the underlying general truth of revelation and separate that from the historical conditions by which the revelation came. "If we can accomplish that, we will arrive at principles that will be true for any time or anywhere in the world."[21]

Just as the gospel must always come to people clothed in a culture, so the original revelation and word of God to humankind could only come clothed in humanity. Pentecostal New Testament scholar Gordon Fee agrees: "God's Word to us was first of all His Word to them. If they were going to hear it, it could only have come through events and in language they could have understood."[22] John Walton, professor of Old Testament at Wheaton College, cautions that the Bible's message "transcends the culture in which it originated, but the form in which the

---

[19] Henricus Renckens, S. J., *Israel's Concept of the Beginning: The Theology of Genesis 1–3* (New York: Herder and Herder, 1964), 42.

[20] Alexander Heidel, *The Babylonian Genesis*, 2nd ed. (Chicago: University of Chicago Press, 1951), 136.

[21] Edwin Lewis, *The Creator and the Adversary* (New York: Abingdon-Cokesbury, 1948), 124.

[22] Gordon Fee and Douglas Stuart, *How to Read the Bible for All Its Worth.* 2nd ed. (Grand Rapids: Zondervan, 1993), 18.

message was imbedded was fully permeated by the ancient culture. This was God's design and we ignore it at our peril."[23]

Genesis 1 is the beginning of that revelation, clothed in the human limitations of the ancient Israelite culture. Jesus came much later, in fulfillment of the promise in Genesis 3:15, as the revelation and Word of God. He came clothed in a human body and lived within the limitations and values of the ancient Mediterranean culture of his time.

From the first to the last, God's Spirit was superintending the process of inspiration ("all Scripture is given by inspiration of God"), just as Genesis 1:2 shows the Spirit of God superintending the preparation for the days of Creation. Through the selection of authors within a chosen culture, the Spirit guided what would be written so that it would convey what God wanted to reveal in ways that would be valid for all time and all peoples. Revelation 5:9 shows that God wants to be known by all cultures and each is able to contribute something to the composite of humanity's knowledge of God's glory. But in God's sovereignty and wisdom, God chose the culture of one people, Israel, to mold them for the purpose of communicating himself to the rest of the world.

Beyond the words of the inspired authors, British Old Testament scholar, Gordon Wenham, speaks of the form in which God's revelation was preserved: "These likewise were conditioned by the culture of the time and place."[24] He goes on to refer to the obvious changes that occurred in Israel's cultural expression of their faith as a result of their experience of the Exile. These modifications, including an increased awareness of God's adversary, were necessary before the Spirit, superintending the course of history and inspiration, would decide the "fullness of time" had been reached for God to send the ultimate revelation of himself—Jesus, the human and divine Word of God.

Catholic theologian Henricus Renckens gives a good example of the doctrine of inspiration in Genesis, which applies to the rest of Scripture as well:

> Genesis will mean more to us if we look at it in the light of the doctrine of inspiration. Through this Israelite speaking to his compatriots, God is speaking—to them and to us. He is not saying more to us than he was saying to them, though we can of

---

[23] Walton, *Lost World*, 22.

[24] Gordon J. Wenham, *Word Biblical Commentary: Genesis 1–15* (Waco, TX: Word Books, 1987), 124.

course understand more and better than they could, now that he has spoken fully in Christ.[25]

Find Out What the Text Originally Meant

Grasping what God is saying to us today depends on understanding what the text originally meant to its author and audience. Understanding the relationship between the meaning to the original audience and to readers today is a key question that is addressed by Vernon Robbins who asks,

> What is the relation of our reading of a New Testament text to the way in which a first-century person might have written or read a text? The answer is that all people choose ways to write and to read a text. For this reason, socio-rhetorical criticism interprets not only the text under consideration but ways people read texts in late antiquity and ways people have interpreted New Testament texts both in the past and in different contexts in our modern world.[26]

Each of the socio-rhetorical textures can be useful in attempting to discover what the text originally meant. Two highly respected Old Testament scholars have clearly stated the importance of discovering the original meaning of the text, one from the evangelical and one from the Jewish tradition:

> The primary task of the Biblical scholar is to unfold the meaning of the text of Scripture as it was originally intended to be understood by the writer of that text.[27]

> The aim of this commentary [on Genesis] is to explain, with the help of an historico-philological method of interpretation, the simple meaning of the biblical text, and to arrive, as nearly as possible, at the sense that the words of the Torah were intended to have for their reader at the time when they were written.[28]

This primary task requires acknowledgement of the limitations of looking back from a contemporary Western (or other) worldview at texts written in ancient times. The worldview of the writers of Scripture

---

[25] Renckens, *Israel's Concept,* 12.

[26] Robbins, *Tapestry,* 39.

[27] Walter C. Kaiser, "The Literary Form of Genesis 1–11," in *New Perspectives in the Old Testament,* ed. J. B. Payne (Waco, TX: Word, 1970), 48.

[28] Cassuto, *Genesis,* 1.

was not that of the Western scientific culture of today. We should not expect, for instance, that the human author and original audience of Genesis knew or cared about our present day scientific astronomy, geology, biology, etc., as French evangelical theologian, Henri Blocher, and physicist-theologian Stanley Jaki emphasize.[29] Old Testament scholar, Terrence Fretheim, gives another perspective by calling attention to evidence in Genesis 1 that the biblical writer had pre-scientific interests in showing an awareness of classification of plants and animals and by addressing questions about how the earth was created. But the answers grew out of "knowledge of the natural world available to them in their culture."[30] The principle must be kept in mind that what was understood by the original author and audience is what the text still means. As Fee and Stuart put it, "a text cannot mean what it never meant."[31] For example, if the author did not originally intend to teach scientific truths, it should not be viewed in any age as teaching scientific truths, which are always in process and subject to change. Fretheim points out that "to claim that God created the world and all that exists is a matter of faith, ... (see Hebrews 11:3) and is not the result of scientific investigation."[32]

Blocher, Jaki, and others feel strongly that the exegesis of Genesis 1 must "free itself from excessive concern with science."[33] Jaki speaks of the "concordist trap" that commentators throughout the ages have fallen into while trying to harmonize the current state of science with what they think Genesis 1 is teaching. For the most part, these authors, including those in the Young Earth camp today, miss important theological truths and the key role of Genesis 1 in the Bible because they are focused on trying to make it mean something it was never intended to mean.

In cautioning against reading into the text meanings that were not originally there, Fee and Stuart mention the Mormon practice of baptizing for the dead (based on their reading of 1 Corinthians 15:29) and the prosperity doctrine of the charismatic movement (taken from 3

---

[29] Henri Blocher, *In the Beginning: The Opening Chapters of Genesis* (Downers Grove: InterVarsity,1984), 27; Stanley Jaki, *Genesis 1 through the Ages* (London: Thomas More, 1998).

[30] Terrence E. Fretheim, *God and World in the Old Testament: A Relational Theology of Creation* (New York: Abingdon, 2005), 27.

[31] Fee and Stuart, *How to Read*, 19.

[32] Fretheim, *God and World*, 27.

[33] Blocher, *In the Beginning*, 27.

John 2) as examples of those who have started with "the here and now and have read into the texts meanings that were not originally there."[34]

The creation science interpretation of Genesis 1 is an additional example of this type of "eisegesis." Based on the presupposition that a biblical account of the creation of the world must be scientifically accurate (or rather, specifically, the Genesis 1 account), they have looked for scientific accuracy in ancient literature and have found it necessary to claim that science is wrong in some respects to support their theory. This is what happened in Galileo's time, resulting in widespread disrespect for God's Word.

The "problem" of science and Scripture is not a major concern in this book, however. Instead, the aim is to discover from the text itself what its original author and audience understood it to mean. The socio-rhetorical approach we are following fits well with Fretheim's approach to the study and interpretation of Scripture:

> The key task, finally, both for that time and for our own, becomes that of integrating materials from various fields into a coherent statement about the created order. In effect, Genesis invites every generation to engage in this same process.[35]

Old Testament scholar, John Sailhamer, stated his intention in writing his book, *Genesis Unbound*, "my desire in this book is to make clear what I am convinced is the central message of the first two chapters of Genesis."[36] In this book we have a similar intention to clarify the central message of the first few verses of Genesis, in addition to the message of the First Epistle of John.

Sailhamer further elaborated on his approach that this book will also follow: "A large part of that task will be dealing with well-worn opinions .... In many cases those opinions are correct and must be incorporated into a proper interpretation; in other cases they are not correct and need to be replaced with a new understanding."[37]

Learn to Hear that Same Meaning within New Contexts

Only after the first task is completed, of uncovering the original meaning of the text, can the question be addressed, what does Genesis 1 (or First John) mean for a specific culture today, and how might participation in international development efforts help restore a

---

[34] Fee and Stuart, *How to Read*, 18.
[35] Fretheim, *God and World*, 28.
[36] Sailhamer, *Genesis Unbound*, 24.
[37] Sailhamer, *Genesis Unbound*, 24.

semblance of God's intentions for the world? Finding the relevance of the text for today in a variety of new contexts is how Fee and Stuart define the hermeneutical task, which comes only after the first step of exegesis has been done.[38] Jewish biblical scholar, Nahum Sarna, draws attention to the distinctive patterns of thought and ways of speaking of the ancient Israelite people. To understand their writings we need to be careful not to confuse their way of speaking, including metaphorical language, with the reality behind the metaphor. Sarna cautions, "the two have to be disentangled from each other and the idea conveyed must be translated into the idiom of our own day."[39] The true meaning of the biblical text for today, for any culture, is what God originally intended it to mean when it was first spoken.

All societies have to answer the question, How shall we bring order out of chaos? People trying to be submitted to God in any culture need to find their own particular implications for how to live in right relationship with God within that culture. The principles of the Bible are timeless and apply in all cultures in addressing these and other questions.

Ask the Right Questions of the Text

Fee and Stuart state that the secret of exegesis is asking the right questions of the text.[40] John Sailhamer[41] and Leon Kass[42] ask many inductive questions of Genesis 1, such as the following:
- What is the meaning of the phrase translated "in the beginning"?
- Why this kind of beginning?
- Is it logically or pedagogically necessary for what comes next?
- What is the overall purpose and theme of the Pentateuch (and the Bible)?
- How do these early chapters prepare us for understanding and appreciating all that follows in the Pentateuch (and the Bible)?

Tremper Longman III, professor of Old Testament at Westmont College, adds the following "most important" question:
- What does Gen 1–2 teach about God, humanity, and the world?[43]

---

[38] Fee and Stuart, *How to Read*, 18.
[39] Nahum M. Sarna, *Understanding Genesis* (New York: Schocken Books, 1966), 3.
[40] Fee and Stuart, *How to Read*, 11.
[41] Sailhamer, *Genesis Unbound*, 82.
[42] Leon Kass, *The Beginning of Wisdom* (New York: Free Press, 2003), 26.
[43] Tremper Longman III, "What Genesis 1–2 Teaches (and What It Doesn't)," in *Reading Genesis 1–2: An Evangelical Conversation*, ed. J. Daryl Charles (Peabody, MA: Hendrickson, 2013), 103.

These are examples of the types of questions that we will be asking as we engage in the hermeneutical spiral, merging exegetical principles with the textures of socio-rhetorical analysis.

Investigate the Contexts

The contexts of the books of Genesis and First John include historical, literary, and biblical contexts.

HISTORICAL CONTEXT (HISTORICAL INTER-TEXTURE)

Authorship. Within the historical context, we can briefly consider the question of the authorship of the first chapter of Genesis and that of First John.

Genesis. Even if the somewhat discredited documentary hypothesis[44] were accepted (that Genesis was patched together from various sources), we could still, as Kass says, "give the redactor the benefit of the doubt and assume that he knew precisely what he was about."[45] In the end, the question of inspiration requires a decision of faith, and whether God inspired a single author or a single editor is irrelevant. The final product of the Book of Genesis is what we have to deal with in deciding how to respond to its truths. Throughout this book, when the question of the authorship of Genesis arises, the assumption will be that Moses wrote the Book of Genesis along with the rest of the Torah or Pentateuch. This is the position taken by such respected Old Testament scholars as Waltke, Sailhamer, Blocher, and many others.[46]

First John. Similarly, the authorship of First John is not crucial to the investigation of the cosmic battle theme. Was John, the disciple of Jesus, the author of First John? This is a much-debated question,[47] but for the purposes of the present study it is not particularly crucial to determine if the author was John the son of Zebedee, another disciple

---

[44] See Cassuto, *Genesis*, 27.

[45] Kass, *Beginning*, 14.

[46] Bruce K. Waltke, "The Literary Genre of Genesis 1," *Crux* 27 (Dec., 1991): 2; Waltke, *Genesis*, 23; Sailhamer, *Genesis Unbound*, 24; Blocher, *In the Beginning*, 34.

[47] Oscar Cullmann gives reasons why "It is impossible to reconcile the picture of the author derived from the content of the Gospel with what we know of John the son of Zebedee" (*The Johannine Circle* [Philadelphia: Westminster Press, 1975], 76). On the other hand, Schnackenburg seems to assume John the son of Zebedee as the author of the Gospel of John (Rudolf Schnackenburg, *The Johannine Epistles: Introduction and Commentary*, trans. Reginald Fuller and Ilse Fuller [New York: Crossroad, 1992], 41).

named John (the elder) to whom Papias of Hierapolis refers,[48] one or more editors from the Johannine school,[49] or even perhaps Polycarp, a bridge person between the apostles and the Early Church whose Letter to the Philippians, in verses 7:1, 2 contains an echo of 1 John 4:3 and possibly other allusions as well.[50] The important aspect of authorship for the purposes of the present study is that an individual or group with knowledge of the original teachings in the Gospel of John wrote or compiled an authoritative document that purports to represent teaching "from the beginning," and that exhibits a central concern about the work of the devil in the world (1 John 2:13, 14; 3:8, 10; 5:19; also see John 12:31; 14:30, 16:11, 33). All the theories of authorship meet these conditions.

Occasion for Writing. What was going on that compelled these authors to put forth these documents? The occasion for the writing of a book is part of its historical context, which also includes the time and culture of the author and his readers, as well as relevant geographical and political factors.[51] In addition to these short descriptions of the occasions for writing Genesis and the First Epistle of John, later chapters will go into more detail.

 Genesis. As Waltke, Kass, Bernard Och, and others have shown, Genesis gave Israel the history of its origins and its connection to the Creator and Lord of history.[52] It introduces the Torah, the biblical teaching about how human beings are to live. In other words, Genesis 1

---

[48] Speaking of his research method, Papias, a church leader in the first half of the second century said, "And if anyone chanced to come who had actually been a follower of the elders, I would enquire as to the discourses of the elders, what ... John or Matthew or any other of the Lord's disciples [said]; and the things which ... John the elder, the disciples of the Lord, say." (Quoted by Martin Hengel, *The Johannine Question* [London: SCM Press, 1989], 17, emphasis added) This seems to show the existence of at least two "John's" who were disciples of Jesus.

[49] Raymond Brown summarizes his well-respected opinion: "I develop the thesis of a Johannine school of writers who shared a theological position and style, to which the evangelist, the redactor [of the Gospel], and the author of the Epistles all belonged" (Raymond Brown, *The Community of the Beloved Disciple: The Life, Loves, and Hates of an Individual Church in New Testament Times* [New York: Paulist Press, 1979], 95.)

[50] Polycarp wrote to the Philippians in 7:1, 2: "For everyone who does not confess that Jesus Christ has come in the flesh is an anti-Christ," which is similar to 1 John 4:3, "every spirit that does not confess Jesus is not from God."

[51] Fee & Stuart, *How to Read*, 19.

[52] Waltke, "Literary Genre," 2; *Genesis*, 22; Kass, *Beginning*, 9; Bernard Och, "Creation and Redemption: Towards a Theology of Creation," *Judaism* 44 (Spring, 1995): 226.

can be taken as an introduction to the documents Moses was providing, under God's guidance, as a sort of constitution for the emerging nation of Israel. As Waltke says, "every political and / or religious community must have a memory of its history that defines and distinguishes it."[53] "To undergird [the] covenant [at Mt. Sinai], an inspired Moses gave Israel this creation story allowing only one God, Creator of heaven and earth, who alone deserves worship, trust and obedience."[54] The people coming out of the chaos of slavery in Egypt would have seen the creation account as God's demonstration of bringing order out of chaos, turning darkness into light. Jewish theologian, Bernard Och, sees Genesis 1, the prologue to the Torah, as affirmation that "God has given the history of his people its meaning through creation."[55]

The nation of Israel emerged in the historical context of many other ancient Near Eastern peoples. Old Testament scholar, Richard Averbeck, gives an example of how an understanding of the Ancient Near East (ANE) relates to understanding the first verses of Genesis:

> A deep, dark, watery abyss was a most natural and understandable starting point for a creation story in the ancient Israelite world. Thus, in Gen. 1 we watch God paint his literary picture of creation and the cosmos step by step, and he paints it against the same standard backdrop as would be normal in the ancient Near East. The picture itself is quite different in many important respects, but there are also similarities to ANE accounts.[56]

These ancient Near Eastern people were all polytheistic. Israel's distinctive mission was to announce that there is one God, Yahweh. This is who was giving them the land God had originally created, as a sending base to make him known to all peoples. The creation account in Genesis reflects the literary forms and mythical imagery of these other nations, although it contrasts with them radically.[57] Cassuto feels "it is not possible to understand the purpose of [Genesis 1] without constant reference to the lore and learning, the doctrines, and traditions of the

---

[53] Waltke *Genesis*, 22.

[54] Waltke, "Literary Genre," 2

[55] Och, "Creation and Redemption," 226.

[56] Richard Averbeck, "A Literary Day, Inter-Textual, and Contextual Reading of Genesis 1–2," in *Reading Genesis 1–2: An Evangelical Conversation*, ed. J. Daryl Charles (Peabody, MA: Hendrickson, 2013), 12.

[57] Allen P. Ross, *Creation and Blessing: A Guide to the Study and Exposition of Genesis.* (Grand Rapids: Baker Academic, 1996), 23.

neighboring peoples."[58] How the Genesis account differed, and where other biblical accounts of creation or chaos were similar but with different meanings will be part of the inner texture word studies of Genesis 1:2.

First John. An understanding of the doctrines and disagreements among the factions in the Johannine community is part of understanding the purpose and occasion for the First Epistle of John. Will the members of the Johannine community continue to walk in love for one another and in belief in Jesus as the Christ, or will they stumble by allowing former members of the community to deceive them into abandoning their faith and their love for each other? This is the pastoral emergency the author of First John is addressing in the context of a cosmic battle that engulfs the whole world. ("The whole world lies in the power of the evil one, 1 John 5:19, ESV).

The seriousness of the community's situation can be illustrated by a humorous story once told by Polycarp. Picture a man about 80 years old named John, a disciple of Jesus, running out of a public bath-house in Ephesus, towel flying, crying out, "Fly, lest even the bath-house fall down, because Cerinthus, the enemy of the truth, is within!" Further imagine a young boy named Polycarp (70–155 C.E.), who would later become one of the bishops of the Early Church, standing by with open mouth as this scene impresses itself on his mind.[59] The moral of this story is found at the end of First John: "Little children, keep yourselves from idols [false teachings and teachers]" (5:21).

In concluding his letter by telling his "little children" to "keep themselves from idols" (1 John 5:21), the author knew his audience would know very well what he meant. He was accusing their opponents of being in the same category with idols—false representations of God, enemies of the truth. A leader in the Johannine community wrote First John to confirm believers in making the right choice to separate themselves from those following false teachings. He expected the recipients of his letter to recognize and repudiate their opponents as being "children of the devil," on the wrong side of the cosmic battle that is going on in the world.

---

[58] Cassuto, *Genesis*, 32.
[59] Irenaeus (120–202 C.E.) recorded Polycarp's story in *Against Heresies* 3.3.4.

LITERARY CONTEXT (INNER TEXTURE)

Recognition of the meaning and purpose of a passage of Scripture requires careful consideration of the literary context. This includes determining the genre, the structure of the book or passage, the meaning of words and their grammatical usage, what figures of speech are used, as well as the place of the text within the rest of the Bible. Identifying the genre of a passage is important since it will determine the way words and figures of speech are understood. "The indications of the literary genre of a text affect its overall reading by showing that the laws of genre have affected its writing."[60]

Genesis. Umberto Cassuto, by his own valuation, was the first commentator on Genesis to give particular attention to the detailed literary rules followed by the biblical authors in various genre, and to take into consideration all the linguistic details of the text, including grammar and figures of speech, for arriving at an understanding of the author's intention.[61] Henri Blocher adds a warning against twisting the grammar to mean something we wish the text would mean.[62] That warning will need to be considered seriously in the analysis of Genesis 1:1, 2.

Commentators generally assign Genesis 1 to the genre of narrative literature[63] although Blocher considers it to be a composite of narrative and other types of prose with a higher degree of structure than is usual for narrative stories.[64] Waltke agrees with Blocher that Genesis 1 is a "literary-artistic representation of the creation. To this we add the purpose, namely, to ground the covenant people's worship and life in the Creator, who transformed chaos into cosmos, and their ethics in His created order."[65]

Biblical narratives are selective in what they tell about within the context of the overall story of the Bible. In *The Art of Biblical Narrative*, Hebrew scholar Robert Alter states, "biblical narrative … is selectively silent in a purposeful way."[66] A narrative such as the creation

---

[60] Blocher, *In the Beginning*, 19.

[61] "This is the first commentary ever written on these sections of the Pentateuch in accordance with the principles that I have outlined above [literary, linguistic, and historical principles]" (Cassuto, *Genesis*, 3).

[62] Blocher, *In the Beginning*, 43.

[63] Kaiser, "Literary Form," 61; Robert Alter, *The Art of Biblical Narrative* (New York: Basic Books, 1981), 112; Wenham, *Genesis*, 37; Ross, *Creation*, 13.

[64] Blocher, *In the Beginning*, 52.

[65] Waltke, "Literary Genre," 9.

[66] Alter, *Biblical Narrative*, 115.

account tells only one part of the overall picture of God's purposes in history. Fee and Stuart elaborate on this trait of biblical narrative: "we have to learn to be satisfied with that limited understanding, and restrain our curiosity at many points, or else we will end up trying to read between the lines so much that we end up reading into stories things that are not there."[67] This caution is particularly appropriate for Genesis 1.

Analysis of narrative and purposeful repetition are two of the aspects of inner texture in a socio-rhetorical approach to a text. We see both of these textures in the structure of the first chapter of Genesis, which establishes a pattern of repeated words and occurrences, organized around the framework of the six days of creation. God's creative word, the report of its effectiveness, God's evaluation of the created entity as "good" (in most cases), and the numbering of each day are the most obvious elements of the structure of this chapter. God said ... God saw ... God separated ... God called ... God made ... God blessed ... God finished ... . There is a stately rhythm in the orderliness of God's creative acts. In regard to this organizing structure, Wenham is disappointed that "one device which our narrative uses to express the coherence and purposiveness of the Creator's work, namely, the distribution of the various creative acts to six days, has been seized on and interpreted over-literalistically."[68]

Among other literary elements, Genesis 1 has a rhetorical pattern in common with other biblical texts in which first the main parts are listed, followed by filling in the details with the particulars of those parts[69] (a pattern also being followed in the structure of the chapters of this book). This pattern is obvious in the parallels between the first set of three days and the second set of three days, in which details about the main parts of creation are filled in, in the same order as they were first listed. Days one and four deal with light and the light-bearing heavenly bodies; days two and five deal with the division of the upper and lower waters and the creatures populating those areas, while days three and six deal with the dry land and those creatures living there. In addition, the first verse of Genesis 1 serves as a general statement about God's creative activity, which is filled in by the details of the six days of creation. In a later chapter, in a word study of "beginning," we will consider arguments for viewing Genesis 1:1 as a title or introduction to the chapter as a whole.[70]

---

[67] Fee and Stuart, *How to Read*, 81.

[68] Wenham, *Genesis*, 39.

[69] Jaki *Genesis*, 3.

[70] Blocher, *In the Beginning*, 62; Walton, *Lost World*, 45.

As one more example of this rhetorical pattern in the book of Genesis, Waltke and his co-author, literary expert Cathy Fredricks, see a pattern of "generalization and particularization" in the structure of the Genesis *toledot* cycles (genealogies accompanied by stories).[71] We will examine this pattern in the word study on the "land."

John Walton further points out that these *toledot* cylces are used eleven times by the author as a literary device to identify the sections of the book of Genesis. "This shows us that the author of Genesis indeed did use initial statements as literary introductions to sections."[72]

These patterns, choices of words, genre, and style, all selected by the author for inclusion in his narrative, are meaningful and helpful for interpreting the passage. A characteristic of biblical narrative literature, according to Robert Alter[73] is the importance of the way words are used. Because the biblical narrative leaves out so many details that might have been included, the author's choice of words and phrases that *are* included can be particularly significant in determining the purpose and meaning of the narrative passage within the overall biblical story. Later chapters will focus in great detail on key words and terms in the first two verses of Genesis to see how God deals with conditions that are opposed to his will.

First John: The pairing of opposites, such as light and dark or love and hate, is one of the prominent literary devices in the First Epistle of John. In addition to this antithetical language, other literary-rhetorical devices in this carefully constructed epistle include chiastic structure, purposeful and progressive repetition of words or phrases, and complex rhetorical transitions. Analysis of these textures in later chapters will be helpful in illuminating the central theme of the cosmic battle in First John.

BIBLICAL CONTEXT (INNER TEXTURE AND SCRIBAL INTER-TEXTURE)

The overall biblical story, and the progressive self-revelation of God, is the ultimate context for any passage of Scripture. Genesis 1 is unique in standing at the beginning of the Bible, serving as a prologue to the biblical story. It gives the setting for the biblical drama and sets the stage for the plot that begins with the entrance of the serpent in the Garden. It gives the necessary background to know why God had to take such drastic steps to correct distortions to his purposes in human

---

[71] Waltke, *Genesis*, 34.
[72] Walton, *Lost World*, 46.
[73] Alter, *Biblical Narrative*, 179.

relationships with other humans, with the created world, and with God himself. The new beginning when God took on human form is the tipping point of the cosmic battle. This will be the focus of a later chapter that looks at the purpose and work of Jesus on earth in the Gospels and in First John.

Genesis: Interpreting Scripture through the lens of other Scripture (an aspect of scribal inter-texture) is advocated by theologian-philosopher-pastor Gregory Boyd: "If we accept the plenary inspiration of Scripture, the Genesis 1 account should be read as a piece of the whole mosaic of Scripture's view of creation, not as the whole picture itself."[74] Henri Blocher[75] also encourages making use of Scripture to illumine difficulties in other Scripture passages, taking advantage of their "common inspiration." This principle allows for interpreting Genesis 1:2 in the light of other biblical accounts of creation which contain some of the cosmic battle themes present in the historical literature of the ancient Near East, an aspect of scribal and historical inter-texture.

Waltke agrees that Genesis needs to be interpreted in light of the whole Bible and asks, "what is the entirety of the Bible all about?"[76] The late missiologist, Ralph D. Winter, would answer that question by saying the Bible is the story of the battle for our planet between the powers of darkness and the kingdom of God. God's purpose throughout Scripture is missiological in nature: to defeat evil wherever it is found and in this way to bring about the glorious triumph of his Kingdom among all the peoples of the earth.[77] This is the ideological assumption we are following, as chapter 3 will describe in more detail, which will influence our interpretation of the prologue of the Bible.

First John: Just as the book of Genesis needs to be interpreted in light of the whole Bible, the same is true for the First Epistle of John. The author claims to have been an eyewitness to "that which was from the beginning, ... the Word of life" (1 John 1:1). This is the first of many strong echoes of the Gospel of John found in the Epistle: "In the beginning was the Word ... and the Word was God" (John 1:1). The

---

[74] Gregory A. Boyd, *Satan and the Problem of Evil: Constructing a Trinitarian Warfare Theodicy* (Downers Grove: InterVarsity, 2001), 220.

[75] Blocher, *In the Beginning*, 17.

[76] Waltke, *Genesis*, 43.

[77] Ralph D. Winter, *Frontiers in Mission: Discovering and Surmounting Barriers to the* Missio Dei, 4th ed. (Pasadena: WCIU Press, 2008), 11, 237.

prologue of the Gospel of John is, in turn, echoing Genesis 1:1: "In the beginning God ... ."

Some of the questions about First John that we can look at in light of the biblical context include:

 • What can we learn about the issues in the text of First John from the other Johannine literature?

 • What can we learn from the rest of the New Testament?

 • From the Hebrew Bible?

 • From Jewish literature of the first century C.E.?

 • From early non-canonical Christian writings which may have influenced the author of First John, or which may have been influenced by this Epistle?

A rich exploration of such texts as the Gospel of John, the Synoptic Gospels, the Hebrew Bible, the *Testaments of the Twelve Patriarchs*, Polycarp's Letter to the Philippians, and Ignatius' Letter to the Ephesians will bring helpful insights to the study of First John and its context.

A key relationship between the First Epistle and the Gospel of John is the finding that at the center of each book is an emphasis on the cosmic battle between the Son of God and the evil one. In each case this central emphasis occurs as part of a similar complex transitional device that we will explore in a later chapter.

Integrating Insights

This brief overview of some of the main points of biblical exegesis and socio-rhetorical analysis has also included background information on the two main texts we will be investigating. This has prepared us to move on into more detailed investigations to see what the original audiences would have understood about the cosmic battle, about chaos, and about the role God intends for his people to play in counter-acting chaos at some level.

In the next chapter we will develop ideological texture in looking at the big picture of the cosmic battle, from a Johannine perspective, in the context of the full biblical story. Following that we will begin looking at the details of the story of the "battle for our planet" in approximate chronological order, but with the approaches described above that take other parts of Scripture into account to illuminate the text and words under consideration. The approach we are following presupposes that what is discovered within one bounded area will be put in dialog with other discoveries, with the intention of integrating the insights to explore the theological texture of the overall cosmic battle theme of Scripture and its application for international development today.

Chapter Three

The Big Picture of Scripture in Ideological Perspective

Images of Precious Stones that Reflect God's Glory and Wisdom

You were in Eden, the garden of God;
every precious stone adorned you:
   carnelian, chrysolite, and emerald,
   topaz, onyx, and jasper,
   lapis lazuli, turquoise, and beryl.
Your settings and mountings were made of gold;
   on the day you were created they were prepared.
You were anointed as a guardian cherub,
   for so I ordained you.
You were on the holy mount of God;
   you walked among the fiery stones.
You were blameless in your ways
   from the day you were created
   till wickedness was found in you.
(Ezekiel 28:13-15)

Fashion a breastpiece for making decisions—the work of skilled hands. ...
Then mount four rows of precious stones on it.
   The first row shall be carnelian, chrysolite, and beryl;
   the second row shall be turquoise, lapis lazuli, and emerald;
   the third row shall be jacinth, agate, and amethyst;
   the fourth row shall be topaz, onyx, and jasper.
Mount them in gold filigree settings.
(Exodus 28:15-20)

The wall was made of jasper, and the city of pure gold, as pure as glass.
The foundations of the city walls were decorated with every kind of precious
stone.
   The first foundation was jasper, the second sapphire, the third agate,
   the fourth emerald, the fifth onyx, the sixth ruby, x
   the seventh chrysolite, the eighth beryl, the ninth topaz
   the tenth turquoise, the eleventh jacinth, and the twelfth amethyst.
(Revelation 21:18-20)

General Overview of the Big Picture

What went wrong? From being adorned with nine precious fiery stones, the angelic being, the guardian cherub, fell into wickedness and became the prince of darkness.[78] When God began working with the people of Israel to win them back to himself, he added three more precious stones to those that had adorned the angelic being, in his instructions for making the high priest's decision-making breastplate. This surely showed that God wanted to share some of his glory and some of his decision-making with humans. Even though God's people have failed time and again to make right decisions, to the point that "the whole world lies in the power of the evil one" (1 John 5:19), this is not the final state of things! At the end of Scripture we see images of the same stones that had adorned the fallen angelic being and the human high priest, incorporated into the foundation of the heavenly city. The original purpose of the stones to reflect God's glory has been restored. In between, a battle has been raging. The cosmic war, a battle for the rulership of God's creation, is reflected in the image at the center of

---

[78] Merrill Unger (*Unger's Commentary On the Old Testament* [Chicago: Moody, 1981], 1:5) and Bruce Waltke ("The Creation Account in Genesis 1: Part 2, the Restitution Theory," *Bibliotheca Sacra* 132 [1975]: 141) agree that these verses apparently are talking about a high-level angelic being before he sinned through pride and became God's adversary.

The Early Church Father, Origen, considered that the texts in Ezekiel 28 and Isaiah 14 have a meaning beyond simply a human figure. Sigve Tonstad points out that Origen "managed to highlight the most important points in Lucifer's 'biography': He 'was Lucifer,' the splendid 'Son of the Morning,' (Isa. 14:12). He 'arose in heaven.' He was 'without sin from the day of his birth' (Ezek. 28:15). He 'was among the cherubim' (Ezek. 28:14). And yet despite his exalted origin and high standing, something went wrong" (Sigve Tonstad, "What the Early Christians Believed: The Reality of the Cosmic Conflict," in *Servant God: The Cosmic Conflict Over God's Trustworthiness* [Loma Linda: Loma Linda University Press, 2013], 76.

Origen specifically states, "Who is there that, hearing such as saying as this, 'Thou wast a signet of likeness and a crown of honour in the delights of the paradise of God,' or this, 'from the time thou wast created with the cherubim, I placed thee in the holy mount of God,' could possibly weaken their meaning to such an extent as to suppose them spoken of a human being, even a saint, not to mention the prince of Tyre? Or what 'fiery stones' can he think of 'in the midst' of which any man could have lived? Or who could be regarded as 'stainless' from the very 'day he was created,' and yet at some later time could have acts of unrighteousness found in him and be said to be 'cast forth into the earth'? This certainly indicated that the prophecy is spoken of one who, not being in the earth, was 'cast forth into the earth, whose 'holy places' also are said to be 'polluted" (*First Principles* I.5.4. cf. *Contra Celsum* 6.43; 6.44).

First John: "The Son of God appeared for the purpose of undoing / destroying the works of the devil" (1 John 3:8). From Genesis to Revelation, the theme of Scripture is God's purpose to win a people for himself back from the rulership of Satan.

We will look at this epic biblical story from the viewpoint of the early Johannine community of believers.

Prior to the Coming of Jesus

Before the appearing of Jesus, according to the Johannine writers, no one had ever seen God (1 John 4:12; John 1:18). These writers believed God wants to be known to people who choose to be in fellowship with him (1 John 1:3, 4; John 1:12), but the people to whom he had chosen to reveal himself in most detail, the people of Israel, did not recognize him, in the form of his Son Jesus, when they saw him. ("He came to that which was his own, but his own did not receive him." [John 1:11].) What was blinding and deceiving them, keeping them from recognizing their Creator (John 1:1-4)? The beginning of Scripture, Genesis 1:1, 2, points to the answer.

The first thing recorded in the Hebrew scriptures, with which the Johannine community would have been very familiar, is that God was having to re-build a world that was in chaos following some sort of disastrous judgment (*tohu wabohu*)[79]. This was apparently due to the sinning of the devil "from the beginning" (1 John 3:8a), prior to the sin of the first humans. Could it be that in an earlier period of time before Genesis 1:1, Satan turned against God and distorted God's good creation into the suffering and violence we now see throughout nature? According to Genesis 1:26, God created humans to take charge of the creation on his behalf. But at some point the devil, who is a liar and has been a murderer from the beginning (John 8:44), deceived the first humans into joining him in rebelling against God's will. The devil's murderous, hateful nature is illustrated by Cain, who was of the evil one and killed his brother because his deeds were evil, while his brother's deeds were righteous (Gen. 4:3-8; 1 John 3:12). The success of the devil's pervasive influence is seen by the fact that the whole world is said to be under the influence the evil one (1 John 5:19), who is called the "ruler of this world" in John 12:31.

God's plan to reverse the evil one's influence (Gen. 3:15) called for humans to freely choose to obey him as their rightful ruler. This plan was delayed numerous times by humans making wrong choices and

---

[79] This will be explained in detail in a later chapter.

experiencing the consequences, such as the Flood, or when the Israelites asked for a human king and ended up in Exile. Each time judgment was followed by a fresh beginning.

Jesus' Life and Death on Earth

Finally, at the right time, God made a radical new beginning: the Word became flesh (John 1:14). Jesus appeared to take away sins and to destroy the works of the devil (1 John 3:5, 8b), loosing people from slavery to sin (John 8:34-36), and making it possible for people to choose obedience to God as their father. (See John 1:12: he gave them the authority or the power to become sons of God.) First John emphasizes two commandments requiring obedience from true children of God: love for one another, and belief in Jesus as the Christ, the Savior of the world (1 John 3:23; 4:14).

The author of First John and his inner circle were eyewitnesses that the Father had sent the Son to be the Savior of the world (1 John 1:1-3; 4:9, 14; also see John 4:42, "we know that this man really is the Savior of the world"). Jesus' ministry began with his baptism by John (1 John 5:6-8; John 1:32-34) and his temptation by the devil, whom he successfully overcame (Matt. 4:10, 11). His ministry included defeating the works of the devil by casting out demons and healing the sick while demonstrating a life of love and obedience to God.

Jesus' life set an example for the believer to follow (1 John 1:7; 2:6; 3:2, 16). His command to his disciples "from the beginning" was to love one another (1 John 4:7, John 13:34, 15:17), one demonstration of which was washing his disciples' feet (John 13:14-16). Not only would his disciples ideally follow his positive example, but they would also experience similar consequences. Jesus warned that since the world hated him, it would hate them also (1 John 3:13; John 15:18-24). But the ruler of this world had no hold on Jesus (John 12:31; 14:30) and ultimately will have no hold on Jesus' followers (see 1 John 5:18 which promises that the evil one does not "touch" the believer). Jesus' successful accomplishment of the Father's will led to the driving out and defeat of the evil one. Jesus appeared to take away sins, which can be defined as opposition to God's will (1 John 3:5), and in doing so, he broke the hold that the devil had on humankind (1 John 3:8b; 5:18). Jesus' atoning death on the cross (1 John 2:2) was the turning point in the battle against Satan.

After Jesus Returned to the Father

As a result of the devil's works being undone in the lives of Jesus' followers, believers are able and obligated to follow his example by laying down their lives for those in need (1 John 3:16, 17). These demonstrations of love are intended to continue in a chain reaction of destroying the devil's works across time and culture by bringing love where there is hatred (1 John 3:11-17), truth where there is falsehood (1 John 4:1-6), and life to overcome death (1 John 3:14). The ideological perspective of this book recognizes that humans were created to join God in rescuing creation from the kingdom of darkness, including the physical and social results of intelligent evil, and in bringing transformation that represents the advance of God's rulership.

The End of History

At the end of the New Testament, in the Book of Revelation, the fulfillment of God's purposes in history is described in terms showing that the state of *"tohu wabohu"* has finally been reversed: there is no more death, crying, or pain. Darkness and night have been permanently replaced with "good" light (see Rev. 21:3, 4; 22:5). By describing the opposite of God's intentions in the context of the Genesis 1 creation account, *"tohu wabohu"* describes the root of the problem and points toward the goal of that creation—a place that can be inhabited by humans in purposeful fellowship with God. An adversary exists that is hostile to life and who opposes God's intentions. The biblical story shows humans are to fight back against the enemy who orchestrates disorder and chaos in opposition to God. The first chapter of Genesis points the way in showing that it is possible to restore order with creativity and patience, showing how to overcome evil with good. As believers follow God's and the Son's example, and as they demonstrate God's love and what God's will is, and what God is like, the peoples of the earth will be attracted to follow that kind of God and experience his blessing. This is the origin and nature of international development.

Particulars:
Developing a Biblical Theology of Bringing Order out of Chaos

All cultures have to answer the question, How shall we bring order out of chaos: in the physical world, in society, in a family, in a relationship, in one's own life? Or as Francis Shaeffer has put it in the title of one of his books, "How shall we then live?"

How should international development workers address the issue of distortions of God's will within a society and its land?

What is God going to do about the evil in this world?

How does God expect his people to live?

"The ability of future generations to make the text answer their questions, without distorting it beyond recognition, is part of the Bible's power."[80] In answer, then, to the questions above, the following interpretive translation of Genesis 1:1-5 is followed by a general interpretive summary of the rest of the chapter. The rationale for the choices made will be shown in the word studies from verses 1 and 2 that will be explained in detail in upcoming chapters. The value of this interpretation of Genesis 1 is its ability to help international development workers address the stumbling block of the "problem of evil," and to point toward the beginnings of a biblical theology of God's desire to bring order out of chaos at many levels.

Interpretive Translation of Genesis 1:1-5 and Summary of Genesis 1

GENESIS 1:1-5

In one of God's new beginnings God re-fashioned everything in nature, as the author of Genesis knew it, because the land had been destroyed and left desolate after the disastrous consequences of conditions contrary to God's will. But God had not given up on the land and its people. The Spirit of God was stirring over the deep chaos that was blanketed by darkness. At the right time God said, "Let there be light," and there it was! God saw that the light was good and he separated the light from the darkness. He called the light "day" and the darkness "night." So after evening, there was morning, one day.

SUMMARY OF THE REST OF THE CHAPTER

The next thing God did was to make some basic structural divisions, to be followed later by filling in the details. God wasn't in a hurry to get everything ready at once. Instead, he worked within the framework of evenings and mornings toward his goal of making a land habitable for humans, who could then continue working with God to fulfill his purposes. Each day saw increasing order brought out of the chaos. Within the rhythm of evening followed by morning, God divided the

---

[80] Aaron Wildavsky, *The Nursing Father: Moses as a Political Leader* (Tuscaloosa, AL: University of Alabama Press, 1984), 12.

upper and lower waters, undoing their mingling and making it possible to distinguish what was good and helpful from what was bad and not conducive to life. Next, God provided for some stability by separating dry land from the lower waters. The existence of the land made it possible for basic subsistence, and now plants and fruit bearing trees were able to thrive. Next, purpose was given to the heavenly bodies (their regular cycles had become visible as the murky atmosphere cleared) to mark the times and seasons in a predictable way, looking ahead toward the need of humans to remember how to take care of the land and to remember to honor their Creator, on whose behalf they would be stewards of the land. After that, moving creatures in the water, air, and land populated the area, with increasing degrees of ability to choose how to use their mobility. Finally everything was ready for God's masterpiece and helper—the first humans whom God made to help him continue the process of bringing order out of chaos and defeating evil. God gave our first parents freedom of choice, hoping they would choose to work with him in obedience, following the pattern he had demonstrated in the process of making their land ready for them. The seventh day was set aside for them and for us to focus on God and to follow God's example of resting from work. God wanted his people to reflect on their relationship to him and to recognize their need to submit to him as the good, orderly, faithful, and trustworthy ruler.

CONTRIBUTIONS OF GENESIS 1 TOWARD A BIBLICAL THEOLOGY OF
   BRINGING ORDER OUT OF CHAOS

Ordinary people, like those for whom Moses wrote the book of Genesis, have always noticed that evil is mingled with good in this world. "Nothing ... can change the fact that in our experience ... there is good and there is evil."[81] "Man has always suspected that behind all creation lies the abyss of formlessness,"[82] wrote German Old Testament scholar, Gerhard von Rad. Although Genesis 1 may have been written to simple, uneducated people who were former slaves, Moses himself was an intellectual who had been well educated in Egypt. He left room in his orderly, calm presentation in Genesis 1 for readers throughout the ages to see that God is not the author of evil.

The tone and language of this chapter reflect the characteristics of God as being orderly and in control, so we have to learn about the opposite of this orderliness, the chaos God was calmly combating,

---

[81] Wenham, *Genesis*, 21.
[82] Gerhard von Rad, *Genesis: A Commentary*, trans. John H. Marks (Philadelphia: Westminster, 1973), 52.

elsewhere in Scripture. A biblical theology needs to account for the role of the devil in the unfolding drama of creation and redemption, thus avoiding attributing evil to God. In the perspective on the cosmic battle in Scripture that this book is developing, there is a special role for humankind. We were created to join God in his mission to defeat the adversary and redeem all creation for the purposes God originally intended for it. In the rest of this chapter we will look in more detail at an ideological perspective of what went wrong before the beginning described in Genesis 1.

BEFORE THE BEGINNING: GOD'S INTENTIONS

Before the beginning, God created something out of nothing. "By faith we understand that the universe was formed at God's command, so that what is seen was not made out of what was visible" (Heb. 11:3). He made "the winds his messengers, flames of fire his servants," "angels ... who do his bidding, who obey his word" (Pss. 104:4; 103:1). In the beginning, that was before this world's beginning, the Word was with God and was God. "Through him all things were made; without him nothing was made that has been made" (John 1:1, 3). "By the word of the Lord the heavens were made, their starry host by the breath of his mouth" (Ps. 33:6). And observing God's creation, the morning stars sang together and all the angels shouted for joy (Job 38:7). Praise echoed in the heavens:

> *Praise him, all his angels;*
> > *praise him, all his heavenly hosts.*
> *Praise him, sun and moon;*
> > *praise him, all you shining stars....*
> *Let them praise the name of the Lord, for at his command*
> > *they were created*
> (Ps. 148:1-5).

The pre-incarnate Son was "the firstborn over all creation. For in him all things were created: things in heaven and on earth, visible and invisible, ... all things have been created through him and for him. He is before all things, and in him all things hold together" (Col. 1:15-17). This was the time of which Jesus said to the Father, "You loved me before the foundation of the world" (John 17:24).

ANGELS AND CREATION

Some have speculated that the world was originally "designed to be the habitation of God's first sinless angelic creatures,"[83] based on Isaiah's claim on God's behalf that God did not create the earth to be empty (*tohu*, inhospitable to life) but he formed it to be inhabited (Isa. 45:18). A further speculation might be that just as God would later lower himself to become human ("the only *begotten* son," among the "sons of God"—see Job 1:6), the only heavenly being to take on a lower order of creation, perhaps God had earlier lowered himself to another less-lower life form. Could it be that God became one of the angels in order to demonstrate to his servants ("winds and flames of fire") how to serve with mutual submission and humility? Evangelical theologian Louis Goldberg's article, "The Angel of the Lord," in *Baker's Evangelical Dictionary of Biblical Theology* states, "The connection between the angel of the Lord and the pre-incarnate appearance of the Messiah cannot be denied." New Testament scholar, Sigve Tonstad explains, "expressing this in admittedly anthropomorphic terms, it is possible that the pre-existent Jesus did not think it below his dignity to appear as an angel or to assume the function of an angel any more than to be a human being."[84]

Did God, as the Angel of the Lord, or as Michael the Archangel, the pre-incarnate Son / the Word, deliberately experience what it was like to be an angel so God could best work with the angels and they with God? Perhaps the Angel of the Lord, or Michael, "the great prince" who would later stand "guard over the sons of [Daniel's] people [Israel]" (Dan. 12:1), worked with another archangel, Lucifer, to fashion the earth out of the basic elements God had created. This speculation finds some support from Martin Luther's understanding of how the world was created. He considered that God (the Father) originally created the earth as an unformed chaotic mass out of nothing that afterwards it was the responsibility of the Son of God "to divide and adorn."[85] In the story we are developing here, we are speculating that the Son of God could have shared that knowledge and responsibility in "creating" with his friends, the angels, just as the Son later shared everything he had learned from his Father with his friends, the disciples (John 15:15).

---

[83] Ross, *Creation,* 719.

[84] Sigve Tonstad, *Saving God's Reputation: The Theological Function of Pistis Iesou in the Cosmic Narratives of Revelation* (London: T & T Clark, 2006), 88.

[85] Martin Luther, *Luther Still Speaking: The Creation; A Commentary on the First Five Chapters of the Book of Genesis,* trans. Henry Cole (1544; repr., Edinburgh: T & T Clark, 1858), 29.

It seems logical to hypothesize that the angels, including Lucifer in his pre-fallen state, assisted in creation, since we know that "wisdom" assisted in creation from before the world began (Prov. 8:12, 23-30; Jer. 10:12), "I [wisdom] was appointed from eternity, from the beginning [*mereshit*], before the world began. When there were no oceans, I was given birth... when he marked out the foundations of the earth, then I was the craftsman at his side" (Prov. 8:23ff.) As God's angelic servants worked with him in creation, they would have been learning how to sculpt the raw materials of the universe. Strange, weird life forms and the slow development of life (according to the "record of the rocks") all lend credibility to the speculation that perhaps God deliberately chose not to use his omniscience and omnipotence to create all life forms instantly, but instead shared creation with beings who were learning as they went along.[86]

Ralph Winter has speculated that life forms were being created by spirit beings whom God was instructing as they were learning to think God's thoughts after him.[87] In this Winter echoes J. R. R. Tolkien's fictional account of the creation of "Middle Earth" in *The Silmarillion* in which the music of the "Ainur" reflects what they are learning of the thoughts of "Iluvatar" and eventually they bring these thoughts into reality.[88]

Some of the raw materials we are speculating that the angels would have worked with in the earth were the precious stones that were associated with Lucifer's original high role and that would later be part of the high priest's breastplate (Ezek. 28:11-15; Exod. 28:17-20). In a pre-creation state these stones had spiritual significance about the role of the king-like or priest-like angelic being who later fell. The fact that the decision-making breastplate of the high priest contains all the stones associated with the guardian cherub hints strongly that they both had decision-making authority. But the high priest's adornment is more glorious, having three additional precious stones, perhaps indicating that humans living in line with God's purposes have more ability to reflect God's glory than the guardian angel who eventually turned his authority toward wrong purposes. There is also a post-creational significance to these stones. In Revelation 21:18-20 the twelve stones in the foundations of the gold city include seven of the original nine (those

---

[86] This speculation presupposes that God created the prototypes of the major categories of life mentioned in the Genesis 1 creation account: vegetation, creatures in the waters, air, and land, each "according to their kind."

[87] Winter, *Frontiers*, 293.

[88] J.R.R. Tolkien, *The Silmarillion* (New York: Ballantine Books, 1977), 3-12.

adorning the guardian cherub), and retain all three of the stones added for the high priest, with two new stones to replace those that were omitted, showing that the Ruler of the heavenly city, Christ the King, has even greater authority and glory than the angels and humans with whom he has shared decision-making authority.

GOD TAKES A RISK: LET US MAKE HUMANS IN OUR IMAGE, WITH FREE WILL

At some point God let the heavenly council know he had determined he wanted to extend heaven's rule to planet earth. God wanted to have creatures on earth that could make free choices, under the guidance and guardianship of the angels (Ps. 91; Heb. 1:14), spirit beings who were already inhabiting and working on the earth under its appointed prince. God would create beings, a little lower than the angels (Ps. 8:5; Heb. 2:7), in God's image (Gen. 1:27), with free will, but who would not live forever if they chose to disobey (Gen. 2:17). Since angels do not experience death, God knew the possibility existed that disobedient angels would have no end to their rebellion against him. God did not want more creatures like that, who might eventually self-destruct, although their self-torment would go on forever in their unending existence. So in God's plan, humans who chose to rebel against God would have to die, to cease to exist.

A DIALOG BETWEEN GOD AND LUCIFER

To be fair, God would have had to point out to Lucifer, the prince and ruler of the earth (see John 12:31), the likelihood that the ruler of a world inhabited by creatures with free choice might end up being rejected by subjects who made rebellious choices. A dialog between Lucifer and God might have looked like this:

God: I want this to be a world suitable for humans to live in where they can make choices to serve me in a riskier environment than what the angels have had. I want to extend my kingdom; I want to see heaven's rule freely chosen on earth.

Lucifer: I'm honored that you chose me above the other angels to be the ruler of these new creatures in my world.

God: The humans might decide they don't want to follow your rules. They might rebel against you, or even try to exile you. I've already taken that risk with giving free will to you angels.

Lucifer: Don't worry, I won't let them disobey me. I'll make sure they follow my rules.

God: The meek shall inherit the earth. My kingdom is not ruled by force.

Lucifer: You made me the prince and ruler of the earth, and I'll do things my way. I'll kill off those who don't want to do what I say. If you could become an angel like Michael, then I, the cherub close to your glory, should be able to become like God and have my humans worship me. "I will ascend to the heavens; I will raise my throne above the stars of God. I will sit enthroned on the mount of assembly, on the utmost heights of Mount Zaphon" (Isa. 14:13).

God (sadly): "You were the seal of perfection, full of wisdom and perfect in beauty.

You were in Eden, the garden of God; every precious stone adorned you: carnelian, chrysolite and emerald, topaz, onyx and jasper, lapis lazuli, turquoise and beryl. ...

You were anointed as a guardian cherub, for so I ordained you.

You were on the holy mount of God; you walked among the fiery stones.

You were blameless in your ways from the day you were created till wickedness was found in you" (Ezek. 28:12-15).[89]

WAR IN HEAVEN

Then there was war in heaven. "Angels which kept not their own principality, but left their proper habitation, incurred the wrath of God" (Jude 6—notice the disregard for separation and boundaries, basic concepts that are built into the creation story). "Michael and his angels had to war against the dragon" (Rev. 12:7, translation by Sigve Tonstad[90]). "The great dragon was hurled down—that ancient serpent called the devil, or Satan, who leads the whole world astray. He was hurled to the earth, and his angels with him" (Rev. 12:9). "How you have fallen from heaven, day star, son of the dawn! [the brightest of the stars that can be seen in the daytime]. You have been cast down to the earth" (Isa. 14:12).

---

[89] This is an ideological issue. Evangelical scholars whose worldview leads them to accept the existence of primeval spirit-beings also tend to accept Ezekiel 28:14-16 as a description of the fall of an originally perfect being due to pride. Those whose ideological presuppositions do not include spirit beings interpret this passage as referring only to a human king. For support for the assumption that this passage is, in part, referring to Lucifer, or Satan, see footnote 78 earlier in this chapter.

[90] Sigve Tonstad, "Revelation, Vision of Healing, Video Lecture 16," May 19, 2013, accessed August 17, 2013, http://www.youtube.com/watch?v=o2JoSh7OGvg.

WAR IN HEAVEN BROUGHT DOWN TO EARTH: EVOLUTIONARY COSMIC
BATTLE

The prince of the earth, Lucifer, now Satan, the dragon, must have
determined to wreak havoc on the earth to make it unsuitable for the
humans God had in mind to create. Satan succeeded in this to some
extent, as seen in Genesis 1:2 when God initiated a new beginning for
the earth or a local land: "Now as for the earth, it was *tohu wabohu*, it
was destroyed and desolate" (author's translation). Ralph Winter
suggested that Genesis 1:1, 2 "actually permits this interpretation:
'When God began His work of rehabilitation he had to deal with a
battered, formless, and darkened earth ....'"[91] It was a mess after Satan
and his angels had been battling with Michael and his angels in
evolutionary cosmic battle. Gregory Boyd quotes theologian-
philosopher Eric Mascall who argues that one major effect of the
angelic fall was "to introduce into the material realm a disorder which
has manifested itself in a distortion of [God's] evolutionary plan."[92]

Contemporary Christian philosopher Alvin Plantinga summarizes a
traditional understanding of the problem of evil: "Satan is a mighty non-
human free creature who rebelled against the Lord long before human
beings were on the scene; and much of the natural evil the world
displays is due to the actions of Satan and his cohorts."[93] Dom Bruno
Webb, who was a Benedictine monk in England during World War II,
agrees:

> So the fallen angels which have power over the universe and
> over this planet in particular, being motivated by an intense
> angelic hatred of God and of all creatures, have acted upon the
> forces of matter, actuating them in false proportions so far as lay
> in their power, and from the very outset of evolution, thus
> producing a deep-set disorder in the very heart of the universe
> which manifests itself today in the various physical evils which
> we find in nature, and among them the violence, the savagery,
> and the suffering of animal life.[94]

---

[91] Winter, *Frontiers*, 108.

[92] Boyd, *Satan*, 300; quoting Eric L. Mascall, *Christian Theology and Natural
Science: Some Questions on Their Relations* (Longmans: Green, 1956), 303.

[93] Alvin Plantinga, "Supralapsarianism, or 'O Felix Culpa'," in *Christian
Faith and the Problem of Evil*, ed. Peter Van Inwagen (Grand Rapids: Eerdmans, 2004),
15.

[94] Dom Bruno Webb, *Why Does God Permit Evil?* (London: Burns, Oates, and
Washbourne Ltd., 1941), 52.

Sociologist Tony Campolo also refers to Satan's use of the evolutionary process:

> Since Satan's fall, he and his followers have been at work perverting and polluting all that God created. Before Adam and Eve were ever created, Satan worked to create havoc throughout creation. One of the consequences of Satan's work is that the evolutionary process has gone haywire. That is why we have mosquitoes, germs, viruses, etc. God did not create these evils. They evolved because Satan perverted the developmental forces at work in nature.[95]

Philosopher-theologian Gregory Boyd gives a biblical defense of the view that Satan and other malevolent cosmic powers have been involved in the evolutionary process. He contends that "the process of evolution may be seen as a sort of warfare between the life-affirming creativity of an all-good God, on the one hand, and the on-going corrupting influence of malevolent cosmic forces, on the other."[96]

A number of other scholars (and literary giants), as well as the post-apostolic fathers, agree that God's good creation has been deliberately distorted by evil intelligent beings. Boyd summarizes: "In apocalyptic tradition, under the leadership of Satan, [his] angels work to afflict the world with earthquakes, famines, hailstorms, diseases, temptations and many other things that are not part of God's design for his creation.[97]

C.S. Lewis wrote, "It seems to me ... a reasonable supposition, that some mighty created power had already been at work for ill on ...planet Earth, before ever man came on the scene."[98]

Bruce McLaughlin wrote in the journal of the American Scientific Affiliation:

---

[95] Tony Campolo, *How to Rescue the Earth Without Worshiping Nature: A Christian's Call to Save Creation* (Nashville: Thomas Nelson, 1992), 38.

[96] Gregory Boyd, "Evolution as Cosmic Warfare A Biblical Perspective on Satan and 'Natural' Evil," in *Creation Made Free: Open Theology Engaging Science*, ed. Thomas Jay Oord (Eugene, OR: Pickwick Publications, 2009), 127. In this chapter Boyd gives five biblical defenses of his "evolution-as-cosmic warfare" thesis: 1) the Bible's clear emphasis on the reality of Satan and other fallen powers, 2) the healing ministry of Jesus in which Jesus frequently confronted evil spirits, 3) Jesus' nature miracles (he rebuked the wind and waves in the same way he rebuked demons), 4) the Bible's *chaoskampf* creation material, and 5) the contrast between descriptions of the ideal and cursed creation.

[97] Gregory A. Boyd, *God at War: The Bible and Spiritual Conflict* (Downers Grove: InterVarsity Academic, 1997), 206.

[98] C.S. Lewis, *The Problem of Pain* (New York: HarperCollins, 1940), 138.

According to Scripture, the universe was originally good and the glory of God is still evident in it (Rom. 1:20). But something else—something frightfully wicked—is evident in it as well. Of their own free will, Satan and other spiritual beings rebelled against God in the primordial past and now abuse their God-given authority over certain aspects of creation. Satan, who holds the power of death (Heb. 2:14), exercises a pervasive, structural, diabolic influence to the point that the entire creation is in bondage to decay. The pain-ridden, bloodthirsty, sinister, and hostile character of nature should be attributed to Satan and his army, not to God. Jesus' earthly ministry reflected the belief that the world had been seized by a hostile, sinister lord. Jesus came to take it back.[99]

Biblical scholar Herschel Hobbs concurs with this thinking: "Any evil force at work in the universe (see Eph. 6:10-13)" may be seen as "works of the devil" (1 John 3:8).[100]

Many of these scholars likely had the thinking of the Early Church father, Origen, in mind, who wrote in about 200 C.E.:

To [demons] belong famine, blasting of the vine and fruit trees, pestilence among men and beasts: all these are the proper occupations of demons, who in the capacity of public executioners receive power at certain times to carry out the divine judgments.[101]

In the story we are developing, the dragon was carrying out his own judgment for his rebellion against God by destroying his own world. Satan and his minions destructively built chaos into the condition of the planet, resulting in random hurricanes, typhoons, tsunamis, earthquakes, asteroidal collisions, and other life-threatening conditions that affect both the innocent and the wicked. In his description of the creation of his fictional physical world, Tolkien envisions something similar in a battle between good and evil spirit beings to fashion a fictional land in preparation for intelligent life:

The Valar [good spirit beings] endeavoured ever, despite of Melkor, to rule the Earth and to prepare it for the coming of the Firstborn; and they built lands and Melkor destroyed them;

---

[99] Bruce McLaughlin "From Whence Evil?" *Perspectives on Science and the Christian Faith* 56, no. 3 (2004): 237.

[100] Herschel Hobbs, *The Epistles of John* (Nashville: Thomas Nelson, 1983), 87.

[101] Origen, *Contra Celsus* 8.31.

valleys they delved and Melkor raised them up; mountains they carved and Melkor threw them down; seas they hollowed and Melkor spilled them; and naught might have peace or come to lasting growth, for as surely as the Valar began a labour so would Melkor undo it or corrupt it. And yet their labour was not all in vain; and though nowhere and in no work was their will and purpose wholly fulfilled, and all things were in hue and shape other than the Valar had at first intended, slowly nonetheless the Earth was fashioned and made firm.[102]

CAMBRIAN EXPLOSION: THE FALL OF SATAN?

Slow fashioning of the earth is also part of the scientific evolutionary story of creation. But at a particular point in time, according to the evidence from the fossil record, there was a sudden proliferation of life on this planet: complete with predators and defense mechanisms.[103] Biologist Andrew Parker states that an external force has to be taken into account to explain the Cambrian explosion, in which there was the sudden development (in the "blink of an eye" in geological terms) of hard body parts in all biological categories of life.[104] Parker's research led him to the conclusion that it was the sudden appearance of vision in one evolving creature at the beginning of the Cambrian period that led to selective pressures for all the various phyla to also develop sight, then hard parts to stab with, "limbs to perform their acts of murder" [because they saw potential food and wanted it!], and hard body parts for defense mechanisms.[105] But what caused the sudden development of eyes and the simultaneous onset of violence in 35 phyla, all within a relatively short period of time? The scientific creation story claims it was evolutionary chance along with selective evolutionary pressures.

Ralph Winter asks, regarding the sudden appearance of violent forms of life, could this be when the fall of Satan occurred?[106] Going still further, we could speculate that Lucifer, whose name means "morning star, light-bearing" (Webster's *Third New International Dictionary*), may have been responsible for the development of vision in early life forms, that he became proud of his accomplishment, contributing to his

---

[102] Tolkien, *The Silmarillion*, 12.

[103] Richard A. Fortey, *Life: A Natural History of the First Four Billion Years of Life on Earth* (New York: Alfred A. Knopf, 1998), 92, 93; Andrew Parker, *In the Blink of an Eye* (Cambridge, MA: Perseus Publications, 2003), 259.

[104] Parker, *Blink of an Eye*, 36.

[105] Parker, *Blink of an Eye,* 276.

[106] Winter, *Frontiers*, 108.

decision to rebel against God. At that point he may have begun turning his creative knowledge into distortions of God's intentions for creation. Winter speculates:

> Once we recognize the extensive distortion of creation ever since the Cambrian Explosion it would seem reasonable that then was when Satan turned against the Creator. He began systematically to distort non-carnivorous life forms into destructively violent, pain and suffering—producing forms of life which would not at all seem to be the kind of thing God would create in the first place.[107]

DEVASTATIONS AND NEW BEGINNINGS

In this ideological perspective, Satan and his minions frequently killed off their own creatures through the evolutionary process. Dinosaurs and other predators made the environment "red in tooth and claw," and uninhabitable by humans. Ralph Winter notes that "these violent forms of life are again and again blotted out by devastations."[108] Expanding a chart from the March 2002 *Scientific American*, Winter has shown a 600 million year timeline that includes 45 major asteroidal impacts that would have destroyed much of life on this planet at many different times in history. One of the largest of these, causing a 112-mile-wide crater in Yucatan, Mexico, was associated with the extinction of the dinosaurs about 65 million years ago,[109] most likely due to the extended period of time when dust in the atmosphere prevented plants from growing, thereby removing the dinosaur's food source.

Approximately coinciding with the extinction of dinosaurs, a new beginning with the Cenozoic Era featured large mammals and hominids (pre-human creatures) as dominant life forms on the planet.[110] We can speculate that in using the evolutionary process, Satan must have decided to fashion beings that would submit to his rules. He was not willing to give them intelligent free choice, so these pre-human creatures, such as Neanderthals, *homo erectus*, *homo habilis*, and

---

[107] Winter, *Frontiers*, xv.

[108] Winter, *Frontiers*, 53.

[109] Peter Schulte, "The Chicxulub Asteroid Impact and Mass Extinction at the Cretaceous-Paleogene Boundary," *Science* 327 (5 March 2010): 1214-18.

[110] William A. Berggren, "Cenozoic Era," *Encyclopaedia Britannica*, February 11, 2014, accessed February 11, 2014, http://www.britannica.com/EBchecked/topic/101936/Cenozoic-Era.; Winter, *Frontiers*, 51.

Australophithecus, were a caricature of the humanity God desired to create.

WAR AGAINST AN INTELLIGENT ENEMY

This evolutionary battlefield is apparently the context in which humans were brought into being. We are in a war against an intelligent enemy. As Gregory Boyd says, "humans are made in the image of God and placed on earth so that they might gradually vanquish this chaos."[111] "Our struggle is not against flesh and blood, but against the rulers, against the authorities, against the powers of this dark world, and against the spiritual forces of evil in the heavenly realms" (Eph. 6:12).

Erich Sauer, a German theologian with an Open Brethren background, postulates that Satan's area of power had been granted to him legally before his fall and that God's plan to take the rulership of the world back from him had to be done "legally" in order to reflect God's justice.[112] This meant, according to Sauer, that God would have to take the rulership of the world back, without force, through the free choices of neutral beings who would have to decide for themselves which ruler to follow. This was obviously a big risk for God, as Gregory Boyd points out.[113] But as Edwin Lewis said, "the very fact of the course of created existence must be accepted as the evidence that it is worth all that it costs."[114] In effect, by creating humans and putting them in charge of a particular part of the world, God was setting up a counter Kingdom and throwing out a challenge to Satan. "This cosmic calling of the new inhabitant of the earth as its deliverer [a human being] demanded that he should have freedom of will," says Sauer.[115] The serpent's insinuation to Eve was Satan's initially successful response to that challenge. But God struck back with a long-term plan, first mentioned in Genesis 3:15, to defeat the dark prince of this world and restore the world to what it was originally intended to be, under the rule of the Creator-King.

In his wisdom God knew that humans would most likely not be able to resist the wiles of the devil without supernatural help. From the foundation of this world, God knew he would need a ruler for the world who was willing to identify with humans, one who was willing to risk being betrayed and killed by those he came to help. Since no other

---

[111] Boyd, *God at War,* 107.

[112] Erich Sauer, *The King of the Earth* (Grand Rapids: Eerdmans, 1962), 73.

[113] Boyd, *Satan,* 86.

[114] E. Lewis, *Creator and Adversary,* 170.

[115] Sauer, *King of the Earth,* 73.

heavenly being would take on the terms of ruling the earth so that creatures of free will could live there under God's and heaven's rule, God himself, in the person of the pre-incarnate Son, had to be willing to take on the risk of being slaughtered. God had chosen, "from the beginning," to work out his purposes in the midst of demonic opposition and to receive into himself "the fiery darts of the Evil One."[116]

THE LAMB

The Lamb was "slain from the foundation of the earth" in the sense that God and the Lamb were both willing to take the risk of being killed by the very people the Messiah was planning to save from the inevitable consequences of their wrong choices. The slaughtered lamb, the victim of violence, was God's paradoxical way of defeating the enemy. As Tonstad says, "when Revelation says that 'no one in heaven or on earth or under the earth was able to open the scroll or to look into it' (5:3) it means that absolutely no one else would have solved the cosmic conflict in this way."[117] In preparing his disciples for his violent death, Jesus was able to say, "now the prince of this world will be driven out" (John 12:31). Through Jesus' life, death, and resurrection, God "has rescued us from the dominion of darkness and brought us into the kingdom of the Son he loves" (Col. 1:13).

IN BETWEEN TIMES AND BACK TO THE BEGINNING

In the meantime, before the new heaven and new earth have become a reality, humans are still participants and victims in the cosmic battle raging on earth. Edwin Lewis states, "The future is always a real future for which God and we must wait, that God does not fear because he has faith in his power to meet it. We are called upon to have faith in the God who has faith in himself."[118]

What, then, is the responsibility of the body of Christ to those in harm's way? What should be the role of Kingdom-minded international development workers in addressing the roots of human problems around the world and what opposition should they expect to face? "Our struggle is not against flesh and blood, but against the rulers, against the authorities, against the powers of this dark world, and against the spiritual forces of evil in the heavenly realms" (Eph. 6:12). In this battle, Jesus has shared his decision-making authority with his people. He has

---

[116] E. Lewis, *Creator and Adversary*, 170.

[117] Sigve Tonstad, "Revelation, Vision of Healing, Video Lecture 8," April 19, 2013, accessed August 13, 2013, http://www.youtube.com/watch?v=Ez7ccbmJZ4A.

[118] E. Lewis, *Creator and Adversary*, 171.

made us to be "a kingdom and priests to serve his God and Father" (Rev. 1:6). We can engage the powers of darkness through international development efforts in order to demonstrate that chaos is not God's will and that love *is* God's will. Just as the precious stones in the foundation of the heavenly city show the splendor of God's glory, Christ's followers serve as God's display window, showing his glory and what Christ's kingdom is meant to look like.

Jesus' coming to the rescue of the earth, his works, and the responsibilities he left with his followers will be the themes of upcoming chapters in this book. In the next chapter we will go back to the beginning of Genesis and explore some of the key terms that have contributed to the interpretation of the cosmic battle proposed here.

Chapter Four

A New Beginning

Images of Beginnings

In the beginning, Lord, you laid the foundations of the earth,
*   and the heavens are the work of your hands.*
They will perish, but you remain;
*   they will all wear out like a garment.*
You will roll them up like a robe;
*   like a garment they will be changed.*
(Heb. 1:10-12a)

Have you ever given orders to the morning,
*   or shown the dawn its place,*
that it might take the earth by the edges
*   and shake the wicked out of it?*
(Job 38:12, 13)

In beginning, God created the heavens and the earth.
As for the earth,
*   it was destroyed and desolate* (tohu wabohu),
*   with darkness on the face of the deep,*
*   but the Spirit of God stirring over the face of the waters.*
Then God said, "Let there be light," and there was light!
And God saw that the light was good (tob).
*   So God slashed a separation between the light and the darkness.*
(Gen. 1:1-4, author's translation)

The one doing sin
*   is of the devil,*
*   because from the beginning,*
*   the devil*
has been sinning.
    (1 John 3:8a, author's translation, retaining the Greek word order)

49

General Overview

"From the beginning" is the focus at the center of the stylistic arrangement of the words of 1 John 3:8a in the original Greek. This careful ordering of the words emphasizes that sin has been an intrinsic part of the of the devil's character, "from the beginning." The Johannine community was very aware that Satan "was a murderer from beginning" (John 8:4). As theologian and philosopher of religion, Stephen Webb, says,

> Satan is the author of violence, hatred, and strife. If Satan was a murderer from the beginning, how far back do we have to go to find evidence of his handiwork? Evidently, wherever we find death and deception, no matter how early in the biblical, biological, and historical record, we find Satan.[119]

"In the beginning" of Genesis chapter one, God is starting over. The devil's character had become clear. God's adversaries had corrupted the world to the point of its being unsupportive of human life. The first two verses of the Bible literally say, "In beginning, God created the heavens and the earth. Now the earth was destroyed and desolate [*tohu wabohu*] and darkness was over the surface of the deep."

A whimsical metaphor in Job 38:12, 13, that could have also occurred to Moses during his years of wandering in the desert, gives some comic relief to this dark picture. It sounds like an allusion to a tent-dwelling nomad shaking the bed bugs out of his sleeping blanket in the morning: "Have you ever given orders to the morning, or shown the dawn its place, that it might take the earth by the edges and shake the wicked out of it?" Think about that as part of what Moses may have had in mind, as a nomad himself, when he reported God saying, "Let there be light!"

In beginning a study of the first two verses of Genesis, Henri Blocher says,

> We must hear [Genesis 1] as the beginning of a symphony whose interpretative and illuminative power transcends all cultural diversity. These pages come to us as the opening pages of the Bible, and the Bible has demonstrated sufficiently that it is not just any ancient book.[120]

---

[119] Stephen Webb, *The Dome of Eden: A New Solution to the Problem of Creation and Evolution* (Eugene, OR: Wipf and Stock, 2010), 150.

[120] Blocher, *In the Beginning*, 16.

The first word of the Bible, *bereshit* ("in beginning"), immediately plunges us into the issue of interpretation. The fact that, in all the thousands of years since this word was chosen by the biblical author, there has not been complete agreement on how to interpret it is a hint that we cannot expect to neatly classify and fully comprehend God's dealings with humankind. As Paul said in writing to the Corinthians, "now we see through a glass darkly" (1 Cor. 13:12). What is the significance of this being the first word of the Bible? In our exegetical assumptions we are postulating that every word of Genesis chapter 1 was chosen with care and for a purpose. Leon Kass asks regarding the Bible's first creation story, "Why this kind of beginning?"[121]

Blocher's statement that "the first verse of Genesis breaks with all the mythologies of the ancient East,"[122] is not quite strong enough. In fact, it is the first *word* of Genesis that throws out a challenge to the worldviews of the ancient Near East. The Bible begins with the word "beginning" which was a foreign concept to the cyclic worldviews of the ancient Near East. History had a beginning: that was new news! And if something has a beginning, it will have an ending. The writer of Hebrews affirms: "In the beginning, O Lord, you laid the foundations of the earth, and the heavens are the work of your hands. They will perish, but you remain; they will all wear out like a garment ..." (Heb. 1:10, 11). The concept of an end to history was not in the worldview of the ancient peoples. Archaeologist and biblical scholar, Jack Finegan, author of *Light from the Ancient Past: The Archaeological Background of the Hebrew-Christian Religion,* states that the big change with Israelite doctrine "was the revelation that time runs on from its beginning into a future that is always new and different. Time moves toward some culmination, the ultimate intent of which cannot be outside the purpose of God."[123]

In his book, *Science and Creation: From Eternal Cycles to an Oscillating Universe*, physicist-theologian Jaki shows that this concept of purposeful history, traced to the very first word of Genesis, was the origin of the cosmology that eventually made it possible for science to arise in Judeo-Christian western culture. By contrast, he says, there has been a stillbirth of science in all cultures throughout history that have had a cosmology that reflects a view of nature caught in an eternal

---

[121] Kass, *Beginning*, 26.

[122] Blocher, *In the Beginning*, 62.

[123] Jack Finegan, *In the Beginning: A Journey through Genesis* (New York: Harper & Brothers, 1962), 16.

cyclic treadmill.[124] Only a belief in a beginning originating from a
rational, orderly Creator could give people the confidence to experiment
and systematically investigate the orderly laws by which the world
operates. John Walton agrees: "the order and function established and
maintained by God renders the cosmos both purposeful and intelligible.
So there is reason or motivation for studying the detailed nature of
creation, which we now call science.[125]

In the creation literature of the ancient Near East there is no parallel
to the opening word of Genesis 1.[126] The epics of the ancient Near East
traditionally opened with the equivalent of the Hebrew word "*beyom*"
meaning "on the day that," or "when."[127] For instance, the Babylonian
creation epic, the *Enuma Elish*, begins, "When on high ...." "Once upon
a time" might be an equivalent contemporary phrase. But the author of
Genesis breaks from that tradition and uses the word "*bereshit*" (literally
"in beginning") as an adverb "standing majestically alone"[128] and
without literary parallel at the beginning of the inspired Word of God.

In addition to conveying a sense of direction and purpose to creation
and history, the biblical context of the opening word of Genesis causes
it to convey something else. Something existed before the beginning. As
evangelical theologian-philosopher Francis Schaeffer says in his book,
Genesis in Space and Time, "although Genesis begins, 'in the
beginning,' that does not mean that there was not anything before
that."[129] Examples from Scripture include:

"You loved me before the creation of the world" (John 17:24).

"[God] chose us in him before the creation of the world" (Eph. 1:4).

"Christ ... was destined before the foundation of the world but was
made manifest at the end of the times for your sake" (1 Pet. 1:19, 20).

Schaeffer continues, "something existed before creation and that
something was personal and not static; the Father loved the Son; there
was a plan, there was communication; and promises were made prior to

---

[124] Stanley Jaki, *Science and Creation: From Eternal Cycles to an Oscillating
Universe* (New York: Science History Publications, 1974), 356.

[125] Walton, *Lost World*, 51.

[126] Bruce Waltke, "The Creation Account in Genesis 1: Part 3, The Initial
Chaos Theory and the Precreation Chaos Theory," *Bibliotheca Sacra* 132 [1975]: 224.

[127] Alexander Heidel, *The Babylonian Genesis*, 2nd ed. (Chicago: University
of Chicago Press, 1951), 95.

[128] Jaki, *Genesis*, 2.

[129] Francis Schaeffer, *Genesis in Space and Time* (Glendale: Regal Books,
1972), 16.

the creation of the heavens and the earth."[130] In imitation of the first words of Genesis, the Gospel of John says, "In the beginning already was the Word and the Word already was with God and the Word already was God. Through him all things were made." (Schaeffer proposes that John 1:1-3 should be translated with the Greek imperfect tense, "already was," rather than "was.)[131]

Wisdom also existed before the beginning: "From eternity I [wisdom] was appointed, from the beginning [*mereshit*], from before the world existed. When there were no deep oceans I was born ... when he marked out the foundations of the earth, then I was beside him as a master craftsman" (Prov. 8:23ff, NET Bible).

In addition to "wisdom" and the relationship between the Father and the Son that existed before the beginning, Ezekiel 28 shows a fallen cherub's existence before the beginning, presumed by many evangelical commentators to be Satan.[132] "You were the model of perfection, full of wisdom and perfect in beauty. ... You were blameless in your ways from the day you were created until wickedness was found in you. So I drove you in disgrace from the mount of God and I expelled you, O guardian cherub ... . Your heart became proud ... and you corrupted your wisdom" (Ezek. 28:12, 15-17). It is important to note the role of this created being in opposing God's created order after his fall. This opposition to God's good intentions for creation, and the results of the opposition, *tohu wabohu*, will be explained in detail in a later chapter.

Genesis chapter 1 opens the biblical record by showing God's intention to relentlessly oppose this opposition to his purposes by starting over as often as necessary. The interpretive translation presented in the previous chapter for verses 1-5 reads:

> *In one of God's new beginnings God re-fashioned everything in nature, as the author of Genesis knew it, because the land had been destroyed and left desolate after the disastrous consequences of conditions contrary to God's will. But God had not given up on the land and its people. The Spirit of God was stirring over the deep chaos that was blanketed by darkness. At the right time God said, "Let there be light," and there it was! God saw that the light was good and he separated the light from the darkness. He called the light "day" and the darkness "night." So after evening, there was morning, one day.*

---

[130] Schaeffer, *Genesis*, 18.

[131] Schaeffer, *Genesis*, 22

[132] Unger, *Unger's Commentary*, 5. Also see the discussion in chapter 3, footnote 78.

To explain the choices made in this interpretive translation and to show how it relates to understanding the purposes of God in history, upcoming chapters will examine in detail many of the key words of the first two verses of Genesis.

Particulars about "Beginnings"

Missiologist-church historian Ralph Winter sees Genesis 1:1 as one of a number of new beginnings in the Bible,[133] each of which comes after a crisis. Other new beginnings in the Bible include:

- Noah's family rescued in the Ark, following the destructive Flood.
- The calling of Abraham, following the confusion of languages.
- The Exodus, following the "nothingness" and despair of slavery in Egypt.
- The restoration of the Jewish people to their land after deportation to Babylon.
- The coming of Jesus, following centuries of apostasy by Israel and the 400 years of an absence of hearing from God (the "inter-testamental" period). Jesus' coming was accompanied by the chaos of Herod's slaughter of the boy babies and Jesus' demonstration of fighting back against chaos by casting out many demons.
- Pentecost, following the confusion of the disciples after Jesus' death, resurrection, and ascension.
- Followers of Jesus becoming new creations in Christ (2 Cor. 5:17), renewed after living lives of slavery to the god of this age.
- The new heaven and new earth, finally ending the groanings of creation (Rom. 8:20-22) and thousands of years of troubled history on this planet.

"Beginning" is a key word for the biblical story and very appropriate as the first word of that story. This opening word of the Bible leaves room for the eternal existence of God prior to any earthly beginning. The author of Genesis does not follow the example of the other creation stories of the ancient Near East that explain the origins of the gods. God always existed from before the beginning and does not need to be explained. "Before anything began to be, God was."[134]

---

[133] Winter, *Frontiers*, 49.
[134] Renckens, *Israel's Concept*, 82.

Translating the Opening Phrases of Genesis 1

But should the opening word *bereshit,* that includes the prefix *"be"* (and does not include the definite article, "the"), be translated "in the beginning" or "in *a* beginning"? Should we take the first verse as an independent clause or as subordinate to the second or third verse? Here is where technical details of the context get complicated, with no consensus. In his commentary on Genesis, John Gibson explains,

> The two first verses of the Bible are so familiar that we rarely give them the attention they deserve. When we do begin to think about what they mean, we find that they are full of difficulties. We will have to spend a long time on them if we wish to do justice to their message for their own age and restate it authentically for our own. Because of some unusual features in the Hebrew, they are difficult even to translate.[135]

Gordon Wenham provides the most complete list of the possibilities for the clause structure of Genesis 1:1-3[136] so his categories will be used as the basis for comparing the views, and the rationale for those views, of several major commentators and scholars.

OPTIONS FOR INTERPRETING THE CLAUSES OF GENESIS 1:1-3 AND
VIEWS OF COMMENTATORS ON EACH OPTION

Gordon Wenham's First Category

Verse 1 is a temporal clause subordinate to the main clause in verse 2: "In the beginning when God created ... the earth was without form...."

Commentators' Opinions

> <u>Wenham</u>: this view was first proposed by Ibn Ezra but has little support. It presupposes the existence of chaotic pre-existent matter before the work of creation began.

Gordon Wenham's Second Category

Verse 1 is a temporal clause subordinate to the main clause in verse 3 (verse 2 is a parenthetic comment): "In the beginning <u>when</u> God created (now the earth was formless) <u>then</u> God said ...."

---

[135] John C. Gibson, *Daily Study Bible Series: Genesis* (Louisville, KY: Westminster, John Knox Press, 1981), 1:14.

[136] Wenham, *Genesis,* 11.

Commentators' Opinions

> <u>Wenham</u>: does not favor this view that was first proposed by the ancient Jewish rabbi, Rashi. This interpretation observes that *berehsit* does not have the definite article "the." It presupposes the existence of chaotic pre-existent matter before the work of creation began.

> <u>Derek Kidner</u>: Grammatically Genesis 1:1 could be translated as introducing a clause completed in verse 3 after a parenthetical verse 2: "When God began to create ... (the earth was without form ...), God said, Let there be light."[137] But Kidner favors the fourth, traditional interpretation, which he considers to be equally valid.

> <u>Robert Alter</u>: Following the source criticism school of thought, Alter assigns Genesis 1 to the priestly "P" author and assumes that he begins his account, according to the general convention of opening formulas for ancient Near Eastern creation epics, with an introductory adverbial clause, "When God began to create heaven and earth ..."[138]

> <u>Terrence Fretheim</u> quotes, with approval, The New Jewish Version: "When God began to create the heaven and the earth— the earth being unformed and void, with the darkness over the surface of the deep and a wind from God sweeping over the water—God said, Let there be light."[139]

> <u>Several other versions</u> of the Bible follow this interpretation: New Revised Standard Version, Good News Translation, and the Living Bible.

Gordon Wenham's Third Category

Verse 1 is a main clause, summarizing all the events described in the chapter. It is a title to the chapter as a whole.

Commentators' Opinions

> <u>Wenham</u>: The third view presupposes the existence of chaotic pre-existent matter before the work of creation began.

---

[137] Derek Kidner, *Genesis: An Introduction and Commentary* (Downers Grove: InterVarsity, 1967), 43.

[138] Alter, *Biblical Narrative*, 142.

[139] Terrence E. Fretheim, *Creation, Fall, and Flood: Studies in Genesis 1–11* (Minneapolis: Augsburg, 1969), 54.

<u>Karl Barth</u>: "The created reality of heaven and earth [is] summarily described in vs. 1."[140]

<u>Umberto Cassuto</u> sees the first verse as an independent sentence that serves as an introduction and majestic summary of the rest of the chapter.[141]

<u>Henri Blocher</u> states that he agrees with Young, Westermann, Waltke, Cassuto, Beauchamp, and von Rad "in retaining the reading of the ancient versions. It avoids ascribing a difficult construction to the text and is more suitable for the first verse of the Bible, the opening of a majestic passage. 'In the beginning God created' acts as a title, as Beauchamp and others have seen."[142]

Blocher does not distinguish between those who see Genesis 1:1 as a title that presupposes a creation before Genesis 1:1 and those who see this verse in the more traditional view as the title for the description of the first act of creation. Both of these views agree that the verse is an independent sentence.

<u>Bruce Waltke</u> examines lexical and grammatical arguments in great detail. He asks, "Is *bereshit* in the construct or absolute state? If it is construct [such as, 'at the beginning,' or 'from the beginning'], then verse 1 is a dependent clause. If it is in the absolute state the traditional rendering will stand."[143] Although Waltke acknowledges that *bereshit* is nearly always used in the construct state, indicating a dependent clause, he feels the one exception in Isaiah 46:10 ("I make known the end from the beginning") shows that the word can legitimately be considered to be in the absolute state in Genesis 1:1, with a temporal meaning. He further argues that if Moses had wanted to be unambiguous he could have used the "infinite construct" as in Genesis 2:4: "When they were created [*behibara*]." Apparently Waltke thinks the author could have chosen to omit the word *reshit* and start the first verse as he ended the passage if his clear intention had been to begin the passage as other ancient literature often began.

---

[140] Karl Barth, *Church Dogmatics Study Edition 13: The Doctrine of Creation*, trans. G. W. Bromiley and et al (London: T&T Clark, 2010), 3:103.

[141] Cassuto, *Genesis*, 20.

[142] Blocher, *In the Beginning*, 62.

[143] Waltke, "Creation Account: Part 3," 222.

Waltke sees no problem with the absence of the definite article. He refers to Alexander Heidel who states that terms like *reshith* (beginning), *rosh*, (beginning), *qedem* (olden times) and *olam*, (eternity), "when used in adverbial expressions, occur almost invariably without the article, and that in the absolute state."[144]

According to Waltke, an even more convincing argument that the word should be understood as an absolute is the fact that "all ancient versions (LXX, Vulgate, Aquila, Targum Onkelos) construed the form as absolute and verse 1 as an independent clause."[145]

Waltke concludes that the chaotic state described in verse 2 existed before the creation spoken of in the Bible, and he understands verse 1 as an independent clause and verse 2 as a circumstantial clause connected with verse 3. "According to this view, verse 1 is a summary statement, or formal introduction, which is epexegeted in the rest of the narrative. It appears to this author that this is the only viewpoint that completely satisfies the demands of Hebrew grammar."[146]

NET Bible: The editors agree with Waltke that the word translated "beginning" is in the absolute state rather than the construct (which would be translated, "when God created"). "In other words, the clause in v. 1 is a main clause, v. 2 has three clauses that are descriptive and supply background information, and v. 3 begins the narrative sequence proper. The referent of the word 'beginning' [of what?] has to be defined from the context since there is no beginning or ending with God."

The NET Bible's editors see the verse as a summary statement of the rest of the chapter, about God's creating the world "as we know it." It is interesting that the editors did not say, "as they knew it" which could only have been the case, since the ancient Hebrews had no concept of the world as we now know it. The editors conclude that Genesis itself does not account for the original creation of matter but this does not deny that the Bible teaches that God created everything out of nothing—it simply says that Genesis is not where that is taught. This view

---

[144] Heidel, *Genesis*, 92.
[145] Waltke, "Creation Account: Part 3," 223.
[146] Waltke, "Creation Account: Part 3," 225, 226.

presupposes matter that existed before the Genesis 1 creation account.

Allen Ross, an evangelical professor of Old Testament at Beeson Divinity School, summarizes this option for interpreting the grammar of Genesis 1:1: "In view of the syntax of the first three verses and the meanings of all the words chosen, the view of Gerhard von Rad seems to carry the most exegetical support. That is, verse 1 is the summary statement of the contents of chapter 1. ... The first day of creation would actually begin with verse 3, although verse 2 provides the circumstances. The chapter records the bringing of creation as we know it out of chaos. For the initial creation, ... one has to look elsewhere in the Bible."[147]

John Walton points out that the phrase repeated at the beginning and ending of the creation story, "the heavens and the earth" (Gen. 1:1; 2:1), indicates that the creation referred to in Genesis 1:1 is recounted in the seven days. "This suggests that verse 1 is a literary introduction to the rest of the chapter."[148]

Richard Averbeck, professor of Old Testament and Semitic languages at Trinity Evangelical Divinity School, states regarding the grammar of Genesis 1:1, "I take it to be an independent clause serving as a title announcing the subject of Gen. 1, not the actual beginning of God's creation work in the chapter."[149]

Gordon Wenham's Fourth Category

Verse 1 is a main clause describing the first act of creation. Verses 2 and 3 describe the subsequent phases in God's creative activity.

Views of Commentators

Wenham: This is the traditional view and he adopted this in his translation. Wenham bases his choice on the presupposition that Genesis 1 has to explain the original creation of everything out of nothing. He rejects the first three options because they "presuppose the existence of chaotic pre-existent matter before the work of creation began."[150]

---

[147] Ross, *Creation*, 723.
[148] Walton, *Lost World*, 45.
[149] Averbeck, "A Literary Day," 10.
[150] Wenham, *Genesis*, 11.

Sailhamer follows this view when he states that no time limitations are placed on that "beginning" period when God created the universe.[151] Therefore the following verses are describing subsequent phases of creation.

Walter Kaiser analyzes verse 1 as an independent clause (for reasons mentioned below), but he does not make clear whether he believes the sentence is functioning as a title or as the first act of creation since he is mainly interested in clarifying the literary style of the chapter (history, myth, etc.). Since Kaiser tends to make conservative choices, I have put his comments under the fourth, traditional, view. Kaiser sees Genesis 1:1 as an independent sentence for these reasons:

a. The Massoretes, in their copies of the Hebrew text, used the symbol that resembles our colon [:] which shows the end of a sentence, indicating their early understanding of the verse as an independent clause.

b. The ancient versions treat the verse as an independent clause.

c. The position of the subject prior to the verb in verse 2 (rather than the usual order of the subject following the verb) indicates that the second verse contains subordinate clauses to verse 3.[152]

Kidner considers the familiar translation, "In the beginning God ..." to be just as valid grammatically as beginning with "When God ..." He favors this fourth view because it affirms "unequivocally the truth laid down elsewhere (Heb. 11:3) that until God spoke, nothing existed."[153]

Todd Beall: "Gen 1:1 is not a title or a summary but instead (since it begins with a verb in the perfect tense) is itself the first act of creation."[154]

---

[151]. Sailhamer, *Genesis Unbound*, 29.

[152] Walter C. Kaiser, "The Literary Form of Genesis 1–11," in *New Perspectives in the Old Testament*, ed. J. B. Payne (Waco, TX: Word, 1970), 58.

[153] Kidner, *Genesis*, 43.

[154] Todd S. Beall, Response to John Collins, "Reading Genesis 1–2 with the Grain: Analogical Days," in *Reading Genesis 1–2: An Evangelical Conversation*, ed. J. Daryl Charles (Peabody, MA: Hendrickson, 2013), 96.

SUMMARY AND EVALUATION OF THE OPTIONS FOR TRANSLATING
  GENESIS 1:1

A number of commentators base their ultimate choice for how to
interpret the grammar on the interpretation that most easily supports
creation out of nothing, rather than implying something existing before
the beginning. This is an example of ideological texture.

With the traditional interpretation (Genesis 1:1 is describing the
origin of the universe out of nothing), either a gap must be
acknowledged between verses 1 and 2 or it has to be said that God
originally created the earth to be *tohu wabohu*—destroyed, desolate, and
inhospitable for life. Since the other planets in our solar system could be
described as inhospitable for life, this may not be as difficult to accept
as some have thought, who have Isaiah 45:18 in mind: "He who created
the heavens, ... who fashioned and made the earth, ... he did not create
it to be empty [*tohu*], but formed it to be inhabited."

It is hard to argue, however, with Bruce Waltke's carefully reasoned
position, seeing Genesis 1:1 as an independent summary statement for
the chapter. In the end, with any of the interpretations, we can
acknowledge that God is the ultimate Creator of everything, some of
that creation has been inhospitable for life either before or after Genesis
1:1, so God fashioned or re-fashioned the earth to be a place where life
could exist.

Scribal Inter-texture Word Studies

According to the ideological perspective we are developing, Genesis
1 is the story of a new beginning. God is re-fashioning the land that was
destroyed and desolate due to conditions contrary to God's will. He is
starting over with a new set of conditions. An inter-textual study of the
Hebrew word *reshit* translated as "beginning" in Genesis 1:1, shows that
interpreting this "beginning" as one among many new beginnings is
compatible with the usage of the word. *Reshit* often refers to an
indefinite period of time at the beginning of a sequence of events rather
than to a specific starting point (for which another Hebrew word exists).
Sailhamer bases his interpretation on this meaning when he says about
the first verse (referring to the original creation of the universe), "no
time limitations are placed on that period."[155]

Examples of the use in the Old Testament of the word *reshit*
(Strong's #7225) include:

The beginning of his kingdom (Gen. 10:10, KJV).

---

[155] Sailhamer, *Genesis Unbound*, 29.

The <u>beginning</u> of my strength. When Jacob blessed his sons he said to Reuben, "you are my firstborn, ... the <u>first sign</u> of my strength" (Gen. 49:3, NIV).

The first of the <u>firstfruits</u> of the land (Exod. 23:19, KJV). (Firstfruits seems to be the most common use of the term *reshit.*)

From the <u>beginning</u> of the year to its end; an indefinite period of time, not an instant (Deut. 11:12, KJV).

Wisdom is the <u>principal</u> thing (Prov. 4:7, KJV).

I [wisdom] was appointed from eternity, <u>from the beginning,</u> before the world began (Prov. 8:22, KJV).

The <u>beginning</u> of strife (Prov. 17:14, KJV; or "starting a quarrel," NIV).

Declaring the end <u>from the beginning</u> (Isa. 46:10, KJV).

In the <u>beginning</u> of the reign of Jehoiakim (Jer. 26:1, KJV).

<u>Early</u> in the reign of Zedekiah (Jer. 49:34, KJV)

You who live in Lachish, ... you were the <u>beginning</u> of sin to the Daughter of Zion [gives a sense of origins] (Mic. 1:13, KJV).

Another word for "beginning" is the word for a definite starting point: *t'ghillah* (Strong's # 8462). Examples of this use in the Old Testament of the word *t'ghillah* include:

Where his tent had been at the <u>beginning</u> (Gen. 13:3, KJV).

Still ill favoured, as at the <u>beginning</u> (Gen. 41:21, KJV).

In our sacks at the <u>first time</u> (Gen. 43:18, KJV).

Which of us shall go up <u>first</u> (Judg. 20:18, KJV).

In the <u>beginning</u> of barley harvest (Ruth 1:22, KJV).

The fear of the Lord is the <u>beginning</u> of wisdom (Prov. 9:10, KJV).

Harris, Archer, and Waltke, in the *Theological Wordbook of the Old Testament,* explain that *reshit* may refer to the initiation of a series of historical events (Gen. 10:10; Jer. 6:1); it may indicate a foundational or necessary condition such as the fear of God (Ps. 111:10; Prov. 1:7); the initiation of a life (Job 8:7); or the best of a group or class of things to be set aside for God ("firstfruits" [Lev. 2:12]).

Considering the evidence for the use of *reshit* and that other words were available to the author if he had wanted to convey a definite starting point, it would seem to be reasonable to postulate that "in the beginning" (or more accurately, "in beginning") refers to an indefinite period of time which could have stretched both backwards, before creation, and forwards into the early events of creation. Since *reshit* does not refer to a definite starting point, the translation, "in one of God's new beginnings" would seem to be a valid interpretation. If the definite article had been used this translation would have been problematic, but since the article is not used, it would seem permissible to suggest that the text may be intentionally ambiguous.

Views of Commentators on Genesis 1:1 as a New Beginning

A number of respected scholars agree that Genesis 1:1 does not refer to the beginning of "everything" but to something more recent—a "relative beginning" or a "new beginning." The following summaries and quotations support this interpretation.

TERRENCE E. FRETHEIM

> "When God began to create the heaven and the earth—the earth being unformed and void, with the darkness over the surface of the deep and a wind from God sweeping over the water—God said, Let there be light" (*The New Jewish Version*).

Fretheim prefers this translation and says this means the time involved would be relative, sometime in the past, but not the absolute beginning of time. "This would appear to be the meaning of the word 'beginning' in Isaiah 46:10 [I make known the end from the beginning (*reshit*)]."[156]

ALLEN ROSS

Three quotations from Allen Ross's substantial volume, *Creation and Blessing*, demonstrate his position on Genesis 1 as a new beginning.

> "In the beginning" is a relative beginning in which the cosmos was reshaped for the latecomer—man. Brought into existence before sin entered the universe (Ezek. 28; Isa. 14), the original earth was designed to be the habitation of God's first sinless angelic creatures (Job 38; Isa. 45). This sinless earth was

---

[156] Fretheim, *Creation,* 54.

evidently the place where sin began in God's hitherto sinless universe in connection with the revolt of Satan.[157]

In the first part of Genesis 1:2, there is ... an ominous, uncomfortable tone. The clauses describe not the results of divine creation but a chaos at the earliest stage of this world. It is not the purpose of Genesis to tell the reader how the chaos came about. ... The expositor must draw some conclusions from other passages with similar descriptions. If one can posit that the fall of Satan (Ezek. 28) brought about the chaos in God's original creation, then Genesis 1 describes a re-creation, or God's first act of redemption, salvaging his world and creating all things new.[158]

The chapter records the bringing of creation as we know it out of chaos. For the initial creation, or original creation, one has to look elsewhere in the Bible. This view ... recognizes that "beginnings" with God are not necessarily absolute beginnings.[159]

JOHN H. SAILHAMER

Sailhamer contributes the insight that he sees two separate time periods in Genesis 1:

1. The absolute beginning when God first created the universe—"no time limitations are placed on that period."[160]

2. Genesis 1:2–2:4a: God prepared the Garden of Eden for humans to live in—"that activity occurred in one week."[161]

As we discussed in the inter-textual word study,

The Hebrew word *reshit* has a very specific sense in Scripture. It always refers to an extended yet indeterminate duration of time—not a specific moment. It refers to a duration of time which falls before a series of events.[162]

God created the universe during an indeterminate period of time before the actual reckoning of a sequence of time began. Other Hebrew words were available to the author to convey the

---

[157] Ross, *Creation,* 719.
[158] Ross, *Creation,* 107.
[159] Ross, *Creation,* 723.
[160] Sailhamer, *Genesis Unbound,* 29.
[161] Sailhamer, *Genesis Unbound,* 29.
[162] Sailhamer, *Genesis Unbound,* 38.

temporal concept of a "beginning." He could have used a Hebrew word similar to the English word "start" or "initial point."[163]

Sailhamer considers Genesis 1:1 to be the description of the original, universal creation, in summary form. So he sees a gap before a local re-creation starts in verse 3 rather than a creation before Genesis 1:1, which is Unger's preference and the view being developed here.

MERRILL F. UNGER

Unger considers that it is "more likely that verse 1 [of Genesis 1] refers to a relative beginning rather than the absolute beginning. The chapter would then be accounting for the creation of the universe as man knows it, not *the* beginning of everything, and verses 1-2 would provide the introduction to it. The fall of Satan and entrance of sin into God's original creation would precede this."[164]

BRUCE K. WALTKE

According to Waltke, "'beginning' refers to the entire created event, the six days of creation, not something before the six days. ... This is a relative beginning. As verse 2 seems to indicate, there is a pre-Genesis time and space."[165] Waltke agrees with the view "that ... sees the chaotic state described in verse 2 as existing before the creation spoken of in the Bible.[166]

RALPH D. WINTER

Like Sailhamer, missiologist Ralph Winter saw Genesis 1 as a description of a local new beginning in the Middle East.[167] In Winter's ideological perspective, this new beginning comes after a major disaster had wiped out life in part of a pre-Genesis 1:1 creation. This disaster may have been the result of judgment, as is the case prior to other biblical new beginnings. In Winter's view, the origin and Fall of Satan and the existence of the vicious life forms seen in the fossil record all belong to this pre-Genesis 1:1 creation. Genesis 1 shows God preparing a land for a new humanity, made in God's image, for the purpose of

---

[163] Sailhamer, *Genesis Unbound*, 40, 41.
[164] Unger, *Unger's Commentary*, 5.
[165] Waltke, *Genesis*, 58.
[166] Waltke, "Creation Account: Part 3," 225.
[167] Winter, *Frontiers*, 318.

working with him to bring order out of chaos and to defeat the intentions of the adversary.

Summary and Looking Ahead

"In beginning," God was demonstrating that chaos is not God's will. Jewish scholar and educator, Leon Kass, notes that,

> Creation is bringing order out of chaos largely through acts of separation, division, distinction. Separating or dividing is the means of addressing and holding at bay the twin unruly conditions of the beginning-before-the-beginning: darkness and the watery chaos.[168]

The image of the dawn shaking the darkness and the wicked out of the earth, just as a Bedouin might shake the bed bugs out of his blanket or garments in the morning, illustrates what God was doing in Genesis 1. The "good" light defeats the feared darkness.

When Moses' original audience heard that "darkness was on the face of the deep," what parallels might they have seen to their own new beginning, their creation as a new people, out of the chaos of slavery? Did they see a similarity between their own experience of being "brought out of darkness" (Ps. 107:14) and the description in the first verses of Genesis of God beginning to create?

How did the original audience hear and understand the introduction to the opening chapter of Genesis, "In beginning, God created the heavens and the earth"? In the next chapter we will explore what it meant for God to "create," both physically and spiritually, and what is encompassed by "the heavens and earth," a literary term that means more than the sum of its parts.

---

[168] Kass, *Beginning*, 32.

Chapter Five
God Created Everything and Every Possibility

Images of Creation

In the beginning God created the heavens and the earth.
(Gen. 1:1)

In the beginning was the Word,
and the Word was with God,
and the Word was God.
He was with God in the beginning.
Through him all things were made;
without him nothing was made that has been made.
(John 1:1-3)

In these last days he has spoken to us by his Son,
whom he appointed heir of all things,
and through whom also he made the universe.
(Heb. 1:2)

Ah Sovereign Lord, you have made the heavens and the earth by your great
power and outstretched arm. Nothing is too hard for you.
(Jer. 32:17)

Create in me a clean heart, O God,
and renew a right spirit within me.
(Ps. 51:10, ESV)

General Overview

What did Moses' original audience hear in the majestic first words
God spoke to them through Moses?

Bereshit bara elohim et hashamayim we'et ha'eretz.

In beginning, God created—EVERYTHING! Every possibility. The
"heavens and the earth" speak of the totality of everything that exists or
could exist—physically, spiritually, relationally. God created land, sky,
and water; he created everything and every possibility that can move

and function in those venues, including people, societies, new hearts—everything![169]

The first verse of the Bible is an introduction not only to Genesis chapter 1, but to the whole Bible. It is an introduction to God's revelation of himself to humankind, given first to God's chosen people who were coming out of slavery in Egypt into a new land that God was preparing for them. The truth spoken Genesis 1:1 is the first thing God wanted his people to be aware of—the first, the principal, the most important (*reshit*): God is the source of everything and of every possibility.

With the recent events of the Exodus foremost in their minds, the Hebrew people would no doubt have seen echoes of those events in the imagery of Genesis 1: the fearful darkness, the watery deep that was a barrier to escaping from the Egyptians, the breath and spirit of God slashing a separation of the waters so the people could walk through on dry land and live. The story of creation was preparing the newly-emerging nation of Israel to understand Moses' explanation of their dramatically changing identity from slaves in Egypt to "a kingdom of priests" (Exod. 19:6) in God's cosmic temple of creation.[170]

When God had finished creating (*bara*), bringing order out of chaos, "he rested on the seventh day from all his work which he had made [*asah*]" (Gen. 2:2, KJV). John Walton describes this climax of creation:

> Deity rests in a temple, and only in a temple. This is what temples [in the ancient Near East] were built for. We might even say that this is what a temple is—a place for divine rest. ... The most central truth to the creation account is that *this world is a place for God's presence*"[171] (emphasis added).

In a later chapter we will look at a Johannine supplement to God's revelation of his purposes and we will see that not only did God create the world to be a place for his presence, but God specifically intends for *people* to be his dwelling place. At the end of history we find this desire fulfilled, that had failed in the first chapters of Genesis: "God's dwelling

---

[169] Gordon Wenham agrees with the translation, "In the beginning God created everything." See Wenham, *Genesis*, 15. Richard Averbeck also supports this interpretation: "The expression 'the heavens and the earth' at the end of v. 1 is a *merismus*; that is, the two opposite parts refer to the whole of the created order" (Averbeck, "A Literary Day," 10).

[170] John Walton sees Genesis 1 as "describing the creation of the cosmic temple with all of its functions and with God dwelling in its midst" (Walton, *Lost World*, 84).

[171] Walton, *Lost World*, 71, 84.

place is now among the people, and he will dwell with them. They will be his people, and God himself will be with them and be their God" (Rev. 21:3).

Particular Word Studies Related to God's Creation of Everything

Bara Elohim *(God Created;* bara: *Strong's # 1254)*

In the context of an adversary that is hostile to God's will for humans and creation to flourish, God exercised his creativity to make it possible for his will to be accomplished. The goal of God's creative activity was a place where his glory could dwell among creatures who would freely choose heaven's rule and, in turn, implement it. God intends that "the earth will be filled with the knowledge of the glory of the Lord as the waters cover the sea" (Isa. 11:9; Hab. 2:14). "God said, 'Let us make [*asah*] mankind in our image, in our likeness, so that they may rule ... over all the creatures ...'" (Gen. 1:26).

An inter-texture study[172] of representative examples of the use of the Hebrew word for "create," *bara*, lends support to the legitimacy of the interpretation of Genesis 1:1 as the introduction to an account of the refashioning of a previously judged and destroyed earth. A concordance search of the Hebrew word *bara* shows that often this word is in the context of re-creating something.

> Create in me a clean heart, O God (Ps. 51:10, ESV).

> In that day ... the Lord ...will cleanse the bloodstains from Jerusalem by a spirit of judgment and a spirit of fire. Then the Lord will create over all of Mount Zion and over those who assemble there a cloud of smoke by day and a glow of flaming fire by night; over all the glory will be a canopy (Isa. 4:2-5).

> I have seen their ways, but I will heal them; I will guide them and restore comfort to Israel's mourners, creating praise on their lips (Isa. 57:18, 19).

> I create new heavens and a new earth (Isa. 65:17).

> When you send your Spirit, they are created, and you renew the face of the ground (Ps. 104:30).

---

[172] See the explanation in chapter two of the textures of socio-rhetorical analysis.

A grammatical study of the word *bara* shows that in the *kal* and *niphal* forms it is always God who creates. But in the *piel* form (added intensity), people are the subject of *bara*, being told to *bereta* (cut down) a forest of trees (Josh. 17:15, 18), to clear the ground and make a place for themselves to live. The reference in Joshua, in the *piel* form, is to bringing order to uninhabitable forest land, turning an uninhabitable land into a well-arranged, cultivated, and life-supporting territory. "The hill country shall be yours, for though it is a forest, you shall <u>clear it</u> (*bara*) and possess it to its farthest borders" (Josh. 17:18, ESV). So this rare use of the word *bara* is also important as another implication of the disorder preceding the creation events that could have been understood by the original audience in hearing Genesis 1:1, 2 spoken aloud. It also hints at the theme repeated throughout Genesis 1 of evening followed by morning: that humans can imitate God in the creative process by making uninhabitable areas become inhabitable, metaphorically causing evening to become morning, darkness to become light, what is chaotic to become ordered.

Other shades of meaning for *bara* come from closely associated, similar-sounding Hebrew words including, *barach* ("bless," mentioned by Gordon Wenham[173]) and *barar* ("cleanse," mentioned by Tayler Lewis[174]). Creation as blessing and creation as cleansing are helpful additional associations that would have possibly been caught by the original listening audience through the similar sounds of the Hebrew words.

The sense of cleansing and purifying combined with the sense of cutting away or slashing what is unhelpful for life (compare Hebrews 4:12: "The word of God is ... sharper than any double-edged sword") is seen in the use of *bara* in Psalm 51:1, ESV: "Create in me a clean heart, O God, and renew a right spirit within me." So creation is a clearing up, a cleansing, a purifying, a bringing into order out of *tohu wabohu,* which we will investigate in great detail in a later chapter.

This conclusion is further confirmed when rare shades of meaning of the synonymous word *asah* "make," are taken into consideration. *Asah* is used synonymously with *bara* in such verses as Genesis 1:26, 31; 2:2, 4 and Jeremiah 32:17. But it can also mean to wash one's feet or to trim one's beard (notice the associations again with cutting and cleaning that are associated with the *piel* form of *bara*):

---

[173] Wenhan, *Genesis*,14.

[174] Tayler Lewis, *The Six Days of Creation; or the Scriptural Cosmology, with the Ancient Idea of Time-World in Distinction from Worlds in Space* (Schenectady: G.V. Van Debogert, 1855), 49.

Wash (*asah*: do / take care of / dress / prepare) one's feet (2 Sam. 19:24).

Trim (*asah*: do / trim) one's beard (2 Sam. 19:24).

John Sailhamer concludes that when Genesis 2:4 says God "made" (*asah*) the heavens and earth (that he had *bara* / created), it means the same as the English expression "to make" a bed.[175] When the land was covered with water it was not inhabitable. God slashed a separation between the waters and commanded the waters below to recede from the land to "make" a place where human life could flourish. The word *bara*, supplemented with the meanings of its *piel* form and its synonym, *asah*, means to put something in good order, to make it right.

In this sense, people today can participate in God's creative activities by doing what we can to put a society or land in good order so that it better reflects the glory and goodness of God—international development.

Hashamayim we'et ha'eretz *(the Heavens and the Earth; Heavens: Strong's # 8064; Earth: Strong's # 776)*

"The heavens declare the glory of God, and the sky above proclaims his handiwork" (Ps. 19:1, ESV).

Like the Psalmist, the original audience of Genesis 1 would have seen the glory of God in creation. "Heavens and earth" evokes the greatness of the Creator God as seen in these examples of the term:

In the beginning God created the heavens and the earth (Gen. 1:1).

The heavens and the earth were completed in all their vast array (Gen. 2:1).

May you be blessed by the Lord, the Maker of heaven and earth (Ps. 115:15).

Lord Almighty, the God of Israel, enthroned between the cherubim, you alone are God over all the kingdoms of the earth. You have made heaven and earth (Isa. 37:16).

As the new heavens and the new earth that I make will endure before me, declares the Lord, so will your name and descendants endure (Isa. 66:22).

---

[175] Sailhamer, *Genesis Unbound*, 107.

> Ah, Sovereign Lord, you have made the <u>heavens and the earth</u> by your great power and outstretched arm. Nothing is too hard for you (Jer. 32:17).

In the majority of uses of this term, the context is that God is the Creator or Maker of "the heavens and the earth," an indication of God's power and authority, extending over other nations. God receives glory and honor, including recognition from leaders of other nations that the God of Israel is unique as the Creator of heaven and earth. His power to help is tied to this phrase. His blessing is special because he is so high above all others that he could create everything. Because God is maker of heaven and earth, "nothing is too hard" for God.

"Heaven and earth" would have conveyed to Moses' hearers and readers more than just the sum of the two main words. As Bruce Waltke says, "it will prove erroneous to study the words 'heavens' and 'earth' in isolation from one another."[176] Gordon Wenham points out that this type of literary term "is characteristic of many languages to describe the totality of something in terms of its extremes. e.g., 'good and bad, 'big and little,' etc."[177] John Sailhamer describes this figure of speech as a "merism" that combines two words that take on a distinct meaning of their own to express a single idea. "A merism expresses 'totality' by combining two contrasts or extremes."[178] He gives an example of a merism in Psalm 139:2: "You know when I sit down and when I rise up" (ESV). The figure of speech means the Lord knows everything about the psalmist. Sailhamer summarizes,

> By linking ... "heavens and earth" the Hebrew language expresses the totality of all that exists. The expression stands for the "entirety of the universe." It includes not only the two extremes but also all that they contain.[179]

Gordon Wenham and Allen Ross are in agreement. Ross says,

> Heavens and earth [is] a poetic expression (merism) signifying the whole universe. Other examples of this poetic device are "day and night" (meaning all the time) and "man and beast" (meaning all created physical beings). "Heaven and earth" thus indicates not only the heaven and the earth but everything in

---

[176] Waltke, "Creation Account: Part 3," 218

[177] Wenham, *Genesis*, 15.

[178] Sailhamer, *Genesis Unbound*, 55.

[179] Sailhamer, *Genesis Unbound*, 56.

them. Genesis 2:4 also uses this expression in a restatement of the work of creation throughout the six days.[180]

Wenham adds that based on this understanding, Genesis 1:1 could therefore be translated, "In beginning, God created everything."[181] This is better than saying "God created the universe," since at the time Moses was writing, the universe as we now know it was unknown. This understanding of "heavens and earth" also raises the thought that God inspired the author to use phrases that can expand in meaning throughout time. What the ancient Hebrews thought "heaven and earth" meant is not the same as what we know today, but both are true.

Commentators often insist that the phrase "heaven and earth" denotes the universe as we know it today, but this is an anachronistic reading of the ancient text. Physicist and Catholic theologian Stanley Jaki bemoans that while Augustine realized that the expression "heaven and earth" was "'carefully chosen by a spiritual man in a manner that is accommodated to unlearned readers or hearers,'" Augustine did not go further and set forth "what 'unlearned men' understood on hearing Genesis 1 recited to them. To this most important task, in which lay the genuine clue to Genesis 1, Augustine failed to address himself."[182] In other words, the original audience hearing Genesis 1 for the first time would not have been thinking in terms of a scientific description of how the universe and planet earth came into existence. Rather they would have taken the term as an idiom for the totality of the visible world, as they knew it, that had its origin with God. The NET Bible illustrates this common mistake among commentators when the editors explain that the first verse of the Bible refers to the beginning of the world as "we" know it, rather than more accurately stating that "heaven and earth" refers to the totality of the world as "they" knew it.

According to John Walton, this totality of "heaven and earth" represents a cosmic temple. The people of the ancient Near East, which would have included the Hebrew people, conceived of deity dwelling in a temple.[183] The Psalmist and the prophet Isaiah inherited this perspective:

---

[180] Ross, *Creation*, 106.

[181] Wenham, *Genesis*, 15.

[182] Jaki, *Genesis*, 86.

[183] "Everyone knew in the ancient world ... to which most modern readers are totally oblivious: Deity rests in a temple, and only in a temple" (Walton, *Lost World*, 71, 72).

Your throne is established from of old; you are from everlasting (Ps. 93:2, ESV).

The Lord has established his throne in heaven, and his kingdom rules over all (Ps. 103:19).

Heaven is my throne, and the earth is my footstool (Isa. 66:1).

"The most central truth to the creation account," says Walton, "is that *this world is a place for God's presence*" (emphasis added).[184]

With the coming of Jesus, God's people became a special, specific place for God's presence. God's people became his temple. "Where two or three are gathered together in my name, there am I in the midst of them" (Matt. 18:20, KJV). "You yourselves are God's temple and ... God's Spirit dwells in your midst" (1 Cor. 3:16). The Johannine community recognized a similar relationship, of God dwelling, or abiding in his people: "If you abide in me and my words abide in you...." (John 15:7, ESV). This shows a reciprocal relationship between God and believers who meet the conditions of belief and love (1 John 4:16). Those who meet these conditions demonstrate evidence of the creation of eternal life in them (see 1 John 2:17: "whoever does the will of God lives forever").

God's people serve as a showcase for what the reign of God should look like, including efforts toward international development to counteract the work of the adversary. In a later chapter we will see that Jesus' appearing on earth was to defeat the works of the devil that are hostile to life and to God's will. God demonstrated his will in the creation of "everything" and every possibility for humans and creation to flourish. In the next chapter we will spend some time exploring the concept of the place God was getting ready for humans to live and flourish.

---

[184] Walton, *Lost World*, 84.

Chapter Six:

Developing the Land

Images of the Land

In the beginning God created the heavens and the earth (eretz). *Now the earth*
(eretz) *was ...*
(Gen. 1:1, 2a)

*And God said, "Let the water under the sky be gathered to one place, and let
dry ground appear." And it was so. God called the dry ground "land"* (eretz)
and the gathered waters he called "seas." And God saw that it was good.
(Gen. 1: 9, 10)

To your descendants I give this land (eretz), *from the Wadi of Egypt to the
great river, the Euphrates—.*
(Gen. 15:18)

*If the hill country of Ephraim is too small for you, go up into the forest and
clear land for yourselves there in the land* (eretz) *of the Perizzites and
Rephaites.*
(Josh. 17:15)

*"This is what the Lord Almighty, the God of Israel, says: 'Tell this to your
masters: With my great power and outstretched arm I made the earth* (eretz),
and its people and the animals that are on it, and I give it to anyone I please.'"
(Jer. 27:4, 5)

General Overview

The account in Genesis 1 of God's making the land helped the
people of Israel see themselves as a community of the people of God,
about to inherit a land made for them by God. The author of the creation
passage certainly knew how to get his readers' and listeners' attention.
The grammar of Genesis 1:2 places a strong emphasis on "the land" by
placing the noun before the verb, which is not usual in Hebrew:
we'ha'eretz hayeta, "now the earth was ...". Allen Ross asks, "Why did
the new nation of Israel need to have this material and to have it written

as it is?"[185] In the particulars section of this chapter we will explore three main possibilities:

1. The people needed to know why the land they were going to enter could legitimately be considered theirs.

2. The process of God's making the uninhabitable "earth" or "land" into a place for people to live serves as metaphor for the creation of a society, the nation of Israel, out of the chaos of slavery.

3. The people could learn important lessons about God and their relationship to him from this creation account.

In addition, we will look at the possibility of understanding Genesis 1 to be referring to a local creation, and the implications of that possibility. A concordance study of the word "earth" reveals that *eretz* can be translated to refer to the whole known earth or to a local area, depending on the context and how the translator thinks it should be interpreted. Within the hermeneutical spiral, in which we keep returning to some of the same words and phrases, after having gathered insights while exploring other aspects of Genesis 1:1, 2, some of the answers to our questions will assume the word *eretz* to refer to the local land. So in order to explore the purposes for which Moses described the *eretz* in Genesis 1:2, we will need to look at the evidence showing it was possible that the original audience would have understood Moses to be referring to a local land, not the whole planet earth and the universe as we know them today, but which were unknown to the ancient Hebrews.

However, in this and later chapters, we will see that the description of a local re-creation, bringing order out of chaos, can also be generalized to apply to the creation of everything else, at both larger and smaller scales. The pattern seen in creation, of overcoming something that was not right with something that was good, is one that God's people can imitate by using the decision-making authority has God delegated to them.

Particular Details about the Land

In exploring the origin of international development we need to take a detailed look in the verse that immediately follows the introduction or title to the creation story, at the first two main words: *eretz* ("land") and *hayeta* ("was," in the emphatic position; root word *hayah*). The emphasis is on the "land." Jewish scholar, Umberto Cassuto, translates

---

[185] Ross, *Creation*, 102.

wa'ha'eretz hayeta: "as for the earth, it was …" and calls attention to the unusual word order. Normally, in Hebrew, the verb precedes the subject, but "whenever the subject comes before the predicate, as here, the intention of the Bible is to give emphasis to the subject and to tell us something new about it."[186]

Scribal Inter-texture Word Studies

We will learn several new things about the importance of the land to the original audience from a detailed study of the first words of Genesis 1:2. As mentioned in chapter two, scribal inter-texture analysis looks at written texts from other parts of Scripture for illumination of the meaning of the text under investigation.

HAYAH (STRONG'S # 1961)

A word study on the verb, *hayah / hayeta* (Strong's #1961), using the *New Englishman's Hebrew Concordance*, shows that this particular verb (from the verb, "to be," in the *kal preterite* form) is often used in association with strong emotions or significant circumstances that need to be particularly noticed or emphasized. Examples include:

Now the earth was *tohu wabohu* … (Gen. 1:2).

Now the serpent was more crafty … (Gen. 3:1).

"I shall be a fugitive and a vagabond on the earth, and it will happen that anyone who finds me will kill me" (Genesis 4:14, NKJV).

The word of the Lord came to [was to] Abram in a vision (Gen. 15:1).

"I am the Lord your God, who brought you out of Egypt to be your God" (Num. 15:41).

We would have become like Sodom, we would have been like Gomorrah (Isa. 1:9).

Now Nineveh was an exceedingly great city, three days' journey in breadth (Jon. 3:3, ESV).

Then he showed me Joshua the high priest standing before the angel of the Lord, and Satan standing at his right hand to accuse

---

[186] Cassuto, *Genesis*, 21.

him. ... Now Joshua <u>was</u> ... clothed with filthy garments (Zech. 3:1, 3, ESV).

In light of these significant, emotionally-laden uses of the verb *hayah/ hayeta*, it seems reasonable to assume that a verse as important as Genesis 1:2, at the beginning of the Hebrew Bible, would also carry the connotation of having a strongly emotional, significant context: "Now the earth was ... ." It calls attention to an important state of the earth that needs to be noticed and understood.

A similar word with the same consonants but different vowel points (Strong's # 1962; *hayyah*) means, "ruin, calamity," which is a further indication that to the original audience, hearing Genesis 1:2 read aloud, the sounds of the spoken Hebrew would have brought to mind images of something with a negative emotional connotation (which we will further explore in the next chapter in a detailed study of the term *tohu wabohu*).

As mentioned earlier, the verb, *hayah / hayeta* in Genesis 1:2, is in the *kal preterite* form. If it were in the passive *niphal* form, it would have been appropriate to translate it "had become," as in Moses' announcement to Israel in Deuteronomy 27:9: "You <u>have</u> now <u>become</u> the people of the Lord your God." But Henri Blocher warns against translating *we'eretz hayeta* as "and the earth became," saying,

> This translation [had become] takes inadmissible liberties with the Hebrew grammar. The only admissible translation is "and or now the earth was," by analogy with constructions that are totally similar in Jonah 3:3 ("now Nineveh was") and Genesis 3:1 ("now the snake was"). Only in defiance of philology may the pseudo-translation "the earth became" act as the basis of the [reconstructionist or gap] theory.[187]

Waltke, a respected contemporary evangelical Hebrew scholar, agrees, pointing to the parallel word construction in Genesis 1:2, Jonah 3:3, and Zechariah 3:3, in which the conjunction, *waw*, is joined to a noun, rather than as usual to a verb, followed by the verb, *hayah*. In Jonah 3:3 ("now Ninevah was") and Zechariah 3:3 ("now Joshua was") the verb *hayah* is translated "was," not, "had become." Waltke concludes, "no modern or ancient versions understand the verb [in Genesis 1:2] in the sense of 'had become.' It would be most unusual for an author to introduce his story with a pluperfect [had become]."[188]

---

[187] Blocher, *In the Beginning*, 43.
[188] Waltke, "Creation Account: Part 3," 227.

But in the end, whether the grammar is taken as meaning "the land was" or "the land had become," the context and the interpretation of that context being developed in this paper indicate that something had existed prior to the conditions described in Genesis 1:2. At the "beginning" of God's creative activity, the earth, or land, was in a negative condition.

ERETZ (STRONG'S # 776)

What was special about "the land," or "the earth" to the people of Israel? Examples of the use of the word *eretz* show that it often refers to a specific local place, an expanse of land that has boundaries, or a country, not always to the whole known world. In fact, in Deuteronomy 4:26, the word is used in both ways.

> In the land of his birth ... (Gen. 11:28).

> To go into the land of Canaan ... (Gen. 11:28, ESV).

> Go from your country, ... to the land I will show you (Gen. 12:1).

> Is not the whole land before thee? (referring to Abram's invitation to Lot to choose the part of the land he wanted to live in, obviously not referring to the whole planet or even the known earth at that time) (Gen. 13:9).

> To your descendants I give this land, from the Wadi of Egypt to the great river, the Euphrates— (a local area circumscribed by its boundaries) (Gen. 15:18).

> I call the heavens and the earth as witnesses against you this day that you will quickly perish from the land that you are crossing the Jordan to possess. You will not live there long but will certainly be destroyed (Deut. 4:26).

> O Lord our Lord, how majestic is your name in all the earth! You have set your glory in the heavens (Ps. 8:1).

With these uses of the word *eretz* in mind, it becomes necessary to apply the exegetical principle of considering what the original audience would have understood by the term in order to interpret the use of this word in Genesis 1:2.

Local Creation

What was Moses' purpose in telling the people about the *eretz* and the need to refashion the negative state of "the earth" or "land" (*eretz*)? To what would the people have thought he was referring? Sailhamer notes, "the medieval Jewish commentator Rashi understood most of the account of Genesis 1 as a direct reference to God's preparation of the promised land."[189] In Rashi's commentary on the Pentateuch he asks,

> What is the reason, then, that [Genesis 1] commences with the account of the creation? Because of the thought expressed in the text (Ps. CXI.6): "He declared to His people the strength of His works (i.e., He gave an account of the work of creation), in order that He might give them the heritage of the nations" for should the peoples of the world say to Israel, "You are robbers, because you took by force the lands of the seven nations of Canaan," Israel may reply to them "All the earth belongs to the Holy One, blessed be He; He created it and gave it to whom He pleased."[190]

Rashi was alluding to Jeremiah 27:5, an understanding of the earth that John Sailhamer feels it would be natural for the people of Israel to have held from their beginning as a nation:[191] "This is what the Lord Almighty, the God of Israel, says: 'Tell this to your masters: With my great power and out-stretched arm I made the earth and its people and the animals that are on it, and I give it to anyone I please'" (Jer. 27:4, 5).

WHAT DID THE ORIGINAL AUDIENCE UNDERSTAND *ERETZ* TO MEAN?

John Sailhamer, a contemporary proponent of the local earth theory,[192] points out that by "paying close attention to how earlier readers understood these two chapters we can gain new insight into the biblical author's intent."[193] In his book, *Genesis Unbound*, Sailhamer states the exegetical assumption we are following in this book:

---

[189] Sailhamer, *Genesis Unbound*, 215.

[190] Morris Rosenbaum and Abraham M. Silbermann, trans., *Pentateuch with Targum Onkelos, Haphtaroth and Prayers for Sabbath and Rashi's Commentary* (London: Shapiro, Vallentine and Co., 1929), 1:2.

[191] Sailhamer, *Genesis Unbound*, 216.

[192] Stephen Webb also advocates reading Genesis 1 as portraying "Eden as a particular place, not the whole of the earth. In other words, there were weeds on our planet, but not in the Garden" (Webb, Dome of Eden, 138).

[193] Sailhamer, *Genesis Unbound*, 11.

> Our task is to read [the first two chapters of Genesis] as the
> author intended them to be understood. ... The primary question
> for any interpreter must always be, What does the text say? ...
> Just because an interpretation is commonly held doesn't mean
> it's correct."[194]

Sailhamer cautions that "today the word 'earth' too easily calls up
images of the whole planet on which we live.[195] The modern view of the
universe should not be allowed to control our understanding of what the
author of Genesis would have meant by "earth." One of Sailhamer's
sources, John Pye Smith, stated in 1854, "a most important inquiry is
the meaning of the word which we render earth."[196] He goes on to point
out that the ancient Hebrews could not have had any conception of the
planet as we know it ("the spheroidal figure of the earth"), so we must
base our understanding of the "earth,"

> in conformity with the ideas of the people who used it. ...
> Frequently it stands for the land of Palestine, and indeed for any
> country or district that is mentioned or referred to. Sometimes
> [*eretz*] denotes a mere plot of ground; and sometimes the soil,
> clay, and sand, or any earthy matter.[197]

Most commentators, without any explanation, simply assume that the
modern conception of the planet is what is meant by *eretz* in Genesis
1:2. But several have some thoughtful comments that can be taken in
support of the local earth theory if the exegetical principle is applied to
their thinking, that the meaning of the words to the original audience is
what it still means today. For instance, the editors of the NET Bible
explain *eretz* as, "this is what we now call 'the earth.' Prior to this the
substance which became the earth (=dry land) lay dormant under the
water." But why would these commentators think of the meaning of the
"earth" in Genesis 1:2 in today's terms? The editors could have better
explained *eretz* as "what they called 'the earth.'" That would have
opened a profitable line of inquiry that relatively few scholars have
taken the trouble to explore.

Gordon Wenham quotes a 19th century commentator, saying,
"According to Stadelmann [author of *Hebrew Conception of the World*],
'the term *eretz* means primarily the entire area in which man thinks of

---

[194] Sailhamer, *Genesis Unbound*, 20.

[195] Sailhamer, *Genesis Unbound*, 58.

[196] John Pye Smith, *The Relation between the Holy Scriptures and Some Parts of Geological Science* (London: Henry G. Bohn, 1854), 250.

[197] Smith, *Relation*, 250.

himself as living, as opposed to the regions of heaven or the underworld."[198] This commentator could just as easily have ended his sentence without the final phrase, which would have been to admit that *eretz* means the area in which people think of themselves as living locally.

Catholic theologian, Henricus Renckens, came close to recognizing the local nature of the creation story in Genesis 1 when he said,

> We have thus in Genesis the story of the creation told from start to finish in function of the actual world as it is empirically observed to be. The creation on the one hand, and on the other the actual world of the author's own observation, are completely bound up together in his mind.[199]

Unfortunately he missed the implications of his insight when he added, "and his world was the same as our own." But the author's world was not the same as our own. It was the land of Israel, not the whole globe, which was unknown at that time.

A LITERARY OBJECTION TO THE LOCAL EARTH THEORY ANSWERED

Bruce Waltke objects to Sailhamer's "novel suggestion" of limiting "the earth" to a local creation, because Waltke is "bound" (as Sailhamer puts it) by his assumption that in Genesis 1:1 "heavens and earth" must refer to the entire cosmos. Waltke objects to the local earth interpretation on the basis of the literary devise of the *inclusio* formed by 1:1 and 2:1.[200]

> In the beginning God created the heavens and the earth (Gen. 1:1).

> Thus the heavens and the earth were completed in all their vast array (Gen. 2:1).

Sailhamer agrees that Genesis 1:1 refers to God creating the universe,[201] but he curiously ignores the use of the literary device of *inclusio,* which is found throughout Scripture. Sailhamer states that "Genesis 1 has a summary title at its conclusion [2:1], making it unlikely it would have another at its beginning."[202] He assigns the second statement to a summary of a local creation, leaving the first

---

[198] Wenham, *Genesis*, 15.
[199] Renckens, *Israel's Concept,* 48, 49.
[200] Waltke, *Genesis*, 59.
[201] Sailhamer, *Genesis Unbound*, 14.
[202] Sailhamer, *Genesis Unbound*, 103.

verse hanging without a connection to the rest of the chapter, in spite of its obvious similarity to Genesis 2:1.[203] With Sailhamer, Waltke assumes that 1:1 refers to the creation of the whole cosmos. But Waltke had the advantage of working with a literary expert, co-author Cathy Fredricks, who recognized the possibility that Genesis 1:1 and 2:1 constitute an *inclusio*. If this argument is accepted, it means that the same meaning must hold true for both Genesis 1:1 and 2:1 and logically then, the narrative in between must also refer to what the summary statements refer to—according to Waltke, the entire cosmos.

However, Waltke's objections to a local creation disappear if we take the original hearers' understanding of the phrase, "heavens and earth" to mean "everything they knew of" (which can be seen as a metaphor standing for the whole earth and cosmos as it began to be more fully explored and known), with the "earth" in verse 2 as the local land, perhaps of Israel. In this interpretation, we can acknowledge the validity of the literary *inclusio* while also recognizing that the first verse functions in two ways: (1) as a title or summary for a local re-creation story and (2) as a statement of universal truth as God begins to reveal himself to his people. As Sailhamer says,

> There is hardly a verse in the Bible that carries as much weight as Genesis 1:1. The whole of the Bible's view of God rests on that single, initial statement. ... The writer wants us to see God as both the Creator of the universe and the One who prepares a land for his people.[204]

LITERARY SUPPORT FOR THE LOCAL EARTH THEORY

Generalizations and Particulars

The second chapter of Genesis clearly describes the preparation of a local place for the first humans to live well. If the first and second chapters of Genesis could be taken as referring to the same creation event, that would lend further support for the local creation theory. Sailhamer mentions a textual device, that is also discussed by Waltke and Fredricks, that we will explore below in detail, as evidence for the theory that first two chapters of Genesis are two versions of the same creation event, that is a local creation. Sailhamer explains,

---

[203] Sailhamer says, "the rest of the chapter is not an elaboration of Genesis 1:1; rather, it is an account of a different and subsequent act of God" (Sailhamer, *Genesis Unbound*, 103).

[204] Sailhamer, *Genesis Unbound*, 92.

The relationship between Genesis 1 and 2 follows a common
pattern seen throughout the further narratives of the primeval
history in Genesis 1–11. ... After a general description of an
event, the author often attaches one which gives more detail
about the same event. ... The link between Genesis 1 and 2
casts considerable light on the author's purpose in these creation
accounts. If chapters 1 and 2 recount the same event, then the
"land" where the Garden of Eden is located in chapter 2 is
identified with the "land' which God makes in chapter 1.[205]

In referring to this textual strategy of details following a general
description in the "primeval history" of the early chapters of Genesis,
Sailhamer seems to be referring to the genealogy, or "*toledot*," sections
of Genesis 1–11. Waltke and his co-author, literary expert Cathy
Fredricks, see, among other patterns in the structure of the *toledot*
cycles, one they call "generalization and particularization."[206]

Original research for this book produced the following summary of
the pattern of generalization followed by particular details in the *toledot*
sections of Genesis.

Toledot of Adam's Descendants

The **general** account of Adam's genealogy (*toledot*) ends with Noah
and his sons (Gen. 5:1-32).
> This is followed by two **detailed** stories:
> - The problem with the Nephilim, and evil among the people in
>   general, leading God to decide to wipe humans from face of
>   the earth (Gen. 6:1-8).
> - An account from Noah's life of how God went about wiping
>   the evil people out while preserving Noah's line (Gen. 6:9–
>   8:22).

A **general** account that names the sons of Noah: "from them came
the people who were scattered over the earth" (Gen: 9:18, 19).
> This is followed by a **detailed** story about Noah and his sons
> when he was drunk, and the consequences of curses and
> blessings (Gen. 9:20-27).

---

[205] Sailhamer, *Genesis Unbound*, 90, 91. Unfortunately, Sailhamer doesn't
acknowledge that Genesis 1:1 can also be seen as a general statement followed by the
particulars of the rest of the chapter.

[206] Waltke, *Genesis*, 34.

Toledot of Noah's Sons

The **general** account of the descendants of Shem, Ham, and Japheth ends with the statement, "from these the nations spread out over the earth after the flood." (Gen. 10:1-32).

> This is followed by the **detailed** account of how that spreading out happened, due to the judgment at the tower of Babel (Gen. 11:1-9).

A **general** *toledot* of Shem is a flashback to two years after the flood, up to the time of Abraham (Gen. 11:10-26).

> This is followed by the **detailed** story of the family of Terah, one of Shem's sons, and the account of how he took Abram and Lot to Haran (Gen. 11:27-32).

Applying the Generalization / Particularization Pattern to Genesis 1

In light of this clear pattern that the author uses in the first eleven chapters of Genesis, it is feasible to assume that the first two chapters could be seen as having a similar pattern of general accounts followed by detailed accounts:

A **general** statement about the refashioning of a locally destroyed area (Gen. 1:1, 2).

> This is followed by the **details** about that re-creation event (Gen. 1:3–2:2).

> Nested within the first chapter are **general** statements about the first three days of creation, the preparation for the "heavens and earth" to be inhabited by living creatures.

>> This is followed by the **details** of the next three days of creation, describing the creation of the living beings for each of the general respective habitats: water, air, and land.

Simultaneously, Genesis 1:2–2:2 serves as a **general** account of creation in relation to chapter 2. Genesis chapter 2 gives the **details** about specific humans and the preparation of a specific land for them to live in.

These examples of general accounts followed by detailed accounts follow a pattern that was common among the ancient Hebrews. Cassuto calls attention to this characteristic of Hebrew thinking: "One should first state the general proposition and then specify the particulars."[207]

---

[207] Cassuto, *Genesis*, 13.

Stanley Jaki gives four pages of examples from the Old Testament of general statements followed by the particulars.[208] P.B. Harner, writing in *Vetus Testamentum*, refers to "the 'holistic' quality of Israelite thinking, the tendency to apprehend a totality and integrate details into the whole."[209] Bruce Waltke claims this tendency and pattern as evidence for his position that the first verse of Genesis serves as a summary statement.

> The evidence seems convincing that verse 1 should be construed as a broad, general declaration of the fact that God created the cosmos and the rest of the chapter explicates that statement. This reflects normal Semitic thought which first states the general proposition and then specifies the particulars.[210]

In summary, this biblical literary pattern of generalization followed by particulars can be seen as corroboration for considering Genesis 2 to be a detailed description of the more general account in Genesis 1, both about a local re-creation. Following the general statements about the creation of humans, Genesis 2 is about a specific human couple in a specific location, the Garden of Eden. The Hebrew word *eretz* in Genesis 1:2, that is usually translated "earth" and understood by many, anachronistically, as "the planet," could be understood instead as being what is described in Genesis 2, which is a local place prepared for the first human couple.

Parallel Grammar Constructions

"The Genesis 1 and 2 narratives are about the same events and have the same setting. What we see God doing in Genesis 2 is merely another perspective on what he does in Genesis 1,"[211] says Sailhamer, who considers that these are both describing a local creation. Further support for Sailhamer's conclusion that the two chapters are describing the same event comes from noticing a grammatical relationship between the first verses of the creations accounts in Genesis 1 and 2.

The summary statement of Genesis 1:1 and the unusual word order in Genesis 1:2 have exact parallels in Genesis 2:4-7, which opens the second account of creation at a detailed level. Each of these passages has an introductory statement that summarizes the rest of the chapter,

---

[208] Jaki *Genesis*, 277ff.

[209] P. B. Harner, "Creation Faith in Deutero-Isaiah," *Vetus Testamentum* 17 (1967): 305.

[210] Waltke, "Creation Account: Part 3," 227.

[211] Sailhamer, Genesis Unbound, 51.

followed by a circumstantial clause that modifies the upcoming verse. This second element in each case follows the non-usual, emphatic pattern "*waw* + noun + verb (*hayah*)," describing a negative state before creation. Finally each creation account, in its introductory verses, brings in the main clause that uses the normal Hebrew verb/subject pattern "waw consecutive + prefixed conjugation form describing the creation."[212] The editors of the NET Bible gives this summary:

> This literary structure [of Genesis 1:1, 2] is paralleled in the second portion of the book: Gen 2:4 provides the title or summary of what follows, 2:5-6 use disjunctive clause structures to give background information for the following narrative, and 2:7 begins the narrative with the *vav* consecutive attached to a prefixed verbal form.

This sounds complex, but is easily illustrated with the following chart:

Comparison of Genesis 1:1, 2 with Genesis 2:4-7

	Gen 1:1, 2	Gen 2:4-7
1. Introductory summary statement	In the beginning God created the heavens and the earth (1:1)	This is the account of the heavens and the earth when they were created (2:4)
2. Circumstantial clause of the pattern *waw* + noun + verb (*hayah*); an emphatic description of a negative state before creation	Now the earth was [*tohu wabohu*] (1:2)	Now no shrub of the field was yet in the earth (2:5, 6)
3. Main clause of the usual pattern *waw* + verb describing the creation	Then God said let there be light ... (1:3)	Then the Lord God formed man. (2:7)

This parallel construction emphasizes the negative condition of the land prior to creation. In Genesis 1:1, 2, this negative state is called, *tohu wabohu*. This phrase, which we will focus on in the next chapter, is at the heart of the discussion about the purposes of God, as indicated in the Bible, for bringing order out of chaos. God's activity in these first

---

[212] Waltke, "Creation Account: Part 3," 225.

two chapters of Genesis is the origin of "international development," making right what is out of order.

Questions about the Land

Knowing that the land had been in a negative state before God starting making it "good" would have been an encouragement to the people of Israel, having recently come out of the chaos of slavery. It would have helped them hold on to the hope that something good could be the end result in their circumstances. In answer to Allen Ross' question, "Why did the new nation of Israel need to have this material and to have it written as it is?"[213] we will explore three main possibilities:

1. The people needed to know why the land they were going to enter could legitimately be considered theirs because God gave it to them.

2. The process of God's making the uninhabitable "earth" or "land" into a place for people to live serves as metaphor for the creation of a society, the nation of Israel, out of the chaos of slavery.

3. The people could learn important lessons about God and their relationship to him from this creation account.

THE NEED TO KNOW THE LAND THEY WERE ENTERING WAS GIVEN TO THEM BY GOD

As Moses was leading the people of Israel to the Promised Land, the people needed to know why the land they were going to enter could legitimately be considered theirs. Social historian Aaron Wildavsky claims, in his anthropological history of the beginnings of the people of Israel (*The Nursing Father: Moses as a Political Leader*),

> The creation is not about just anybody. It rationalizes one of the most important claims Moses made for this people—the land of Israel is theirs by right because the Owner gave it to them.[214]

In this he echoes Rashi's assertion, which is based on Jeremiah 27:5, as mentioned earlier: "Should the peoples of the world say to Israel, 'You are robbers, because you took by force the lands of the seven nations of Canaan,' Israel may reply to them 'All the earth belongs to the Holy One, blessed be He; He created it and gave it to whom He pleased.'"[215]

---

[213] Ross, *Creation*, 102.
[214] Wildavsky, *Nursing Father*, 80.
[215] Quoted by Rosenbaum, *Pentateuch* 1:2.

John Collins, professor of Old Testament at Covenant Theological Seminary, adds another perspective on what the people of Israel needed to know about the land:

> They are going to live in the promised land .... They need to be reassured this is God's world, the land is God's land, and God has the right to instruct human beings how to live and how to use his stuff.[216]

METAPHOR FOR THE CREATION OF A SOCIETY

Knowing how to live well in the land was essential for the new people of Israel whom God was "creating" into a new society out of the chaos of slavery they had recently escaped. A local creation story could be seen as a metaphor or commentary on the creation of a society.[217] Robert Alter, in *The Art of Biblical Narrative*, explains that in biblical literature:

> "Recurrence, parallels, and analogy are the hallmarks of reported action in the biblical tale. The use of narrative analogy, where one part of the story provides a commentary on or a foil to another should be familiar from later literature [such as a Shakespearian double plot]."[218]

Moses spoke and wrote the books of the Pentateuch, or Torah, to provide a commentary and background information for the emerging nation. Waltke states,

> A nation consists of a common people, normally sharing a common land, submissive to a common law, and led by a common ruler. The book of Genesis is concerned principally in identifying both the people who submit to God's commands and the land that sustains them.[219]

The narration of God's creation of the land would have helped the Israelites see themselves as the people of God (a common people), about

---

[216] Collins, "Reading Genesis 1–2," 90, 91.

[217] We can also view Genesis 1 as a local creation story that serves as a metaphor for the creation of everything and every possibility. What is thought to be included in that "everything," is a concept that has expanded over time as people have learned more about their environment. But this account does not give a record of something unknown and un-thought of by the audience at the time it was spoken and written.

[218] Alter, *Biblical Narrative*, 180.

[219] Waltke, *Genesis*, 45.

to inherit a common land made for them by God. The laws they were to follow were the focus of the Torah for which Genesis 1 serves as an introduction. It is clear from the first chapters of Genesis (and from the accounts of the Exodus, and even in the first two verses of Genesis) that God intended to be their only and all-powerful ruler in the land they were going to inhabit.

The importance to the people of the ancient Near East of the origin and organization of a society sharing a common land is hard for modern people to realize. Today we are asking questions about the physical world and some look for answers to such questions in Genesis 1. But "to the ancients, human society organized in a particular place was [what was important],"[220] and this was reflected in their creation stories. Catholic theologian J. Clifford explains,

> In the Akkadian epic, Enuma Elish, ... the exaltation of Marduk among the gods is parallel to the organization of Babylonian society. The Bible too contains similar cosmogonies by which a society is established in a particular place.[221]

The imagery of Genesis 1 would have been a lens through which the people of Israel could interpret their recent experiences in the Exodus. The story of the formation of the people of Israel into a nation begins with emphasis on the negative, chaotic conditions under which they were living in slavery in Egypt, just as Genesis 1:2 begins with emphasis on the negative, chaotic condition of the land before God started making it inhabitable. In making a people for himself,

> God reacts to Pharaoh's anti-creational designs by unleashing forces of nature to punish and destroy. The moral chaos of human enslavement is countered by the natural chaos of Divine retribution.[222]

This is the equivalent of *tohu wabohu*, as the land is described in Genesis 1:2. The implications of this parallel will be explored in detail in the next chapter. God corrects the societal conditions that can be described as *tohu wabohu* as the people of Israel cross through the Red Sea. Accounts of the escape of the people of Israel from slavery in Egypt are often described in terms that echo themes from the Genesis creation account. As they confront and overcome the challenge of

---

[220] J. Clifford S.J. "The Hebrew Scriptures and the Theology of Creation," *Theological Studies* 46 (1985): 509, 510.

[221] Clifford, "Hebrew Scriptures," 509, 510.

[222] Och, "Creation and Redemption," 8.

crossing the Red Sea the people experience personally what Moses described regarding God's preparation of the land. Parallel themes include chaotic conditions (*tohu wabohu*), darkness (*hosek*), the feared deep (*tehom*), the Spirit or wind of God (*ruach*), the waters (*mayim*), the heavens or sky (*shamayim*), and dry ground (*yabbahshah*). The following passages demonstrate the parallels between the Creation and Exodus accounts.

Preparation of the Land through Creation

> Now the earth (*eretz*) was formless and empty (*tohu wabohu*), darkness (*hosek*) was over the surface of the deep (*tehom*), and the Spirit of God (*ruach elohim*) was hovering over the waters (*mayim*) (Gen. 1:2).

> And God said, "Let the water (*mayim*) under the sky (*shamayim*) be gathered to one place, and let dry ground (*yabbahshah*) appear." And it was so (Gen. 1:9).

Preparation of a New Society through the Exodus

> [Slavery is a form of societal chaos (*tohu wabohu*)].

> Moses stretched out his hand toward the sky (*shamayim*), and total darkness (*hosek*) covered all Egypt for three days (Exod. 10:22).

> With your mighty arm you redeemed your people, the descendants of Jacob and Joseph. The waters (*mayim*) saw you, O God, ... and writhed; the very depths (*tehom*) were convulsed. ... Your path led through the sea, your way through the mighty waters (*mayim*) (Ps. 77:15, 16, 19).

> You blew with your wind (*ruach*) (Exod. 15:10).

> The waters (*mayim*) were divided and the Israelites went through the sea on dry ground (*yabbahshah*) (Exod. 14:21, 22).

The Hebrew word for "dry," used repeatedly in the Exodus accounts, is the same word used in Genesis 1:9 when God separates the inhospitable waters and causes dry land to appear. This word (Strong's # 3004) is relatively rare and is used mainly in the contexts of the Exodus, crossing the Jordan, and the creation story of Genesis 1. As Moses originally spoke the word *yabbahshah* to his audience in Genesis 1:9, it is likely that the people would have identified at an emotional level with the term for dry land, the miracle that led to their last-minute rescue. This reminder of their recent experience with the Red Sea would have tied together in their thinking the creation or "making" of the land with the creation or making of themselves as a people. In both cases, life was only possible because of a mighty act of God in pushing back the waters to make a dry, life-sustaining place.

Jonah experienced a small-scale personal version of this same life-sustaining act of God. Further support for the parallels between the physical creation and the creation of the people of Israel is seen in Jonah 1:9 where he says, "I am a Hebrew and I worship the Lord, the God of heaven, who made the sea and the dry land (*yabbahshah*)." (Later the fish spits Jonah out on the dry land.) Here Jonah is claiming his heritage as a Hebrew, and the way he supports his claim is to refer to the two most basic and formative acts of God in the origin of the Hebrew nation: the creation of "everything" (heaven, sea, and dry land), and the origin of the Hebrew people by their passing through the sea on dry land. Jonah's speech shows his understanding, as a Hebrew familiar with the Torah, that deliverance from the sea is tied to God's creation of the nation of Israel and his creation of "everything."

In the Exodus, Yahweh creates a way through the sea by separating the water from the land by his wind / spirit / breath (*ruach*), not allowing "the deep" (*tehom*, see Psalms 77:16; 106:9; Isaiah 51:10; 63:13) to keep his people from their land. In the Genesis creation account, God's wind (*ruach* / spirit) is blowing over the water (earlier called "the deep"), preparing it for the major separation of bringing forth the "dry" (*yabbahshah*, Genesis 1:9, 10), the same word used for the result of God's wind in Exodus 14:16, 22, 29 and 15:19.[223]

Movement from a state of chaos and trouble, including social disorganization, to a state of peace in the land, is the pattern Richard Clifford sees in the poetic accounts of the Exodus in Psalm 77:15-19; 78:42-55 and Exodus 15. "To the ancients, the primary focus is on describing the cosmos from the point of view of what assumptions are necessary if human beings are to live optimally in the world."[224] Clifford is describing the purpose and goal of international development, which had its origins in the beginning history of the nation of Israel as God prepared a land in which they could potentially live well.

---

[223] Israel's deliverance from the sea, with God drying up a path through the sea, foreshadows the fulfillment of history when God will dry even the smallest amounts of salty tears (Rev. 21:4), representative of the troubles and chaos the ancient Hebrews traditionally associated with the sea.

[224] Clifford, "Hebrew Scriptures," 510, 511.

IMPORTANT LESSONS ABOUT LIVING WELL IN THE LAND

A description of what is necessary to live well in the world is exactly what is found in Genesis 1. Old Testament scholar, Richard Averbeck summarizes,[225]

> The way of telling this creation story was determined and shaped by God's concern that they know him as the only true God, that they know the kind of good God he is, and that they live well for him within his good creation.

From the description of the uninhabitable condition of the land in Genesis 1:2 and the subsequent acts of God to prepare the land as a place for humans to leave peacefully, the people would have learned important lessons about God and their relationship to him. The intentional emphasis on the word "land" in verse 2 would have focused attention on the covenant that God was making through Moses with the people, of which the land was a visible representation. Sailhamer highlights the link between the land and obedience:

> Like a loving father, "in the beginning" God gave His children a place to dwell, a good land, filled with divine blessings. So also in his covenant with Israel at Sinai, God again promised to give them a "good land" where they could enjoy his blessing and have fellowship with Him. They had to remain faithful and obedient, however.[226]

The lesson learned by the link between land and covenant is that obedience is necessary; otherwise judgment on the land and loss of the land will follow. This is what the ancient Rabbi Resh Lakish taught, as quoted by Hebrew scholar, Robert Alter:

> The Torah was given to Israel: "to teach us that the Holy One made a condition with all created things, saying to them, 'If Israel accepts the Torah, you will continue to exist. If not, I shall return you to welter and waste [*tohu wabohu*]'" (Babylonian Talmud: Shabbat 88A).[227]

We could easily view the rest of the Old Testament as a commentary on this relationship between the land and obedience to the covenant. Psalm 37 gives three examples of how the ancient people interpreted their relationship to the land and the covenant:

---

[225] Averbeck, "A Literary Day," 8.
[226] Sailhamer, *Genesis Unbound*, 73.
[227] Alter, *Biblical Narrative*, ix.

A little while, and the wicked will be no more; though you look for them, they will not be found. But the meek will inherit the land (*eretz*) and enjoy peace and prosperity (Ps. 37:10, 11).

Those the Lord blesses will inherit the land (*eretz*), but those he curses will be destroyed (Ps. 37: 22).

Hope in the Lord and keep his way. He will exalt you to inherit the land (*eretz*); when the wicked are destroyed, you will see it (37:34).

To emphasize the importance of not incurring God's judgment through disobedience, the *tohu wabohu* condition of the land at the time of the creation events serves as advance warning. We will explore the meaning and implications of this term in detail in the next chapter.

LESSONS FOR TODAY

The value for us today of seeing Genesis 1 as the record of a local event, inspired by God to be preserved for posterity, is that it can serve as an example or metaphor for the chaos that has occurred repeatedly throughout time in different parts of the earth, and for the spiritual chaos of evil that all peoples of all times have had to deal with. Chaos caused by evil intentions always lurks in the background, as von Rad has pointed out.[228] It is the theme of Scripture that God deals creatively with the results of evil. As Joseph said to his brothers, "You intended evil against me, but God meant it for good" (Gen. 50:20). In the next chapter we will look at the first hint in Scripture that God has to deal with conditions that are in opposition to his intentions for his people.

---

[228] von Rad, *Genesis*, 52.

Chapter Seven

Tohu Wabohu: Destroyed and Desolate

Images of Chaos

As for the earth,
> *it was destroyed and desolate* (tohu wabohu),
> *with darkness on the face of the deep,*
> *but the Spirit of God stirring over the face of the waters.*
(Gen. 1:2, author's translation)

Edom's streams will be turned into pitch,
> *her dust into burning sulfur;*
> *her land will become blazing pitch!...*
From generation to generation it will lie desolate;
> *no one will ever pass through it again.*
The desert owl and screech owl will possess it;
> *the great owl and the raven will nest there.*
God will stretch out over Edom
> *the measuring line of chaos* (tohu)
> *and the plumb line of desolation* (bohu).
(Isa. 34:9-11)

I looked at the earth, and it was formless and empty (tohu wabohu);
> *and at the heavens, and their light was gone.*
I looked at the mountains, and they were quaking;
> *all the hills were swaying.*
I looked, and there were no people;
> *every bird in the sky had flown away.*
I looked, and the fruitful land was a desert;
> *all its towns lay in ruins before the LORD, before his fierce anger.*
This is what the LORD says: "The whole land will be ruined,
> *though I will not destroy it completely.*
Therefore the earth will mourn and the heavens above grow dark,
> *because I have spoken and will not relent,*
I have decided and will not turn back."
(Jer. 4:23-28)

General Overview

Something opposite to God's intentions exists and is described in Genesis 1:2 where the condition of the earth (prior to the creation events beginning with verse 3) is described as *"tohu wabohu."* In speaking of verse 2, Karl Barth said that this is "one of the most difficult in the whole Bible" to interpret, and he called the term *tohu wabohu* "notorious" to translate and understand,[229] so it should not be a surprise that this chapter will be much longer and more complex than earlier chapters.

In the "Particulars" section of this chapter we will see a variety of translations of this term, from "destroyed and desolate" to "topsy turvey," or, traditionally, "formless and void." An exegetical study of the Hebrew figure of speech, *tohu wabohu*, shows that the term describes both circumstances that are the cause of judgment and the consequences experienced as a result of judgment, which is often simply a withdrawal of God's protection of a society from the evil tendencies of humankind. Scott Moreau's description of the variety of evils experienced in the human condition is also a good assessment of the meaning and connotations of the term *tohu wabohu.*

> Diseases, natural disasters, famines and droughts, accidents, socio-political disorders, economic oppressions and the like could be either the consequences of divine judgment, satanic assaults, human sinfulness, or some combination of these factors.[230]

When a portion of the world is drastically and violently upside down from God's intentions, Scripture shows that God often decides to shake that world through judgment and start over with a person or people who are open to his leading.[231] Since judgment is always associated in

---

[229] Karl Barth, *Church Dogmatics*, 3:102.

[230] A. Scott Moreau et al., *Deliver Us from Evil: An Uneasy Frontier in Christian Mission* (World Vision International, 2002), 9.

[231] Examples of God's new beginnings in Scripture include the Genesis 1 Creation account, the Flood, the calling of Abraham, the Exodus, the return from Exile, the coming of Jesus the Messiah, and the final new beginning described in the Book of Revelation, the new heaven and the new earth.

Scripture with the word *tohu*,[232] it is logical to assume that the first occurrence of the word in Genesis 1:2 would have had the same connotation. In fact, it is likely that this would have been the original use of the term that other writers of Scripture had in mind in their own use of the term. It might seem natural to ask, then, what could have been in existence before the Genesis 1 creation account that God would have seen a need to judge? Merrill Unger represents a conservative evangelical understanding that the first verses of Genesis may speak of a judged earth that is about to be re-created:

> Genesis 1:1, 2 evidently describes not the primeval creation *ex nihilo*, ... but the much later refashioning of a judgment-ridden earth in preparation for a new order of creation—man. The Genesis account deals only with God's creative activity as it concerns the human race in its origin, fall, and redemption.[233]

> God did not create the earth in the state of a chaos of wasteness, emptiness, and darkness (Isa. 45:18). It was reduced to this condition because it was the theater where sin began in God's originally sinless universe in connection with the revolt of Lucifer (Satan) and his angels (Isa. 14:12-14; Ezek. 28:13, 15-17; Rev. 12:4). The chaos was the result of God's judgment upon the originally sinless earth.[234]

The term *tohu wabohu* is not limited, however, to a description of the physical condition of the land before the creation events of Genesis 1. Satan is still active in this world deceiving people into ongoing rebellion and violence. *Tohu wabohu* can also describe rebellion and chaos at a societal level or at a personal level with regard to physical or spiritual conditions. We will see that the conditions described as *tohu wabohu* are never God's will and that he wants to work through his people to correct these conditions. ("Be fruitful and multiply, and subdue the earth" [Gen. 1:28].) Gregory Boyd uses a vivid word picture to describe the role of humanity: "Creation was birthed in an infected incubator, and humanity was given leadership over this earth as the means of killing the infection."[235]

---

[232] See the summary later in this chapter of the uses and meanings of this term. (The word, *bohu*, never occurs alone, perhaps because it was coined to rhyme with *tohu*.)

[233] Merrill F. Unger "Rethinking the Genesis Account of Creation," *Bibliotheca Sacra* 115 (January–March 1958): 28.

[234] Unger, *Unger's Commentary*, 5.

[235] Boyd, *God at War*, 110.

The whole theme of Scripture is to fight back against opposition to God's intentions. This is the biblical worldview demonstrated throughout Israel's history, in the prophets' interpretation of that history, in Jesus' activity and words, and in the descriptions of living in God's Kingdom found in the Epistles of the New Testament. Where God's rule and reign is not acknowledged and his will is not being done, *tohu* describes the conditions. As a description of the opposite of God's creational intent and the root of human problems, the figure of speech, *tohu wabohu*, also contains within itself the solution to those problems. By bringing order out of chaos, God was overcoming evil with good (Hebrew, *tob,* a word play with the similar-sounding *tohu*).[236] *Tohu* and the emphatic term *tohu wabohu* describe something that is not God's will. Each occurrence of the word *tohu* is in the context of a state of the land or of humans that God wants to see corrected. It implies the existence of evil, of opposition to God's will, and chaos.[237] God's way of dealing with the physical condition of the earth described in Genesis 1:2 gives direction to his followers for dealing with the roots of human problems at physical, personal, community, and spiritual levels. God's people have the privilege of allowing God's Spirit (*ruach elohim*) to work through them to demonstrate his glory in fighting back against *tohu,* the conditions societies and people encounter when they are in opposition to God's will.

Particular Details about the Term and Conditions of *Tohu Wabohu*

Significance of the Term Tohu Wabohu

The Hebrew figure of speech, *tohu wabohu*, startles the listener or reader with its rhyming quality and calls attention to the fact that something surprising and significant is being said, possibly something unexpected that will throw the reader and listener off balance. In this chapter we will develop the proposition that this rhyming pair of words is a key to understanding the purpose and drama of Scripture. The term serves as the beginning of the framework for the whole Bible, showing that God's purpose in history is to reverse judgment and usher in the eternal Sabbath rest, the *shalom*, that is the goal of creation. The last

---

[236] Sailhamer, *Genesis Unbound*, 63.

[237] The comments of biblical scholar, Charles Moeller, align with the findings here: "The arts inspired by the diabolical are characterized by the representation of disorder, of a cosmic chaos" (Charles Moeller, "Introduction," in *Satan*, ed. Bruno de Jesus-Marie O.C.D [New York: Sheed and Ward, 1952], xv.)

chapter in the Bible, Revelation 22, provides the other end of the
biblical framework (an *"inclusio,"* as literary-minded biblical scholars
call it), showing that history, the story of the inter-relationships between
God, his adversary, and humans, has reached its goal: "No longer will
there be any curse ... There will be no more night ... God will give
them light. And they will reign for ever and ever" (Rev. 22: 3, 5).
Finally, God's intentions in creating humans will be accomplished.

But in between, the failure of the first human couple to choose to
follow God's ways has resulted in conditions that can be labeled *tohu
wabohu*. This is a compound term that occurs only one other time in the
Old Testament (Jer. 4:23), while the rhyming word pair occurs in one
additional place (Isa. 34:1). The word *tohu* alone occurs 16 times, but it
must be kept in mind that the compound term, as a figure of speech, will
mean something more than the sum of its component parts. To arrive at
a satisfactory meaning for this rare term the following process will be
followed:

1. A review of relevant literary considerations

2. An examination of the context of the passages in which *tohu* or
tohu wabohu is used

3. A summary of the word associations found with these terms

4. A review of a number of major commentators' opinions

5. A rationale for the most helpful translation

6. A concluding discussion of the application of the concept at
various levels.

Literary Considerations

A review of relevant literary considerations for this phrase includes
noticing the importance of the sounds of words in Hebrew, the
significance of the use of figures of speech and rhyme, and the role of
parallelism in Hebrew writings for determining the meanings of obscure
terms.

The original audience must have heard Genesis 1 spoken aloud as
part of the oral literature of ancient Israel. Everett Fox, a specialist in
Near Eastern and Judaic Studies, points out that the "Hebrew Bible
originated largely as a spoken literature [and] must be translated with
careful attention to rhythm and sound."[238] Moses' listeners, who had
recently escaped from the chaos of slavery and non-entity in Egypt and
had experienced deliverance from the destructive waters of the Red Sea,

---

[238] Everett Fox, trans., *In the Beginning: A New English Rendition of the Book
of Genesis, Translated with Commentary and Notes* (New York: Schocken Books,
1983), ix.

would have been caught up in the imagery evoked by the words and sounds of Genesis 1:1, 2. Their own recent experience would have caused them to resonate with the word play and meaning of the rhyming *"tohu wabohu"* and the assonance of *"ruach / merachepet"* (the consonant and vowel sounds in *merachepet* ("stirring") echo the sound of *ruach* ("spirit").[239] The juxtaposition of these two sets of word plays must have been a reassuring sound to the people of God as Moses began to explain to them how their God had prepared a place for them to live by bringing order and goodness out of a land that was *tohu wabohu*—destroyed and desolate, turned upside down (that's like us! they would have recognized)—and that he had never left that land (or the people) without the presence of his *ruach merachepet* (spirit stirring).

A PLAY ON WORDS AND FIGURES OF SPEECH

Word plays and the assonance of deliberate repeated sounds would have caught the attention of the original audience, alerting them to notice that something out of the ordinary was being said. Perhaps the rhyme gave a playful, as well as memorable, twist to the depiction of anti-creational chaos. Job seems to do something similar in his description of the feared sea monster, Leviathan, in Job 41:5: "Can you pull in leviathan with a fishhook? ... Can you make a pet of it?" Perhaps by the very sound of the words he was inspired to choose, *tohu wabohu*, Moses was reassuring the people that God has chaos under control and that even conditions contrary to God's will can be turned to his good purposes.

Closely related to the sounds of the words is the use of figures of speech, which can include deliberate plays on the sounds of words, as with *tohu wabohu*. In his lengthy volume, *Figures of Speech Used in the Bible*, Anglican clergyman and biblical scholar, Ethelbert Bullinger, points out that figures of speech draw the attention of the reader or listener to an important statement and cause the reader to ask why "the words have been used in a new form, what the particular force of the passage is, and why we are to put special emphasis on the fact stated or on the truth conveyed."[240] Michael Fishbane, a scholar of Judaism and rabbinic literature, points out that the "justification for the utilization of

---

[239] J. S. Kselman, "The Recovery of Poetic Fragments from the Pentateuchal Priestly Source," *Journal of Biblical Literature* 97 (1978): 164.

[240] E. W. Bullinger, *Figures of Speech Used in the Bible, Explained and Illustrated* (Longdon: Eyre & Spottiswoode, 1898), vi.

puns and allusions in exegesis lies in the acknowledged independent and efficacious power of words. They are pregnant with meaning."[241]

We will examine the meaning of *tohu wabohu* from the perspective of two figures of speech: hendiadys (which includes the compound nature of the term) and paronomasia (which includes the rhyming quality of the term and the possibility that it is intended to be a pun). Each of these will shed light on the interpretation of this rhyming figure of speech, *tohu wabohu*.

Hendiadys

Webster's Dictionary defines "hendiadys" as "'one by two': the expression of an idea by two nouns connected by 'and,' instead of by a noun and an adjective." The *Oxford English Dictionary* gives this definition: "a figure of speech in which a single complex idea is expressed by two words connected by a conjunction." We need to understand something about the word *tohu*, and if possible about the word *bohu* (which is never used apart from *tohu*), before we can know what the author had in mind in joining these words together, although we can be sure that the compound phrase will mean more than the just the sum of its parts.

Waltke gives these examples of hendiadys: "dribs and drabs, spic and span, hem and haw," and says the hendiadys, *tohu wabohu*, signifies "utter chaos." "[The land] was uninhabitable and uninhabited, 'unformed and unfilled.'"[242] Just as Waltke's examples contain words coined for the purpose of the compound expression, we will later consider the likelihood that "*bohu*" is not a real word, but one created to rhyme with "*tohu*," to draw the listener's or reader's attention to something unusual and even startling that is being said.

Paronomasia and Rhyme

Bullinger and Fishbane both refer to this unusual pair of rhyming words as the figure of speech known as "paronomasia,"[243] "a word play, especially a pun, to call by a different name" (*Webster's Dictionary*). The *Oxford English Dictionary* points out that paronomasia comes from the Greek words meaning "after naming." Paronomasia means "to alter slightly in naming; a playing on words that sound alike; a word-play; a pun." The entry gives an example of a book title from 1888 that is "cleverly paronomastical": *A Cursory History of Swearing*. The

---

[241] Michael Fishbane, "Jeremiah IV 23-26 and Job III 3-13: A Recovered Use of the Creation Pattern," *Vetus Testamentum* 21 (1971): 161.

[242] Waltke, "Literary Genre," 4.

[243] Bullinger, *Figures of Speech*, 306; Fishbane, "Jeremiah," 161.

whimsical and rhyming quality of a paronomasia is something to keep in mind in determining the meaning of *tohu wabohu*. The rhyming quality of the term *tohu wabohu* comes from a slight alteration of the sound of the first word (changing the "t" to "b"), combined with the Hebrew conjunction "*wa*" (and). Later we will look at evidence that the word *bohu* may have been invented for the purpose of rhyming with *tohu* by altering a similar-sounding Hebrew word with a compatible meaning.

We can see the value of rhyme for illuminating the meaning of the biblical text in a passage related to Genesis 1:2. In Isaiah 45:18, the use of rhyme calls attention to something significant the author wants the reader to notice, and perhaps because of its close relationship to Genesis 1:2, the rhyme may be indirectly giving us another example of the meaning of the full phrase, *tohu wabohu*. In the Hebrew it can be seen that Isaiah 45:18 is a poem that rhymes and has the same number of syllables, something that is not necessary or usual in Hebrew poetry:

> *Lo tohu bera'a*
> *Lasebet yesara*

> He did not create it to be [*tohu*]
> But formed it to be inhabited.

Since most Hebrew poetry does not rhyme, the fact that this is the second occurrence of rhyme in association with the word *tohu* indicates something significant is being said that needs extra thought. Could it be that Isaiah introduced this word play because he had the rhyming sound of *tohu wabohu* in mind when he chose to use the word *tohu* in this context? In that case then, we would have a fourth (implied) context for the term *tohu wabohu*. This playful rhyme in Isaiah 45:18 shows that God wants to turn the conditions upside down that are described by the rhyming words *tohu wabohu*. He wants to reverse the judged state of the land (described earlier in Isaiah 45), to make it inhabited and life-giving. The context shows that Cyrus, as God's servant, is going to rebuild what God had allowed to be destroyed.

PARALLELISM

Isaiah 45:18 also gives an excellent example of parallelism, a common literary device in Hebrew poetry. In determining the meaning of each of the words separately as well as the term *tohu wabohu* as a whole, the use of parallelism is a key exegetical tool. An example of the usefulness of this tool is found in determining the meaning of *tohu* in

Isaiah 45:18. The four lines in parallel structure are related to each other in this way:

> (A) He who fashioned and made the earth (*eretz*)
> (A') He founded it
>
> (B) He did not create it to be (*tohu*)
> (B') But formed it to be inhabited.

Lines A and A' are obviously synonymous, both referring to the making of "the earth" / *eretz*. Lines (B) and (B'), are also synonymous. "Not ... *tohu*" is paired with "inhabited," giving us a clue to the meaning of *tohu*: empty or uninhabited or perhaps purposeless and meaningless.

This example from Isaiah 45:18 shows how parallelism can help determine the meaning of *tohu wabohu* in Genesis 1:2:

> As for the earth,
> (A) it was *tohu wabohu*
> (B) with darkness on the face of (the) deep
> (C) but the Spirit of God stirring over the face of the waters.

With these three lines we need to ask if parallelism is involved, and if so, which lines are parallel to each other, and in what relationship. The repetition of the phrase, "the face of," seems to indicate that it would be appropriate to consider these lines as a form of parallelism, typical in Hebrew poetry.[244] This supposition is further supported by the fact that the last word of both lines (B) and (C) is about water ("the deep" / *tehom* and "waters" / *mayim*). Assuming we are dealing with parallelism, which type of parallelism is intended in lines (B) and (C): synonymous, synthetic, or antithetic? It would be practically blasphemous to consider lines (B) and (C) to be synonymous, in which case "darkness" would be equated with "Spirit of God." Synthetic parallelism seems inappropriate as well: the concept of the Spirit of God does not add to our understanding of what it means for darkness to be on the face of the deep. The third option, antithetical parallelism, fits the context very well. The Spirit of God is the antithesis of darkness. God has not left his land or his people totally without his presence, even in the midst of darkness.

It could also be argued that lines (A) and (B) exhibit synthetic parallelism in relationship to each other, with "darkness" and "deep" serving as an elaboration of the meaning and connotations of "*tohu*

---

[244] Kselman, "The Recovery," 69.

wabohu." Darkness is a common biblical symbol of evil and it is the first thing God corrects in Genesis 1 as he sets about overcoming evil with good. Both the words, "darkness" / *hosek* and "deep" / *tehom*, would no doubt have sent shivers of remembered horror down the spines of Moses' listeners. They had just escaped from slavery (societal *tohu wabohu*) in the land of Egypt where the plague of darkness had helped change Pharaoh's mind about letting them go. Darkness was also associated with the last plague of the killing of the first-born sons during the night in all the Egyptian households. Moses' audience had just escaped from the "deeps" of the feared sea by the *ruach* of God (Exod. 15:10) separating the water and making a dry path, followed by the drowning of their enemies. There is no doubt but that the imagery conjured up by the language in the parallelism of Genesis 1:2 would have meant to Moses' audience that the land "at the beginning," before God started making it livable, was an ominous, hostile place.

These various literary devises used in the Hebrew language are helpful for coming to a better understanding of the term *tohu wabohu.* Applying what we have learned about the ancient Hebrew interest in assonance, paronomasia, and parallelism, to the word *bohu,* which occurs only three times in the Old Testament and always combined with *tohu,* will help us eventually arrive at a useful interpretation for the combined term. The ancient Hebrews' delight in sound-alike words will be a factor in determining the origin and meaning of the single word, *bohu.*

PROPOSED ETYMOLOGY OF *BOHU*

These literary considerations, including the question of whether the term was purposely coined just to rhyme with "*tohu,*" indicate a need to study the origin of the word "*bohu.*" Old Testament scholar and linguist, David Tsumura, and others suggest several possibilities for the origin of the word *bohu.*

Review of Etymologies of Bohu

Arabic: *bahiya* "to be empty." The Brown, Driver and Briggs *Hebrew-English Lexicon* suggests this etymology, as does Tsumura:

> This Arabic term is used to describe the empty or vacant state of a tent or house that contains nothing or little furniture or goods.

Thus it has basically a concrete meaning rather than an abstract meaning such as "nothingness" or "emptiness."[245]

Akkadian: *bubutu* "Emptiness, hunger." Tsumura lists several reasons why W. F. Albright's suggestion of this origin of the term is not valid. Tsumura's objection is based on an error by Albright in attributing the definition of "emptiness, hunger" to the Akkadian term, which has other meanings according to linguistic sources.[246] Tsumura is of the opinion that "many of the errors made in interpreting the biblical text we are dealing with [Genesis 1:2] stem from faulty etymology."[247]

Phoenician: Karl Barth proposes a possible "connexion with the Phoenician and Babylonian goddess Bau who is for the Phoenicians a personification of night as the arch-mother of man, and simply means a 'vacuum.'"[248] Tsumura, however, states that he finds no evidence that the Hebrew term had any connection with the Phoenician divine name Baav, the goddess of night, "except for their possible common derivation from the root, *bhw*."[249]

Tsumura concludes,

> In the light of the above discussion, Hebrew *bohu*, though still lacking definite etymology, seems to be a Semitic term based on the root *bhw* and possibly a cognate of Arabic *bahiya* "to be empty."[250]

A New Proposal for the Etymology of Bohu

Tsumura's etymology of *bohu* agrees with the contextual studies, found in the next section, in which associations of emptiness and darkness (night) are seen repeatedly in connection with *tohu* and *tohu wabohu*. But I would like to propose a further, original etymological study, looking to Hebrew cognates, rather than other languages, as a more likely source for the origin and meaning of the term. This original etymological study is patterned after the example of Tsumura who goes

---

[245] David Toshio Tsumura, *Creation and Destruction: A Reappraisal of the Chaoskampf Theory in the Old Testament* (Winona Lake, IN: Eisenbrauns, 2005), 13.

[246] David Toshio Tsumura, "The Earth in Genesis 1," in *"I Studied Inscriptions from Before the Flood": Ancient Near Eastern, Literary, and Linguistic Approaches to Genesis 1–11*, ed. Richard S. Hess and David Toshio Tsumura (Winona Lake, IN: Eisenbrauns, 1994), 313.

[247] Tsumura, *Creation and Destruction*, 4.

[248] Karl Barth, *Church Dogmatics*, 3:104

[249] Tsumura, "The Earth," 314.

[250] Tsumura, "The Earth," 315.

into great detail in his etymological studies to examine possible cognates for *bohu* (and separately for *tohu*) in closely related languages of the ancient Near East. Tsumura's example of informed speculation was the motivation for the following study.

Considering the associations of similar meaning and similar sounds I would like to propose the theory that *bohu* is a word invented by the author of Genesis 1:2 (the term later being copied by Isaiah and Jeremiah in anti-creational contexts) to rhyme with *tohu* and to carry the meaning of "emptiness" in both the abstract and concrete senses, and conveying a state of being "mixed up" or "upside down."

The line of reasoning begins with Jeremiah 8:16, 19, a passage that contains several words and themes often associated with *tohu wabohu*: shaking or trembling, disaster as a result of judgment, worthless idols, vain things. "At the neighing of their stallions the whole land trembles [shakes]. They have come to devour the land and everything in it. ... Why have they aroused my anger with their images, with their worthless foreign idols? [with their vanities = *be'hehvel*]" (Jer. 8:16, 19).

A Hebrew word with a meaning similar to that proposed for *bohu*, *hahval* (Strong's #1891), has an abstract meaning associated with the interpretation of "emptiness," namely, "vain" or "worthless" things (empty of meaning). The phrase "with their vanities," *be'hevel*, with the prefix for the preposition, "with / *be*," sounds very much like the vowel sounds of *wabohu* with the consonants in jumbled order, keeping in mind that in Hebrew the "v" and the "b" sound are somewhat interchangeable. As was previously mentioned, paronomasia means "to alter slightly in naming," so it would seem to be a valid exercise to follow Tsumura's examples in which he speculates on how one word can gradually evolve into other forms.[251] The word *bohu* could have been invented and combined with *tohu* through the following mental steps, based on similar sounds and similar meanings of the words involved. Starting with *be'hehvel* (vanities, things empty of purpose), the following stages could have taken place:

1. Switch the "v" and the initial "h" of *"hehvel"* = *be'vehhel*
2. Change the "v" sound to the closely related "b" = *be'behhel*
3. Change "with / *be*" to "and / *wa*" = *wa'behhel*
4. Drop the "l" sound = *wa'behhe*
5. Change the vowels to cause the newly coined term to rhyme with *tohu* = *wa'bohu*.

---

[251] Tsumura, *Creation and Destruction*, 16, 17, 42-45.

Another example of how this same word could have been played with to come up with "bohu," with fewer steps and more obvious connections, comes from 2 Kings 17:15 (KJV): "they followed <u>vanity</u>, and became <u>vain</u> (*wahebalu*)" (Strong's # 1891). In this case the root word already has the conjunction, "*waw / wa*," and in this grammatical form the "v" sound is already "b," so only three stages would be needed for it to evolve into "*wa'bohu*":

1. Drop the syllable, "*he*" = *wabalu*

2. Exchange the "l" sound for the dropped "h" = *wabahu*

3. Make the minor correction in the vowel sound to cause the newly coined term to rhyme with *tohu* = *wa'bohu*

These suggestions are in keeping with the figure of speech known as paronomasia, mentioned by Bullinger and Fishbane in relation to *tohu wabohu*, as mentioned earlier. If the German Old Testament scholar, Claus Westermann, and Hebrew scholar, Robert Alter, are right, that *bohu* is a made-up word,[252] and if others are right that it means "vain" or "empty," then *hahval* (Strong's # 1891) could well be the word it was based on. "The second word of the pair [*tohu wabohu*] looks like a nonce term coined to rhyme with the first and to reinforce it,"[253] says Alter. And if *bohu* is a made-up word, that would explain why it does not occur by itself anywhere in Scripture.

If this etymological proposal is accepted, the mixed-up origin of the phrase already hints at the meaning of the term *tohu wabohu*, communicating by its sound a mixed up, disordered state of being. The original word in 2 Kings 17:15 that was "mixed up" in creating the new term is in the context of the people falling under judgment for going after the vain or worthless thing / *ha'hahval* (idols) (Strong's # 1891). As a result, they themselves became vain, worthless / *wahebalu* (Strong's # 1891). If we consider the phrase *tohu wabohu* (a variation of *tohu wehabalu*) to be a pun, we could speculate that former inhabitants of the earth or land (prior to Genesis 1:1, 2; cf. Ezekiel 28:15-17) had similarly followed vain things and themselves became worthless (*wehabalu*).[254] Describing the condition of the earth with the mocking rhyme, *tohu wabohu*, would have communicated to Moses' listeners that something had gone wrong, was out of order, contrary to God's intentions. The land was worthless (empty of meaning) for God's

---

[252] Alter, *Biblical Narrative*, 17.

[253] Alter, *Biblical Narrative*, 17.

[254] Compare Jesus' understanding of this principle in Matthew 5:13: "You are the salt of the earth. But if the salt loses its saltiness, … it is no longer good for anything [it is worthless], except to be thrown out and trampled underfoot."

purposes, before he began making things right through the orderly creation events.

Examination of the Context

The concept of being "worthless" or "useless" is often associated with the contexts of the terms, *tohu* and *tohu wabohu*. Frequently the context is a description of the land as a howling, trackless waste. These are descriptions of conditions the prophets predicted for the nations that God has judged or will judge. In light of these frequent uses of the terms we are investigating, it seems reasonable to consider that Genesis 1:2 is also describing the condition of a land that had fallen under judgment. It is not just neutral material waiting passively to be acted upon as some commentators claim.

We will examine the context for each separate occurrence of *tohu* and *tohu wabohu* for further insights into the meaning and significance of this term. Following an inductive analysis of each passage, a listing of the passages according to the usage of the *tohu* will summarize the most important findings. The goal of this study is to understand the usage of the term in Genesis 1:2 and the contribution this understanding makes toward recognizing that chaos is not God's will. The passages in which the word *tohu* occurs demonstrate that God intends to correct what is out of order, turning what is worthless into something life-giving and purposeful. This is also the best understanding of working with God through international development.

The word *tohu* occurs in the following passages. Those in which it occurs as part of the compound term *tohu wabohu* are indicated with an asterisk: Genesis 1:2*; Deuteronomy 32:10; 1 Samuel 12:21 (2x); Job 6:18; 12:24; 26:7; Psalm 107:40; Isaiah 24:10; 29:21; 34:11*; 40:17; 40:23; 41:29; 45:18, 19; 49:4; 59:4; Jeremiah 4:23* For each of these passages, starting with Deuteronomy 32:10, the following categories of information will help us compare the context and usage of the terms:

1. The primary meaning of *tohu* or *tohu wabohu*.

2. Any parallel terms (indicated by the geometric sign, //).

3. A brief description of the broader context of the verse—in most cases, the rest of the chapter in which it occurs.

4. Motifs or word associations within that broad context.

5. What is out of order or in opposition to God's intentions.

6. How God corrected this opposition and demonstrated his will.

DEUTERONOMY 32:10 (*TOHU*)

In a desert land he found him,
* in a barren and howling waste* [tohu].
He shielded him and cared for him;
* he guarded him as the apple of his eye.*

1. Primary meaning: barren and howling waste.

2. // to desert land or wilderness.

3. Broader context: recounting the history of God's care for his people when he found them wandering in the wilderness.

4. Motifs:

> Desert / howling waste / barren
> Care / shield / eagle stirring its nest
> "Apple of his eye" (the literal translation of the Hebrew)
> No foreign gods

5. What is out of order or in opposition to God's intentions: God's people were wandering in a barren land that could not support life.

6. How God corrected this opposition and demonstrated his will: "He shielded him and cared for him; he guarded him as the apple of his eye, like an eagle that stirs up its nest and hovers over its young, that spreads its wings to catch them and carries them aloft. The Lord alone led him; no foreign god was with him" (Deut. 32:10-12).

1 SAMUEL 12:21 (*TOHU*, 2X)

Do not turn away after useless idols [tohu; vain things]. *They can do you no good, nor can they rescue you, because they are useless* [tohu].

1. Primary meaning: useless idols / vain things.

2. The translations for *tohu* ("useless") are // to each other.

3. Broader context: God made the people his own; serve God faithfully; if you persist in evil you will be swept away (with the useless things).

4. Motifs:

> Useless
> Idols
> Vain things
> Idols cannot rescue
> Creation of a people
> God will not reject the faithful
> Evil doers swept away

5. What is out of order or in opposition to God's intentions: Samuel is warning God's people against going back to putting their hope in something useless (idols).

6. How God corrected this opposition and demonstrated his will: because the people repented, Samuel says, "For the sake of his great name the Lord will not reject his people, because the Lord was pleased to make you his own" (1 Sam. 12:22).

JOB 6:18: (*TOHU*)

Caravans turn aside from their routes;
  they go off into the wasteland [tohu; *nothing*] *and perish.*

1. Primary meaning: wasteland / nothing.

2. // to distressed, disappointed (not finding water), perish.

3. Broader context: undependable people are like water not flowing; those hoping for water will perish.

4. Motifs:

> wasteland
> nothing
> undependable as intermittent streams (flood / drought)
> darkened (by thawing ice)
> perish / distressed / disappointed

5. What is out of order or in opposition to God's intentions: Job's "friends" are undependable people who are like an intermittent stream that deceives people into turning aside to look for water and perishing because there is no water to support life.

6. How God corrected this opposition and demonstrated his will: Job had stated God's will (in negative form) a few verses earlier: "Anyone who withholds kindness from a friend forsakes the fear of the Almighty" (Job 6:14).

JOB 12:24: (*TOHU*)

He deprives the leaders of the earth of their reason;
  he makes them wander in a trackless waste [tohu].

1. Primary meaning: wilderness / through a waste (trackless; without a path).

2. // to deprived of reason // to grope in darkness // stagger like drunkards.

3. Broader context: by his wisdom and power God controls the waters, leading to drought or flooding; he reveals deep things of darkness (makes fools out of counselors' advice, resulting in their experiencing chaotic internal conditions) and brings the deep shadows (of death) into the light. All this is a metaphor to describe how God will deal with false advisors.

4. Motifs:

> wisdom / power / control
> waters / drought /flooding
> wilderness / trackless waste
> darkness (metaphorical)
> deep shadows of death (metaphorical)
> insanity
> darkness (literal)
> drunken staggering

5. What is out of order or in opposition to God's intentions: false advisors are wandering without direction or reason.

6. How God corrected this opposition and demonstrated his will: Job is confronting his accusers again, and had stated God's will prior to this description of what happens to leaders and advisors who are not aligned with God's ways. Instead of relying on their own wisdom, people need to recognize that "to God belong wisdom and power; counsel and understanding are his" (Job 12:13).

JOB 26:7: (*TOHU*)

He spreads out the northern skies over empty space [tohu];
  he suspends the earth over nothing.

1. Primary meaning: empty place.

2. // to "nothing."

3. Broader context: "death writhes [shakes] … and destruction [Abaddon] lies uncovered"; God is undoing destruction through re-creation. In this context, God's "battle" with the deep and the sea monster Rahab is metaphorical of his bringing order out of chaos by separating the waters above and below and separating light and dark.

4. Motifs:

> death
> writhing or trembling (shaking)
> destruction lies uncovered

creation theme (separating waters, separating light and
     darkness)
void / nothing / empty place
darkness
quaking (pillars of heaven)
sea monsters killed (Rahab cut in pieces)
storm calmed
breath (*ruach*) of God

5. What is out of order or in opposition to God's intentions: where
there used to be something there is nothingness / empty space.

6. How God corrected this opposition and demonstrated his will:
God responds to emptiness with creation: "He spreads out the northern
skies over empty space; ... He marks out the horizon on the face of the
waters for a boundary between light and darkness" (Job 26:7, 10).

PSALM 107:40: (*TOHU*)

... he who pours contempt on nobles
  made them wander in a trackless waste [tohu].

1. Primary meaning: wander in a waste (without a path); void place
(trackless waste).

2. // to pouring contempt on nobles (see Job 12:24 = deprived of
reason, equivalent to chaos).

3. Broader context: recounting the history of God's people and God's
rescue when they called to him out of darkness and distress; God turned
life-giving land into a salt waste because of the wickedness of those who
lived there; later he turned that desert back to fruitfulness with water and
people; leaders who oppressed the people were made to wander in the
trackless waste; needy were helped (justice).

4. Motifs:
          wander in a waste (without a path / trackless waste)
          void place
          cry for help
          saved from distress
          darkness / gloom
          sea
          works of the Lord
          deep (not *tehom*)
          storm calmed
          desert

fruitful land
wickedness

5. What is out of order or in opposition to God's intentions: leaders who oppressed God's people are wandering without direction in a trackless waste.

6. How God corrected this opposition and demonstrated his will: "he lifted the needy out of their affliction and increased their families like flocks. The upright see and rejoice, but all the wicked shut their mouths. Let the one who is wise heed these things and ponder the loving deeds of the Lord" (Ps. 107:41-43).

ISAIAH 24:10: (*TOHU*)

The ruined [tohu] *city lies desolate;*
   the entrance to every house is barred.

1. Primary meaning: ruined; city of confusion is broken down.

2. // to the entrance to every house is barred.

3. Broader context: a prediction of judgment to come; the Lord is going to lay waste the earth and devastate it (vs. 1) because the people have defiled the land; analogies are given from agriculture, from the floodgates of heaven, and the earth being shaken; the earth reels like a drunkard; all imply chaos.

4. Motifs:

        city of confusion is broken down
        ruins
        empty
        lay waste
        devastate
        defiled (by the people)
        disobedience
        curse
        guilt
        desolate
        beaten
        flood
        shake
        drunkard (reels)
        rebellion

5. What is out of order or in opposition to God's intentions: the desolate city is ruined because the people had rebelled and violated God's ways and a curse consumed the land.

6. How God will correct this opposition and demonstrate his will: "in that day the Lord will punish the powers in the heavens above and the kings on the earth below. ... The moon will be dismayed, the sun ashamed; for the Lord Almighty will reign on Mount Zion and in Jerusalem, and before its elders—with great glory" (Isa. 24:21, 23).

ISAIAH 29:21: (*TOHU*)

... those who with a word make someone out to be guilty,
   who ensnare the defender in court
   and with false testimony [tohu] *deprive the innocent of justice.*

1. Primary meaning: empty pleas; a thing of naught (no account); false testimony; an empty assertion.

2. // ensnare the defender in court.

3. Broader context: woe to David's city; judgment and destruction are coming. Those who try to hide their plans from the Lord are working in darkness. God will turn things upside down (vs. 16). God will help the humble. The ruthless who take advantage of the innocent (through false testimony) will be cut down and disappear.

4. Motifs

> great depths (metaphorical)
> hide
> woe
> darkness
> upside down
> formed / make (potter and clay)
> fertile field
> gloom
> blind will see
> ruthless / mockers / evil
> vanish / disappear / cut down
> guilty
> depriving the innocent of justice
> false testimony / empty pleas or assertions / a thing of naught
>   (no account)

5. What is out of order or in opposition to God's intentions: ruthless people had been using false testimony to deprive the innocent of justice.

6. How God will correct this opposition and demonstrate his will: "in that day ... the humble will rejoice in the Lord; the needy will rejoice in the Holy One of Israel. The ruthless will vanish, the mockers will disappear, and all who have an eye for evil will be cut down" (Isa. 29:18-20).

ISAIAH 34:11: (*TOHU WABOHU*)

The desert owl and screech owl will possess it;
  the great owl and the raven will nest there.
God will stretch out over Edom
  the measuring line of chaos [tohu]
  and the plumb line of desolation [bohu].

1. Primary meaning: measuring line of confusion, chaos; and the plumb line of desolation, emptiness.

2. // to nothing there to be called a kingdom; // to all her princes [leaders] will vanish away.

3. Broader context: judgment against the nations (not Israel; Edom is specifically referred to in connection with the measuring lines of *tohu wabohu*). They will be measured with a plumb line that is empty (weightless) and desolate. Kingdoms will vanish. The formerly inhabited area will become a wilderness inhabited only by wild animals.

4. Motifs:
> heavens will be dissolved
> streams and land become pitch [dark; a description of the
>   results of a volcanic eruption]
> desolate
> desert
> (howling) owl
> the measuring line of chaos (*tohu*)
> and the plumb line of desolation (*bohu*)
> nothing there to be called a kingdom
> uninhabited (implied)
> princes will vanish

5. What is out of order or in opposition to God's intentions: a place meant to be occupied by people has been turned into a desert where only wild animals and birds can live; civilization is ruined and unable to be rebuilt. God has made the plumb line useless (*tohu*) by making the stones empty (*bohu*) that should have weighted the line to make it possible to measure a true straight line for building purposes.

6. How God will correct this opposition and demonstrate his will: "the desert and the parched land will be glad; the wilderness will rejoice and blossom. ... Be strong, do not fear; your God will come, ... he will come to save you. Then will the eyes of the blind be opened and the ears of the deaf unstopped. Then will the lame leap like a deer, and the mute tongue shout for joy. Water will gush forth in the wilderness and streams in the desert" (Isa. 35:1, 4-6).

ISAIAH 40:17, 23: (*TOHU*)

Before him all the nations are as nothing;
  they are regarded by him as worthless [tohu]
  and less than nothing. ...
He brings princes to naught
  and reduces the rulers of this world to nothing [tohu].

1. Primary meaning: vanity, worthless; nothing.

2. // to nothing, less than nothing (vs. 17); // to brings princes to naught (vs. 23).

3. Broader context: God's comfort for his people; turning the desert into a highway for God; caring for people as for loved animals. The context of creation is referred to and the greatness of God in relationship to the nations and their rulers is emphasized. They are as nothing in comparison.

4. Motifs:
> desert / wilderness
> highway / straight paths (opposite of writhing and twisting)
> shepherd
> measured
> waters
> nothing / as dust on scales or drop in bucket
> worthless
> idols
> beginning / earth founded
> strength given to weary
> eagles' wings

5. What is out of order or in opposition to God's intentions: the nations and their rulers and judges are less than nothing and worthless. They are not fulfilling their God-given purposes.

6. How God will correct this opposition and demonstrate his will: God demonstrates what right leadership looks like: "See, the Sovereign

Lord comes with power, and he rules with a mighty arm. …He tends his flock like a shepherd: He gathers the lambs in his arms and carries them close to his heart; he gently leads those that have young. … Those who hope in the Lord will renew their strength. They will soar on wings like eagles; they will run and not grow weary, they will walk and not be faint" (Isa. 40: 10, 11, 31).

ISAIAH 41:29: (*TOHU*)

See, they are all false!
  Their deeds amount to nothing;
  their images are but wind and confusion [tohu].

1. Primary meaning: confusion / vanity.

2. // to deeds amount to nothing.

3. Broader context: God is the helper of Israel. He will rescue them from their enemies who are as nothing to God and will make the land watered and fruitful. The idols are less than nothing. God wasn't able to find a prophet who wasn't false to tell these things to the people.

4. Motifs:

> ends of earth
> fear (the Lord)
> tremble
> servant (chosen by God)
> strengthen / help
> righteous
> rage /oppose
> ashamed / disgraced / as nothing / perish
> rivers flow / springs / pools of water
> barren / desert
> idols
> less than nothing
> worthless
> detestable
> stirred up one from the north
> false
> deeds amount to nothing
> images are wind / vanity / confusion

5. What is out of order or in opposition to God's intentions: the idols and gods are false and cannot give answers or help.

6. How God corrects this opposition and demonstrates his will: "'I am the Lord your God who takes hold of your right hand and says to

you, Do not fear; I will help you. Do not be afraid, ... little Israel, do not
fear, for I myself will help you,' declares the Lord, your Redeemer, the
Holy One of Israel" (Isa. 41: 13, 14).

ISAIAH 44:9: (*TOHU*)

All who make idols are nothing [tohu],
    and the things they treasure are worthless.
Those who would speak up for them are blind;
    they are ignorant, to their own shame.

1. Primary meaning: graven images (or those making them) are
vanity / nothing.

2. // to worthless.

3. Broader context: Israel is God's chosen people. He will pour his
Spirit on them, as pictured by watering the dry ground. Idols are
worthless. The imagery of creation is applied to Israel; the people and
their sins are forgiven; cities will be rebuilt.

4. Motifs:

> dry ground / thirsty land
> Spirit
> offspring / descendants
> flowing streams
> established ancient people (creation of people)
> tremble (do not)
> makers of idols are nothing
> worthless
> blind / ignorant
> shame
> servant Israel
> creation of people, Israel
> redeemed
> inhabited
> creation of physical world described
> stretched out heavens
> false prophets
> overthrow learning of wise / nonsense
> restore ruins
> build up city
> dry up the watery deep

5. What is out of order or in opposition to God's intentions: idols are
worthless and those who value them are ignorant and blind.

6. How God corrected this opposition and demonstrated his will: "this is what the Lord says—Israel's King and Redeemer, the Lord Almighty: 'I am the first and I am the last; apart from me there is no God. ... You are my witnesses. Is there any God besides me?' No, there is no other Rock; I know not one" (Isa. 44:6, 8).

ISAIAH 45:18, 19: (*TOHU*, 2X)

For this is what the Lord says—
he who created the heavens,
    he is God;
he who fashioned and made the earth,
    he founded it;
he did not create it to be empty [tohu]*,*
    but formed it to be inhabited—
he says:
"I am the Lord,
    and there is no other.
I have not spoken in secret,
    from somewhere in a land of darkness;
I have not said to Jacob's descendants,
    'Seek me in vain [tohu]*.'*
I, *the Lord, speak the truth;*
    I declare what is right.

1. Primary meaning: created the earth not in vain, to no purpose (vs. 18); he didn't say "seek me" in vain (falsely, to no purpose) (vs. 19).

2. // to inhabited (vs. 18); // to speak the truth / declare what is right (vs. 19).

3. Broader context for both verses: God creates light and darkness, brings both prosperity and disaster, according to the way the people relate to God's ways. He created the world, sets Cyrus in place to carry out his plans to rebuild the city and to destroy those who make and worship idols. God means for the earth to be inhabited and for Jacob's descendents and all the earth to seek him.

4. Motifs:

> anointed
> light
> darkness
> prosperity
> disaster
> creation of earth and mankind

righteousness / ways straight
rebuild city
set exiles free
makers of idols
disgraced / put to shame
not to be empty
inhabited
not in secret
not in land of darkness
descendants
seek me
not in vain
speak truth / what is right
turn and be saved
ends of earth
no other God
righteousness
strength

5. What is out of order or in opposition to God's intentions: God did not create the world for no purpose (he created it to be inhabited and sustain life) and he did not tell Jacob's descendents to seek him without having a purpose in mind.

6. How God corrected this opposition and demonstrated his will: "I, the Lord, speak the truth; I declare what is right. ... Turn to me and be saved, all you ends of the earth; for I am God, and there is no other. ... Before me every knee will bow; by me every tongue will swear" (Isa. 45:19, 22, 23).

ISAIAH 49:4: (*TOHU*)

But I said, "I have labored in vain;
  I have spent my strength for nothing at all [tohu].
Yet what is due me is in the Lord's hand,
  and my reward is with my God."

1. Primary meaning: spent my strength for nothing.

2. // in vain / for no purpose / nothing.

3. Broader context: the prophet is addressing the far away peoples, telling them the Lord has called him to be a prophet to them, but he feels like he has labored for no purpose (*tohu*). God tells the prophet he will not only help Israel, but all other nations as well, giving them the opportunity to be set free.

4. Motifs:

> servant of the Lord
> islands / distant nations / ends of the earth / Gentiles
> God's "making" of his servant (from birth)
> arrow / quiver (as a tool for God to use)
> strength
> spent to no purpose
> nothing
> Lord's hand / reward
> restore
> salvation
> covenant
> desolate
> inheritance
> captives made free
> darkness
> not hunger, thirst
> desert
> compassion
> guide
> springs of water

5. What is out of order or in opposition to God's intentions: the prophet thinks he has spent his strength for no purpose.

6. How God corrected this opposition and demonstrated his will: God gives the prophet a larger purpose in life, one that perhaps has more hope of success and less frustration: "It is too small a thing for you to be my servant to restore the tribes of Jacob and bring back those of Israel I have kept. I will also make you a light for the Gentiles, that my salvation may reach to the ends of the earth" (Isa. 49:6).

ISAIAH 59:4: (*TOHU*)

No one calls for justice;
  no one pleads a case with integrity.
They rely on empty arguments [tohu], *they utter lies;*
  they conceive trouble and give birth to evil.

1. Primary meaning: they trust in vanity / rely on empty arguments and speak lies.

2. // to conceiving trouble and giving birth to evil.

3. Broader context: sins have separated people from God; justice is not being done; people are relying on false testimony, condemning the

innocent. In the midst of this metaphorical darkness, God stepped in to bring salvation and righteousness, in the context of battle.

4. Motifs:

> save / hear
> iniquities, sin
> separated
> justice
> integrity
> empty arguments
> lies
> trouble
> evil
> shed innocent blood
> ruin
> destruction
> no peace
> no justice
> no righteousness
> darkness
> deep shadows
> intercede
> salvation
> righteousness as a breastplate
> helmet of salvation
> garments of vengeance
> wrapped in zeal as in a cloak

5. What is out of order or in opposition to God's intentions: the people have rejected truth and justice and are trusting in vain, worthless things (*tohu*). They are speaking lies, and giving birth to evil deeds.

6. How God intends to correct this opposition and demonstrate his will: "the Lord looked and was displeased that there was no justice. He … was appalled that there was no one to intervene; so his own arm achieved salvation for him, … He put on righteousness as his breastplate, and the helmet of salvation on his head. … 'The Redeemer will come to Zion, to those in Jacob who repent of their sins,' declares the Lord" (Isa. 59:15-17, 20).

JEREMIAH 4:23: (*TOHU WABOHU*)

I looked at the earth,
  and it was formless [tohu] *and empty* [bohu];
and at the heavens,
  and their light was gone.

1. Primary meaning: earth (land) was ruined, the opposite of creation (*tohu wabohu*).

2. // to heavens: their light was gone

   // to mountains: quaking and hills swaying

   // to no people

   // to every bird in the sky had flown away

   // to the fruitful land was a desert

   // to all its towns lay in ruins.

3. Broader context: return to me Israel; God is sending an agent from the north to destroy the people of Israel. The towns will be ruined and will become desert. This is because God's people foolishly refuse to know and obey him. Their moral values are completely reversed. "They are skilled in doing evil; they know not how to do good" (vs. 22). Symbolically or literally the earth has become empty, shaken, ruined (shattered) because of the Lord's anger against evil. Creation is being undone in a sense. The earth will mourn and the heavens will be dark because of this punishment on God's people.

4. Motifs:

> doing evil
> destroyer of nations
> lay waste the land
> towns ruined
> without inhabitant
> scorching wind
> barren heights
> desert
> judgment
> whirlwind
> clouds
> eagles
> conduct
> disaster
> destroyed
> fools / no understanding / do not know me

evil
earth formless and empty
light gone (darkness)
mountains quaking
no people or birds
desert
mourn
heavens grow dark
towns deserted / no one lives in them

5. What is out of order or in opposition to God's intentions: the land is ruined and unable to sustain life as a result of judgment on the people who are skilled in doing evil. The land is shaken up, as in an earthquake or volcanic eruption.

6. How God wants to correct this opposition and demonstrate his will: the only hope for the people toward whom these disasters are headed is to return to serving God: "'If you, Israel, will return ... to me,' declares the Lord. 'If you put your detestable idols out of my sight and no longer go astray, and if in a truthful, just and righteous way you swear, "As surely as the Lord lives..." [then God's judgment will not fall on them like fire] with no one to quench it'" (Jer. 4:1, 2, 4).

Passages Categorized by the Usage of Tohu *or* Tohu Wabohu

Another way to look at the meaning of the terms, *tohu* and *tohu wabohu*, is by grouping them in categories according to similar usage. In the context studies above, it is possible to discover six categories for the way "*tohu*" or "*tohu wabohu*" is used, outside of Genesis 1:2:

1. *TOHU* AS A LITERAL DESERT BUT USED AS A SPIRITUAL METAPHOR

Deuteronomy 32:1 (desert: where God found the people he created "out of nothing")
> Job 6:18 (wasteland: describes undependable "comforters")
> Job 12:24 (trackless waste: metaphor to describe how God will deal with [false] advisors, rulers who lose their sanity as a result of judgment, as was the case with Nebuchadnezzar)
> Psalm 107:40 (trackless waste: metaphor for pouring contempt and judgment on unjust leaders)

2. *TOHU* TO REPRESENT WHAT IS WORTHLESS, USELESS, AS NOTHING

1 Samuel 12:21 (useless idols do you no good)
Isaiah 40:17 (nations and its rulers are as nothing to God)

Isaiah 41:29 (molten images are wind and confusion)

Isaiah 44:9 (graven images, or those making them, are vanity, nothing, worthless)

Isaiah 49:4 (I have spent my strength for nothing, no purpose)

3. *TOHU* REFERS TO A PLACE THAT IS RUINED AND UNINHABITED

Isaiah 24:10 (ruined city lies desolate)

Isaiah 45:18 (he did not create the earth to be ruined or empty, but to be inhabited)

4. *TOHU* INDICATES VAIN SPEAKING THAT IS FALSE

Isaiah 29:21 (ensnare the defender in court with empty pleas / speaking what is false)

Isaiah 45:19 (I did not speak in vain [falsely], I speak the truth; I declare what is right)

Isaiah 59:4 (they trust in vanity / rely on empty arguments and speak lies)

5. *TOHU* DESCRIBES AN EMPTY PLACE, A DESTROYED AREA

Job 26:7 (spreads out skies over the empty space: over death and destruction that lie naked and uncovered)

6. *TOHU WABOHU* DESCRIBES SOMETHING THAT IS DESTROYED AND UPSIDE DOWN FROM GOD'S INTENDED ORDER

Isaiah 34:11: (The opposite of creation and building construction are described as judgment)

Jeremiah 4:23: (Towns are ruined, deserted, without inhabitants. The opposite of creation and building construction are described as judgment. The people are skilled at doing evil; don't know how to do good. "Their moral values are completely reversed."[255])

Summary of Themes Associated with Tohu *and* Tohu Wabohu

This study shows that the following general themes are associated with *tohu* or *tohu wabohu*, indicating the understanding the ancient Hebrews would have had when they heard that the land God was making for them was "*tohu wabohu.*"

---

[255] Charles L. Feinberg, *Jeremiah: A Commentary* (Grand Rapids: Zondervan Regency Reference Library, 1982), 53.

• Cities or kingdoms are being torn down
• Everything is upside down from God's intended order: the land is desert-like, not supporting life; no people
• The opposite of God's will and of creation is described
• The tone is of mourning and desolation
• Some type of judgment is described or implied

Following are the most common themes and primary meanings of *tohu* and *tohu wabohu* discovered in the context studies. These terms are always used in a context of judgment:

Darkness
Shaking
Water in negative connotations: flood or lack of it in drought
Creation imagery
Refuge, care, shield
Destruction
Desert, wasteland
Worthless (idols, foreign gods)
Justice
Building, city
Evil
Inhabited or not
Vain, nothing, no purpose
Ends of the earth
Judgment (associated with *tohu* in every case)

Barth summarizes the impact of these connotations of *tohu wabohu* for interpreting Genesis 1:2: "There is only 'chaos.' ... According to this phrase the situation in which the earth finds itself is the very opposite of promising. It is quite hopeless."[256]

Commentators Views in Ideological Perspective

Before summarizing the conclusions reached through these inductive studies of the contexts and word associations of *tohu* and *tohu wabohu*,

---

[256] Barth, *Church Dogmatics*, 3:104

we will expand the conversation beyond the biblical author and the current interpreter to include past interpreters of the text. This is a feature of exploring the ideological texture of a text. Vernon Robbins points out,

> All people choose ways to write and to read a text. For this reason, socio-rhetorical criticism interprets not only the text under consideration but ways people read texts in late antiquity and ways people have interpreted ... texts both in the past and in different contexts in our modern world.[257]

In order for this comparison and conversation to take place, we need to examine the presuppositions of the conversation partners. The Pontifical Biblical Commission has openly acknowledged the variety of perspectives from which contemporary interpreters approach the biblical text: "philosophical, psychoanalytic, sociological, political, etc." [258] DeSilva points out that "cultural studies, postcolonial criticism, and feminist criticism have ... raised our awareness of how biblical interpretation is a political and ideological act." [259] According to which lens the interpreter uses, the answers to questions brought to the text will receive differing answers. This requires looking carefully and critically at the biases and beliefs of the interpreter of a text. Robbins clarifies the importance of the conversation partners and their unique backgrounds:

> The primary subject of ideological analysis and interpretation is people. ... The issue is the social, cultural, and individual location and perspective of writers and readers. Ideological analysis of a text, then, is simply an agreement by various people that they will dialogue and disagree with one another with a text as a guest in the conversation.[260]

In consulting other parties in this conversation, with the passages of Scripture above as the "guest" and topic of the conversation, we will review and critique the opinions of various commentators through the ages, in chronological order. We will evaluate how these commentators'

---

[257] Robbins, *Tapestry*, 39.
[258] Pontifical Biblical Commission, "The Interpretation of the Bible in the Church," accessed April 11, 2008, http://www.ewtn.com/library/CURIA/PBCINTER.htm#3.
[259] David A. deSilva, *An Introduction to the New Testament: Contexts, Methods and Ministry Formation* (Downers Grove: InterVarsity, 2004), 25.
[260] Vernon K. Robbins, *Exploring the Texture of Texts: A Guide to Socio-Rhetorical Interpretation* (Valley Forge: PA: Trinity Press International, 1996), 95.

insights and conclusions relate to the themes being developed in this book, and why or why not their conclusions might be either valid or incomplete.

RASHI (ABOUT 1100)

Rashi was a Jewish biblical commentator of the Middle Ages who was born and lived in France. In his commentary on Genesis, Rashi translates *tohu wabohu* as "desolate and void." Rashi explains that the word *tohu* signifies astonishment and desolation, "for a person would have been astonished and amazed at its emptiness." This agrees with Bullinger's explanation about figures of speech which call the audience's attention to something unusual or startling that is being said. *Bohu,* Rashi says, "signifies emptiness and empty space."[261] Rashi approached his interpretation of Genesis from the standpoint of why God gave these words to the original audience. He viewed the creation story as the story of the creation of the local promised land. His explanation of the term fits well with the other usages of the term in the Old Testament and does not preclude seeing "the land" as a place that has experienced God's judgment.

MARTIN LUTHER (1544)

Luther takes other uses of the terms in Scripture into account in reaching his conclusion that *tohu* means "nothing, "so that a *Tohu* earth, means, in its simple reality, that which is … 'empty' or 'destitute;'— where there is no way, no distinction of places, … no animals, no men." Luther compares this with Isaiah's description of the threatened destruction of the earth, "There shall be stretched upon it the line of *Tohu* (nothingness); and the plummet of *Bohu* (emptiness)" (Isa. 34:11), which indicates there will be no people, animals, or houses left. "All things [will be] hurled into chaos and confusion"[262]

Luther considers that *tohu wabohu* is part of the description of the first day of creation, when God created the earth as an unformed mass that was afterwards separated by the Word ("and God said."). "For this was the office of … the Son of God—to divide, and to adorn, that chaotic mass which was produced from nothing."[263] Although Luther forces verse 2 into the pattern of the six days of creation, his suggestion that God first created the earth as a chaotic and confused mass is

---

[261] Morris and Silbermann, trans., *Pentateuch,* 1:2.
[262] Luther, *Still Speaking,* 28.
[263] Luther, *Luther Still Speaking,* 29.

intriguing. Luther is apparently saying the Father gave the Son this "unformed mass" as the material to work with in making the earth. ("Without him nothing was made that has been made" [John 1:3].) This fits well with the ideological speculation in chapter 3 that the Son worked along with the angels to shape the earth out of the basic elements that only God could create out of nothing.

Luther's use of the phrases, "unformed mass" and "emptiness" (and later Calvin's "formless and empty"), may have been responsible for the choice made by the translators of the King James Version more than two centuries later to use the phrase, "without form, and void" for *tohu wabohu.* The ways in which this traditional wording has been understood in recent times is far removed from Luther's understanding of the negative connotations of "unformed," which is closer to "chaos and confusion," than to passive matter waiting to have its details filled in for the first time.

JOHN CALVIN (1554)

Calvin's discussion of *tohu wabohu* ("formless and empty"), like Luther's, lends itself to the speculation that the angels may have worked with the Son to fashion the details of the earth out of the shapeless chaos of the original condition of the earth. Calvin believed that,

> The world was not complete at its commencement, as it now is, but ... it was created an empty chaos of heavens and earth. ... When God in the beginning created the heavens and the earth, the earth was empty and waste.[264]

However, Calvin goes on to confuse the usage and context of the word *tohu* with the compound figure of speech, *tohu wabohu,* when he says, "the Hebrews use *tohu* and *bohu* when they designate anything empty and confused, or vain and worth nothing." The studies above of the occurrences of these terms have shown that it is the single word *tohu* that sometimes has the connotation of "vain" or "worth nothing." These are not appropriate descriptions for something God created, although they do describe conditions resulting from some destructive event.

A valuable insight from Calvin, that helps support the ideological perspective this book is developing, is his comment that, "were we now to take away from the earth all that God added after the time alluded to here, we would have this rude and unpolished, or rather shapeless,

---

[264] John Calvin, *Genesis*, ed. Alister McGrath and J. I. Packer (Wheaton: Crossway Books, 2001), 17.

chaos."[265] This would be one way to describe what can happen when
God withdraws his blessing from a place where the opposite of God's
will is being done. Perhaps Barth, as we will see later, was building on
Calvin's insight when Barth suggested that the state of the earth before
it was shaped and formed matches the description of the earth after
divine judgment.

JOHN PYE SMITH (1854)

British theological tutor John Pye Smith translates *tohu wabohu* as
"without form and void," apparently following the King James
translation of a century earlier. But he gives an original description of
the physical condition of the earth that is implied by Genesis 1:2. He
proposes the possibility that the state of *tohu wabohu* was produced in a
local area by a natural disaster such as an earthquake or volcanic
eruption.

> Extreme darkness has been often known to accompany such
> phenomena. This is the unforced meaning of the two words
> rendered 'without form and void.' Those words [*tohu vabohu*]
> are elsewhere in the Hebrew Bible used to describe ruined
> cities, wild wastes of desert-land, and figuratively any thing that
> is empty, unsubstantial, or useless.[266]

Smith's contribution to the history of the exegesis of this passage is
to go back to the thinking of Rashi, who was closer in both time and
culture to the original Hebrew audience. With Rashi, Smith recognizes
the possibility that Genesis 1 is describing God's preparation of a local
area in which his people could live. Smith adds the insight that the land
had previously been destroyed. He applies the description of judgment
on the land of Edom in Isaiah 34, summarized as *tohu wabohu*, to the
interpretation of the same phrase in Genesis 1:2. He reasons that if
Isaiah uses the term *tohu wabohu* to summarize cataclysmic events
("Edom's streams will be turned into pitch," [Isa. 34:9]), then something
similar must be true of the land in Genesis 1:2.

American missiologist Ralph Winter was also a proponent of seeing
this verse as a description of a local area that was "destroyed and
desolate," due to some cataclysmic event. Winter proposed that perhaps
a small asteroid had caused the destruction and darkness spoken of in
verse 2.[267] Biblical and Hebrew scholar, John Gibson, also suggests the

---

[265] Calvin, *Genesis*, 18.

[266] Smith, *Relation*, 248.

[267] Winter, *Frontiers*, 257.

contexts of the Isaiah and Jeremiah passages describe something violent, such as "the desolation or confusion left behind by an earthquake or a whirlwind or an invading army."[268]

TAYLER LEWIS (1855)

Like John Pye Smith and the King James Version, the conservative professor of Oriental languages, Tayler Lewis, translates *tohu wabohu* as, "without form and void." He sees the term as referring to "irregularity of dimension and the deficiency of gravity, denoting not so much an absolute as relative want of weight." He bases his conclusion on Isaiah 34:11 which speaks in terms of measurement with the line of confusion and the stones of "emptiness." He speaks of *bohu* in this context as, "no weight to the plumb stone or to the stones used for weighing in balances."[269] This is an arbitrary translation, however. The context of Isaiah 34 indicates that the stones were useless for the purpose of building construction, and in fact they were for the opposite purpose, to represent building demolition. A "wrecking ball," might be a better translation than stones with no weight.

While Lewis and the other older commentators all stayed true to versions of Luther's traditional translation, "formless, and empty or void," they compared the implications from the other passages in the Old Testament where the term *tohu* or *tohu wabohu* was used. They were all well aware that something that was not God's will was being described in Genesis 1:2.

UMBERTO CASSUTO (1944)

For Jewish Old Testament scholar, Umberto Cassuto, *tohu wabohu* means "without form or life."[270] "The unformed material from which the earth was to be fashioned at the beginning of its creation ... [was] a chaotic mass, without order or life."[271] Like Luther, Cassuto sees verses 1 and 2 as part of the work of God in creation on the first day, with Genesis 1:2 describing the unformed raw materials from which God later brought order and life. "In this chaos of unformed matter, ... the whole material was an undifferentiated, unorganized, confused, and lifeless agglomeration. It is this terrestrial state that is called *tohu wabohu.*"[272]

---

[268] Gibson, *Daily Study Bible,* 32
[269] T. Lewis, *Six Days,* 58.
[270] Cassuto, *Genesis,* 21.
[271] Cassuto, *Genesis,* 23.
[272] Cassuto, *Genesis,* 20.

Unlike some of the other scholars, Cassuto does not point to other occurrences of the word *tohu* in the Old Testament to show the source of his choices for interpreting *tohu wabohu* as implying chaos. This is because he objects to finding the meaning of *tohu wabohu* by seeking to understand the meanings of the component words. He gives the illustration of "broadcast" in which the separate meanings of "broad" and "cast" would not be particularly helpful in explaining the term to someone unfamiliar with the word.

> Any one who does not know what "broadcast" denotes will not be able to guess the connotation of the word from its separate elements of "broad" and "cast." For the same reason it is profitless to compare other passages in which either of the words *tohu* or *bohu* occurs.[273]

However, Cassuto's argument fails to take into account the figure of speech known as a "hendiadys," mentioned in connection with *tohu wabohu* in Genesis 1:2 by both Waltke[274] and Wenham.[275] Because *tohu wabohu* is a figure of speech in which two separate words are joined with a conjunction, Cassuto's argument using the single word broadcast does not seem applicable. Especially in an oral culture, such as that of the ancient Israelites, an understanding of the meaning of each of the separate words seems important for understanding what connotations the original audience would have caught from hearing the sounds of the compound word.

Cassuto's contribution to the understanding of the term *tohu wabohu* is that this is a state in which life does not exist. Like the commentators before him, he recognizes that the unformed or formless matter is in a state of chaos.

KARL BARTH (1945)

"There is only chaos," Barth says of Genesis 1:2. Barth translates *tohu wabohu*, "waste and void," and says, "there is absolutely nothing in Genesis 1:2 that demonstrates God's will"[276] Barth draws his conclusions from the two other occurrences of the compound term in the

---

[273] Cassuto, *Genesis*, 22.
[274] Waltke, "Literary Genre," 4.
[275] Wenham, *Genesis*, 15.
[276] Barth, *Church Dogmatics*, 3:104

Old Testament. "All the horrors of the approaching final judgment are summed up in the vision of Jeremiah 4:23: 'I beheld the earth, and lo, it was *tohu wa-bohu*, and the heavens, and they had no light.'"[277] Barth sees a similar negative situation in Isaiah 34:11 and concludes, "Thus the condition of the earth depicted in v. 2 is identical with the whole horror of the final judgment."[278]

Unfortunately Barth does not follow through on this insight and denies that there is intelligent opposition to God's will that would be "able in its own power as a matter or a hostile principle to oppose His operations."[279] Without a devil in the picture, Barth's explanation is contradictory. There is horror and judgment, but no apparent reason why something could go wrong that would need to be judged.

BERNARD RAMM (1954)

Unlike Barth, evangelical Baptist theologian and apologist, Bernard Ramm, does not want to acknowledge that Genesis 1:2 implies anything resembling a state of judgment. Instead he chooses to attribute a positive connotation to *tohu*, meaning lack of form, and *bohu,* meaning lack of content. This is a departure from the understanding of earlier commentators, giving a new meaning to the traditional English translation of "formless and void" that avoids the connotations of chaos.

> A marble block and a crumbled statue are both formless. The former is in a state, which awaits a form, and from that formlessness emerges the image. When God made the earth he made it like a marble block out of which He would bring the beautiful world.[280]

This interpretation allows Ramm to use the term *tohu wabohu* as an outline for the narration of the creation events. But Ramm ignores the context of the other uses of the term where *tohu* and *bohu* certainly do not refer to something passive waiting to be acted upon. Rather, the opposite is true—the term refers to a situation in which God has already exercised judgment and the result has been chaos, confusion, and emptiness.

---

[277] Barth, *Church Dogmatics*, 3:104

[278] Barth, *Church Dogmatics*, 3:105

[279] Barth, *Church Dogmatics*, 3:104

[280] Bernard Ramm, *The Christian View of Science and Scripture* (Grand Rapids: Eerdmans, 1954), 203.

MERRILL F. UNGER (1958, 1981)

On the other hand, Unger, a Dallas Theological Seminary professor of Old Testament until his death, recognizes the existence of a counterforce that was responsible for the conditions described in Genesis 1:2 that were definitely not God's will, as Barth had pointed out.

> God did not create the earth in the state of a chaos of wasteness, emptiness, and darkness (John 38:4, 7; Isa. 45:18). It was reduced to this condition because it was the theater where sin began in God's originally sinless universe in connection with the revolt of Lucifer (Satan) and his angels (Isa. 14:12-14; Ezek. 28:13, 15-17; Rev. 12:4). The chaos was the result of God's judgment upon the originally sinless earth.[281]

Unger makes two important contributions to this conversation about the interpretation of *tohu wabohu*: 1) He allows for the existence and activity of the devil prior to the events of Genesis 1, and 2) he represents a conservative evangelical understanding that the first verses of Genesis may speak of a previous creation, that had come under judgment and been destroyed, and is now about to be re-created:

> Genesis 1:1, 2 evidently describes not the primeval creation *ex nihilo*, … but the much later refashioning of a judgment-ridden earth in preparation for a new order of creation--man. The Genesis account deals only with God's creative activity as it concerns the human race in its origin, fall and redemption.[282]

ERICH SAUER (1962)

Sauer, a German theologian with an Open Brethren background, notes regarding *tohu wabohu* that "in both other occurrences [Isaiah 34:11 and Jeremiah 4:23] it means a destruction which is the result of a divine judgment. … In both cases it has the passive meaning of being made desolate and empty."[283] Although Sauer recognizes the work of Satan in the world, he does not want to endorse the Gap or Restitution theory that postulates an earlier creation, implied between verses 1 and 2, that was destroyed due to rebellion. He asks how it would be possible that the angels would rejoice "at the foundation of the world if this creation had at the first been formless and empty, desolate, and

---

[281] Unger, *Unger's Commentary*, 5.

[282] Unger "Rethinking," 28.

[283] Sauer, *King of the Earth*, 232.

chaotic?"[284] In the ideological perspective developed earlier in chapter 3, the response to this question is that Genesis 1 is not talking about the original creation of the world out of nothing, when "the morning stars sang together and all the angels shouted for joy" (Job 38:7).

Because Sauer does not have in mind the possibility that the earth was a battleground where God's enemy had been active prior to the events of Genesis 1, for the definition of the term he has to fall back on "their usual sense of 'formlessness,' and 'emptiness' as a simple description of the original form of the earth at the beginning of creation."[285] However, the "usual sense" he refers to is not the result of contextual studies in Scripture, but rather the traditional translations given by Luther, Calvin, and the King James Version of the Bible. Those earlier commentators unanimously saw that "formless and empty" implied a state of chaos and confusion.

DONALD G. BARNHOUSE (1965)

Barnhouse, a well-known Presbyterian theologian and pastor, was a proponent of seeing a gap in time between the first two verses of Genesis. He offers several possibilities for the translation of *tohu wabohu* in Genesis 1:2: without form, void, waste, desolate, empty, wreck, ruin. Barnhouse prefers the last two as an alliterative phrase and notes that "in French there is a common expression which translates our idea of topsy-turvy: it is *tohu-bohu*—an expression transliterated from the Hebrew of this second verse of Genesis."[286]

Barnhouse speaks of an "invisible war [that] had broken out against the background of a perfect creation"[287] He sees this accounting for the origin of evil; an enemy rebelled against the Creator prior to the creation about which God said that it was "good." Barnhouse astutely asks, "if the Lord ... saw that all was good, whence did this enemy creep in?"[288] The description of the earth as a "wreck and ruin" shows the aftermath of a battle. Barnhouse's ideas lend support to the ideological perspective this book is developing, but as we saw in the previous chapter, it is not grammatically appropriate to say the earth "had become" *tohu wabohu*. Therefore, instead of a gap between verses 1 and 2, we simply need to see verse 1 as a summary statement for the whole chapter, and verse 2

---

[284] Sauer, *King of the Earth*, 232

[285] Sauer, *King of the Earth*, 234.

[286] Donald G. Barnhouse, *The Invisible War* (Grand Rapids: Zondervan, 1965), 15.

[287] Barnhouse, *Invisible War*, 16.

[288] Barnhouse, *Invisible War*, 18.

as describing the conditions when God began to set right what had gone wrong before verse 1. "As for the earth [or land], it was *tohu wabohu*"—it was in a chaotic condition that had no form or order; it was empty of life.

TERRENCE E. FRETHEIM (1969)

Contrary to Barnhouse's proposal of a war in the background of creation, Old Testament Lutheran scholar, Terrence Fretheim, takes the perspective in his early work, *Creation, Fall, and Flood: Studies in Genesis 1–11*, that Genesis 1 represents a transformation of the Israelites' worldview away from the polytheistic assumption that the "present world is the result of a terrible battle."[289] Therefore, while Fretheim acknowledges some similarities to the Babylonian creation epic, such as the watery chaos and darkness at the beginning, he emphasizes the differences and says, "chaos plays little role."[290] Fretheim avoids the issue of the where the chaotic situation came from that is described in Genesis 1:2 by saying that "the origin of this undefined mass is not raised by the author of Genesis 1. The writer is interested only in the creation of the *organized* universe."[291]

As a result of this perspective, Fretheim says *tohu wabohu* is

> … that in which nothing can be distinguished or defined, with the added idea of desolateness or abandonedness (chaos). This is simply a definition of the words "deep" and "waters" which also occur in this verse. This is the unformed material from which most of the earth was now to be fashioned.[292]

This "unformed material" was not neutral, however. Fretheim goes on to say that, "for all the peoples of the ancient Near East, water in large quantities was always a suggestion of the power of evil."[293] Fretheim's contribution to this ideological dialog is that the creation story, with the inclusion of Genesis 1:2, would have illustrated for the Israelites coming out of slavery in Egypt that God is able to overcome evil with good.

Fretheim further points out that "chaos does not cease to exist when it has been ordered. It remains as a threatening possibility to the created

---

[289] Fretheim, *Creation*, 49.
[290] Fretheim, *Creation*, 49.
[291] Fretheim, *Creation*, 52.
[292] Fretheim, *Creation*, 57.
[293] Fretheim, *Creation*, 57.

order."[294] This perspective helps us realize that only in the new heaven
and new earth will there no longer be any threatening circumstances
such as those represented by the sea (Rev. 21:1). In that day, the sea will
be glassy and smooth (Rev. 4:6; 15:2) and there will be no more
darkness or night (Rev. 22:5). Chaos will be finally eliminated.

GERHARD VON RAD (1972)

Von Rad was a German Lutheran pastor, university professor, and
Old Testament scholar, who lived through the two world wars. His
experiences undoubtedly influenced his readiness to note that "man has
always suspected that behind all creation lies the abyss of
formlessness."[295] He sees *tohu wabohu* as referring to this abyss of
formlessness that "all creation is always ready to sink into."[296] Von Rad
cautions against putting too much reliance on the mythologies of the
Israelites' neighbors in interpreting Genesis 1:2, although he concedes
that "the Hebrew word for 'primeval flood' *(tehom)* probably has a
linguistic affinity with Tiamat, the Babylonian dragon of chaos."[297] But
he is not willing to assume that the word *bohu* is related to the
Phoenician mother-goddess, Baau. Instead he defines the meaning of
bohu as "emptiness, desolation," without explaining how he arrived at
that definition. He associates *tohu* with the concept of the wilderness
and cites two of the passages in which *tohu* has that particular meaning
but he does not address how the other two occurrences of *tohu* and *bohu*
together might relate to Genesis 1:2.

Von Rad sees verse 2 as a step backward from verse 1, but refutes
the "restitution" or "gap" theory: "The assumption ... of a cosmic
Lucifer-like plunge of the creation from its initial splendor is
linguistically and objectively quite impossible."[298] We addressed this
objection in discussing Sauer's objections to the "restitution" or "gap"
theory. But von Rad lends support to the pre-Genesis 1 creation theory
when he says that verse 2 speaks of a "reality that existed in a
preprimeval period."[299] There is no logical reason why that "preprimeval
period" could not have been something good and glorious when it was
first created, so that the "morning stars sang together" as that event
unfolded.

---

[294] Fretheim, *Creation,* 54.
[295] von Rad, *Genesis,* 52.
[296] von Rad, *Genesis,* 52.
[297] von Rad, *Genesis,* 50.
[298] von Rad, *Genesis,* 50.
[299] von Rad, *Genesis,* 51.

BRUCE K. WALTKE (1975, 1991, 2001)

Waltke is an evangelical professor of Old Testament and Hebrew who has held prestigious professorships in Old Testament at Dallas Theological Seminary and Westminster Theological Seminary, among other institutions. His preferred translation of *tohu wabohu* is "formless and void," and he rejects the implication that Genesis 1:2 describes the aftermath of destruction or judgment. For Waltke, the negative state of the earth reflects a situation in which the earth is not producing life. It is unformed and unfilled; the opposite of creation.

Waltke's detailed analysis of this term deserves a detailed critique. He gives an extremely thorough analysis of *tohu wabohu*, showing exactly what it means in the context of the other two Old Testament passages where the term is used, then concludes that it means something different in Genesis 1, namely, formless and void, not the aftermath of destruction due to God's judgment.

In the second part of his 1975 *Bibliotheque Sacre* series,[300] Waltke states that it is fallacious reasoning to think that because the judgment coming on the land in Jeremiah takes the form of dismantling creation that therefore the pre-creative state itself is the result of God's fury and judgment. But we can see Waltke's own reasoning as fallacious. He is attributing a false position to other thinkers by assuming that their conclusion (regarding the aspect of judgment in Genesis 1:2) is based on a logic model similar to "if $a = b$, then $b = a$." This position can be shown as follows:

If anti-creation as a form of judgment in Jeremiah 4:23 = *tohu wabohu*

    then

tohu wabohu in Genesis 1:2 = pre-creation as a form of judgment.

However, it is not necessary to attribute this logic to those who endorse this interpretation. They are not necessarily saying that because the judgment looks like the dismantling of creation in Jeremiah, that that is the reason a pre-creation chaos must also be a dismantled creation that was the result of God's judgment. (In the other occurrence of *tohu* and *bohu* used together, in Isaiah 34:11, the result of judgment is the dismantling of civilization rather than of creation.) The focus is not so much on the creation-like state, although that helps legitimize the passage as an appropriate similar context. It is simply a case of taking the few occurrences of a unique term and noticing that in each of the

---

[300] Waltke, "Creation Account: Part 2," 141.

other occurrences, it is in the context of judgment and negative conditions (as are all the occurrences of the single word *tohu*). To disregard the meaning discovered in those contexts is not good exegesis.

Waltke seems to decide that the only other two uses of *tohu* and *bohu* together are irrelevant for his purposes because he wants to use *tohu* and *bohu* as an outline for the rest of the chapter: first the broad form is stated (vs. formless) then the details are filled in (vs. unfilled). This desire to use the phrase as an outline brings a western, literary mindset to the text and imposes a meaning that is not necessarily there (or not the only meaning). It also causes Waltke to be inconsistent in his exegesis, since he recognizes the existence of Satan before the Genesis 1 creation,[301] yet does not want to attribute a meaning to *tohu wabohu* that would imply judgment on Satan's activities. Instead, he concludes that *tohu wabohu* denotes a state of material devoid of order, or without being shaped or formed into something"[302]

In a more recent publication, Waltke describes *tohu wabohu* as

> an antonym to the "heavens and the earth," signifying something uncreated or disordered (Jer. 4:23-27). …
> Chronologically, this must describe the state of the earth prior to verse 1, as it would be a contradiction to represent the creation as formed cosmos and the earth as unformed.[303]

Waltke's interpretation implies the pre-existence of this unformed matter. But Waltke doesn't follow through on the logic of his own position. Did God create the pre-Genesis 1:1 matter in a state of lifelessness, as with the other planets of our solar system? Or did something subsequently turn the original earth (or land) into chaos, resulting in the absence of life-supporting conditions? Given that the earth (or land) was disordered, how did it get that way? Did judgment play some role in this pre-creation period? It is hard to understand why Waltke would balk at considering the state of the earth in Genesis 1:2 to be the result of evil and / or judgment. He ignores the hints from the contexts of all the other occurrences of the word *tohu* in Scripture (including the other two in which *tohu* is combined with *bohu*). He even mentions in Part 1 of his *Bibliotheque Sacre* series that the basic thought of the Old Testament is that Yahweh will triumph over all his enemies

---

[301] Waltke, "Creation Account: Part 2," 141.

[302] Waltke, "Creation Account: Part 2," 144.

[303] Waltke, *Genesis*, 59.

in the establishment of his rule of righteousness.[304] Where did those enemies come from? It would make sense that the first verses of the Bible would introduce a theme so basic and prevalent, even if in a veiled and low-key way so as not to sound as if Yahweh were competing with the gods of the other ancient Near Eastern creation accounts. Through all the biblical creation accounts (or allusions to creation), in fact, it seems not to be a big problem to Yahweh that Satan and chaos are at large in the world. God knows he has the adversary on a leash, unlike humans who cannot control the forces of evil. God asks Job, "Can you pull in Leviathan with a fishhook? ... Can you make a pet of it... or put it on a leash?" (Job 41:1, 5).

Waltke apparently lacks an appreciation for the adversarial element in creation. Although he notes that the absence of the sea and of darkness in the new heaven and new earth (Rev. 21, 22) "suggests that the deep and darkness in verse 2 are less than desirable and were not called into existence by the God of order and goodness,"[305] he fails to say where the conditions of verse 2 came from, if not from God.

In the end, Waltke's arguments are inconsistent and academic. He sorts out the grammar of verses 1, 2, and 3, as we saw in earlier chapters, but he fails to acknowledge or address the interpretive implications of that grammar. All his grammatical arguments over whether verse 1 is an independent or dependent clause, and whether verse 2 is dependent on verse 1 or on verse 3, in the end don't make much practical difference. We still have to interpret what these verses mean, not just clarify the sentence structure. Regardless of the clauses' dependency structure, the first three verses of Genesis clearly mean that God created everything that is known, he started in Genesis 1 with something that existed but that was in an anti-creational form (no order; in chaos, uninhabitable), and he used that as the raw material to shape the land or world.

JOHN C. L. GIBSON (1981)

Scottish minister, theologian, and Hebrew scholar, John C. L. Gibson, chose two sets of alliterative pairs of nouns, "chaos and confusion" or "desolation and disorder," "to catch in English the weird flavor of the Hebrew *tohu wabohu*."[306] He points out that "in the other two passages with the phrase *tohu wabohu*, ... "nearly all of the images

---

[304] Bruce Waltke, "The Creation Account in Genesis 1: Part 1, "Introduction to Biblical Cosmology," *Bibliotheca Sacra* 132 [1975]: 36.

[305] Waltke, "The Creation Account: Part 3," 221.

[306] Gibson, *Daily Study Bible,* 32.

are violent ones and make us think of the desolation of confusion left behind by an earthquake or a whirlwind or an invading army rather than of mere emptiness."[307] In his discussion about the various categories of the use of the word *tohu* (his categories are similar to the categories arrived at inductively earlier in this chapter), Gibson interacts with other interpreters who think of "empty" as a summary term for *tohu* and / or *bohu*:

> One could argue that these senses are linked together by the central idea of "emptiness," but I think it is more likely that all of them go back to a proper association of the word with the creation story. Whatever was considered to be like chaos was called in Hebrew *tohu*.[308]

Gibson does not follow up on his insight that the reason the prophets used *tohu wabohu* in the contexts of Isaiah 34 and Jeremiah 4 was because they saw a similar association with the term in the creation story. If he had explained this similar association he might have supported the pre-Genesis 1 creation and judgment theory.

GORDON WENHAM (1987)

British Old Testament scholar, Gordon Wenham, explains that *tohu wabohu* is an example of a "hendiadys," that literally means, "waste and void." He translates the figure of speech as "total chaos."

> This frightening disorganization is the antithesis to the order that characterized the work of creation when it was complete.... Here and in Isaiah 34:11 and Jeremiah 4:23, *tohu* is coupled with *bohu* "void," where, as the context shows, the dreadfulness of the situation before the divine word brought order out of chaos is underlined.[309]

Wenham does not elaborate on why something "dreadful" came into existence in the first place. His contribution to this ideological conversation is to agree with the common theme of "chaos," and his emphasis on the lack of order implied by the context of *tohu wabohu*. Wenham points out that the rest of verse 2 confirms this: darkness and the deep covered everything. But starting in verse 3, orderliness characterizes the pattern of the creation sequence.

---

[307] Gibson, *Daily Study Bible,* 32.
[308] Gibson, *Daily Study Bible,* 32.
[309] Wenham, *Genesis,* 15, 16.

JON LEVENSON (1988)

Levenson, a professor of Jewish studies at Harvard University, extends the meaning of *tohu wabohu* beyond the merely physical conditions of the earth to take it as

> … an affirmation that God as the creator of the world is directed against the forces that oppose him and his acts of creation—the forces of disorder, injustice, affliction, and chaos, which are, in the Israelite worldview, one.[310]

He objects to viewing the traditional King James translation of *tohu wabohu*, "formless and void," as saying that "void" is the "nothing" out of which God created the world. Levenson's point is that people in the ancient world would have "identified 'nothing' with things like disorder, injustice, subjugation, disease, and death."[311]

> When order emerges where disorder had reigned unchallenged, when justice replaces oppression, when disease and death yield to vitality and longevity, this is indeed the creation of something out of nothing. It is the replacement of the negative by the positive.[312]

Levenson contributes the understanding that Genesis 1 illustrates the principles that God brings good out of evil, which aligns with the international development theme of this book and Sailhamer's insight that *tohu wabohu* becomes *tob*, good. In the last section of this chapter we will explore the concept of *tohu* at a personal and individual level, with the finding that motifs and themes associated with *tohu* are also associated with "the heart." God wants mental and spiritual turmoil and disorder to yield to rightly ordered relationships with God and fellow humans. These are initial steps that are always necessary for successful international development.

DAVID STACEY (1993)

In his commentary on Isaiah 34, Old Testament scholar and archaeologist, David Stacey, says, "The words chaos and jumble

---

[310] Jon Levenson, *Creation and the Persistence of Evil: The Jewish Drama of Divine Omnipotence* (San Francisco: Harper & Row, 1988), xix.

[311] Levenson, *Creation*, xxi.

[312] Levenson, *Creation*, xxi.

translate *tohu* and *bohu*, words that appear in Genesis 1:2 with the meaning 'without form and void'."[313] This is another example of a biblical scholar who thoroughly explains the meaning of *tohu* and *bohu* in Isaiah and Jeremiah, but gives a different meaning for the original use of the term in Genesis 1.

Stacey brings out the helpful point that the immediate context of Isaiah 34:11 describes the results of volcanic activity. "Edom's streams will be turned into pitch, her dust into burning sulfur; her land will become blazing pitch! It will not be quenched night and day; its smoke will rise forever" (Isa. 34:9, 10). He suggests this could also be an allusion to the judgment on Sodom and Gomorrah. "Then the Lord rained down burning sulfur on Sodom and Gomorrah ... and [Abraham] saw dense smoke rising from the land, like smoke from a furnace" (Gen. 19:24, 28).[314]

Stacey probably bases his interpretation of "chaos and jumble" for *tohu wabohu* on the list of unlikely animals he calls attention to, some of which cannot even be definitely identified by scholars. (Another commentator, Christopher Seitz, sees in this chapter, in which the animals' mates are mentioned three times, an allusion to the chaos of Noah's flood.[315]) The stories from Israel's history of Sodom and Gomorrah and of Noah's flood serve as illustrations of what *tohu wabohu* looks like: chaotic conditions that cannot support life, the result of a disaster and God's judgment.

BERNHARD ANDERSON (1994)

Anderson, an American United Methodist pastor and Old Testament scholar, wrote with the realities of World War II in mind. Like Levenson, he sees *tohu wabohu* as representative of the chaos faced in life at many levels. He sees the "chaos and desolation" of Genesis 1:2 as not just a statement about primeval times, but as a statement about a present possibility.[316] This is a valuable contribution to the ideological conversation, showing that others confirm that the creational pattern of bringing order out of chaos has application for today.

---

[313] David Stacey, *Isaiah: Chapters 1–39* (London: Epworth Press, 1993), 209.

[314] Stacey, *Isaiah*, 209.

[315] Christopher R. Seitz, *Isaiah 1-39. Interpretation: A Bible Commentary for Teaching and Preaching* (Louisville: John Knox Press,1993), 237.

[316] Bernhard Anderson, *From Creation to New Creation: Old Testament Perspectives* (Minneapolis: Fortress, 1994), 11.

ALLEN ROSS (1996)

Biblical scholar Allen Ross, formerly of Dallas Theological Seminary and editor of the New King James Version, explains in his contribution on Genesis in the *Bible Knowledge Commentary,* that *tohu wabohu* means a chaos of wasteness, emptiness, and darkness.[317] Ross recognizes the context of judgment in Isaiah 34:11 and Jeremiah 4:23 and contributes to this conversation by acknowledging that this same context applies to Genesis 1:2.

> Genesis gives no explanation for the chaos, but we may gather from the words used and from parallel passages that is was a judgment on rebellion, that Satan was somehow involved, and that oppressive evil existed instead of the fullness of life.... Something is drastically wrong at the outset. The earth was "waste and void" or "formless and empty."[318]

In addition, Ross points out that it is only after God corrects the conditions of Genesis 1:2, through a re-creation, that things can be called, "good."

> Essentially the work of creation is a correction of chaos. Emptiness, formlessness, darkness, and the deep are replaced or altered with a creation that is pronounced good and is blessed by God.[319]

JOHN SAILHAMER (1996)

Sailhamer has taught Old Testament in a number of evangelical colleges and seminaries and served on the editorial committees for two recent Bible translations. In his book, *Genesis Unbound*, he states that the correct sense of the Hebrew term *tohu wabohu* is "uninhabitable" and "wilderness." He claims that *tohu wabohu* would never have been translated "formless and void" or "formless and empty," except for the Greek concept of "primeval chaos."

> The sense of the Hebrew phrase suggests something quite different, a sense which some early translators identified quite clearly. Early non-Greek versions such as the Aramaic Targums show no trace of the concepts found in the LXX. One early Aramaic Targum translates *tohu wabohu* as "desolate without

---

[317] Allen P. Ross, "Genesis," in *Bible Knowledge Commentary: Old Testament*, ed. John F. Walvoord and Roy B. Zuck (Colorado Springs: David C. Cook, 1983), 11.

[318] Ross, *Creation*, 75, 105.

[319] Ross, *Creation*, 74.

human beings or beasts and void of all cultivation of plants and of trees."[320]

Sailhamer concludes that "the Hebrew expression *tohu wabohu* refers simply to a 'wilderness' that has not yet become inhabitable for human beings (Deut. 32:10)."[321] Notice, however that the passage he cites uses only the term *tohu.* Sailhamer has not taken into consideration what added insights can be gained from the rhyming figure of speech, *tohu wabohu.* He does however, have an insight into another word play in the original Hebrew: *tohu* and *tob. Tohu* describes the land before it was *tob* / good.[322] (Even better, this could be an ellipsis showing God's solution for the negative conditions of the land: *tohu wabohu* becomes *tob*)

GREGORY BOYD (1997)

Theologian-philosopher-pastor, Gregory Boyd, retains the traditional translation of *tohu wabohu,* but invests it with negative connotations, as did Luther, Calvin, and many others who see the term referring to "chaos."

> The earth became (or had become) formless and empty. These are usually pejorative terms in Scripture, denoting something gone wrong, laid waste, or judged. ... This theory postulates a prehumanoid world of indefinite duration about which we know nothing more than that it somehow became a battlefield between good and evil and was consequently made into a total wasteland."[323]

Boyd joins Ross, and the perspective being developed in this book, in recognizing the earth as a battlefield or the scene of a rebellion, with the resulting chaos described as *tohu wabohu.*

ROBERT ALTER (2004)

Robert Alter is an American professor of Hebrew language and comparative literature at the University of California, Berkeley, and author of *The Art of Biblical Narrative,* for which he received the National Jewish Book Award for Jewish Thought. Alter endorses the

---

[320] Sailhamer, *Genesis Unbound,* 63.
[321] Sailhamer, *Genesis Unbound,* 63.
[322] Sailhamer, *Genesis Unbound,* 63.
[323] Boyd, *God at War,* 108.

validity of the ancient translation of *tohu wabohu* in the Babylonian
Talmud by Rabbi Resh Lakish:

> The Torah was given to Israel: "to teach us that the Holy One
> made a condition with all created things, saying to them, 'If
> Israel accepts the Torah, you will continue to exist. If not, I
> shall return you to welter and waste [*tohu wabohu*]'"
> (Babylonian Talmud: Shabbat 88A).[324]

By quoting Rabbi Resh Lakish with approval, Alter indirectly
supports the view that judgment is implied by the term *tohu wabohu*. In
addition, in speaking of returning Israel to the condition of *tohu
wabohu*, Alter and the ancient rabbi seem to be implying that the
original use of term in Genesis 1 applied to a local land and the people
of that land. "All created things" alludes to the creation story, and the
return of Israel to a "welter and waste" indicates that they were in that
condition before the covenant made with them by the Holy One. In the
perspective we are developing in this book, this would refer to the chaos
of slavery out of which God brought the people of Israel into the land
that was previously also a "welter and waste."

TERRENCE E. FRETHEIM (2005)

Terence Fretheim is professor of Old Testament at Luther Seminary.
We noticed in a discussion his earlier work, *Creation, Fall, and Flood*,
that he thinks of *tohu wabohu* as representing chaos and that this chaos
has lingered after the events of the creation story in Genesis 1. He also
pointed out that the ancient peoples associated evil with large quantities
of water, such as "the deep," in Genesis 1:2.

In his later work, *God and World in the Old Testament: a Relational
Theology of Creation*, Fretheim denies that verse 2 implies a reality that
is "evil." although he acknowledges, "yet in some sense 'chaos'
persists."[325] He backs himself into a theological corner with his concern
that if we admit that God shows violence in dealing out judgment for the
supposed evil represented by *tohu wabohu*, that will give humans the
justification for violence toward each other.[326] We will look at the
problems that arise from three positions that Fretheim takes: (1) verse 2
does not imply evil; (2) after God declared his creation to be "good,"
some chaos persists, and "such elements of disorder are 'good'";[327] (3)

---

[324] Alter, *Biblical Narrative*, ix.
[325] Fretheim, *God and World*, 44.
[326] Fretheim, *God and World*, 309.
[327] Fretheim, *God and World*, 44.

God does not use violence in his judgments, otherwise people would feel free to imitate that characteristic of God.

These positions force Fretheim to change the plain meaning of "good," and to attribute disorder and chaos to God. This is the inevitable result of the "absence of a Satanic opponent to God's will," as missiologist Ralph Winter liked to point out to his audiences.[328] "Once Satan is in the picture," Winter believed, no amount or kind of harsh or heartless evil should be unexpected in any quarter."[329]

Fretheim is inconsistent. He does not deny God's use of force in judgment in Israel's history, but in his attempt to avoid attributing violence to God (and therefore legitimating it for God's people), he denies the possibility of violence in judgment being associated with the condition of *tohu wabohu* in Genesis 1. He comes close to rescuing God's character from legitimated violence when he points out that God gave humans the responsibility to work creatively within the remaining disorder after the creation events. He adds,

> Human beings could, however, be so irresponsible with respect to this task that ... life would revert more and more toward the situation of Gen. 1:2. What is important to stress here is that such consequences are the effect of *creaturely* irresponsibility and God's judgmental response and not that of some evil forces.[330]

Along with Fretheim, the perspective in this book intends to avoid attributing violence, disorder, or evil to God. Fretheim gives the helpful insight that violence is a natural consequence of irresponsible creaturely choices. To be consistent he would need to be willing to admit the existence of non-human creatures whose choices, according to Origen,[331] make a difference in calamities of non-human origin, such as earthquakes and volcanic eruptions. Fretheim seems unwilling to acknowledge the existence of non-human created beings who used their free choices to rebel against God prior to the events of Genesis 1, with *tohu wabohu* and evil as the result.

In his objections to the "*Chaoskamph*" theories of the Near Eastern religions being attributed to God, and his attempt to avoid saying God fights back against evil (as the gods in the ancient myths did), Fretheim would have benefited from the perspective of Anglican theologian, J.

---

[328] Winter, *Frontiers*, 31.
[329] Winter, *Frontiers*, 205.
[330] Fretheim, *God and World*, 44,45.
[331] Origen, *Contra Celsus* 8.31.

Stafford Wright. Wright proposed that references to mythical battles and chaos monsters in the ancient stories may be "preserving a primeval truth that underlies the biblical conception of the fall of Satan and the warfare between Satan and God."[332]

If Fretheim could have allowed for evil forces in his reasoning he could have blamed the chaos and evils we find in this world on the free choices of powerful beings who corrupted, in an earlier creation, what God had intended for good. People and the earth still experience the consequences of those choices unless God specifically holds back destructive events. All God has to do in order to bring judgment is to withdraw his hand of protection over a society or land.[333] The position being developed in this book is that Genesis 1 describes the result of God withdrawing his protection over a local land (verse 2), and then God's subsequent orderly restoration of that chaotic area to being life-giving again.

Genesis chapter 1 initiates the biblical theme that God overcomes evil and disorder with good, meaning that which is functioning properly.[334] Fretheim is right to want to say that God does not fight back against evil with violence and more evil.

DAVID TOSHIO TSUMURA (1988, 1994, 2005)

Like Fretheim, the Japanese theologian David Tsumura disagrees with the *Chaoskampf* interpretation of Genesis 1:2 and the implication that there is something evil in existence for God to overcome. His preferred translation of *tohu wabohu* is a desert-like, uninhabited place, a waste land. He also agrees with the translation, "emptiness," but denies that this has anything to do with "chaos." He sees the term in Genesis 1:2 as referring to the earth in a state without life, uninhabited, empty.

Tsumura, like Waltke, goes into great detail in several different publications about the origin and meaning of the term *tohu wabohu* and in the end does not wrestle with the core issue, what is the significance of the meaning of this term? How does the exegetical process bring us closer to understanding God's ways and purposes with humankind? Tsumura does not give any help in this direction.

---

[332] J. Stafford Wright, "The Place of Myth in the Interpretation of the Bible," *Journal of the Transactions of the Victorian Institute* 88 (1956): 27.

[333] Bernhard Anderson agrees (*Creation to New Creation*, 36): "Unless God's power upholds the creation, the waters of chaos would seep in and the earth would return to the precreation watery void, as at the time of the flood (Gen. 7:11; 8:2)."

[334] Walton, *Lost World*, 51.

In his article, *"Tohu* in Isaiah 45:19," Tsumura gives an excellent comprehensive exegetical study of *tohu*[335] but he does not address the question, in that or in any of his other writings, whether *tohu wabohu* taken as a figure of speech means something different than each of the words separately.

Tsumura's approach to discovering the meaning of the term *tohu wabohu* in Genesis 1:2 is through a detailed semantic investigation through literary analysis (context, examination of the terms in other passages, parallelisms, figures of speech) and etymology, looking for Ugaritic, Akkadian, and Arabic roots. His etymological approach provided several examples that we followed in the original etymological research reported earlier in this chapter on the meaning of *tohu wabohu*. His listing of categories for the meaning of the word *tohu* as it is used in each context, and his own detailed analysis of each passage, set an example for further inductive and contextual studies. Tsumura's extensive use of parallelism to arrive at possible meanings for disputed terms was a very helpful example.

Through his inductive study, Tsumura reached an original insight. He discovered confirmation in parallel structures in Genesis 1:2 and Jeremiah 4:23 that *tohu wabohu* is related in some way to *hosek* / darkness (or "no light"). Tsumura says this had never been noticed by commentators before. "In this case, the term *tohu* corresponding directly to *hosek* 'darkness' probably means 'desolation.'"[336] The following diagram illustrates Tsumura's complex reasoning. In these examples, A and B are closely related, as are X and Y.[337]

Genesis 1:2:
    (A) Now the earth
        (X) was formless and empty (*tohu wabohu*),
        (Y) darkness was over the surface
    (B) of the deep.

Jeremiah 4:23:
    (A) I looked at the earth
        (X) and it was formless and empty (*tohu wabohu*)
    (B) and at the heavens,
        (Y) and their light was gone.

---

[335] David Toshio Tsumura, *"Tohu* in Isa 45: 19," *Vetus Testamentum* 38 (1988): 361-64.

[336] Tsumura, "The Earth," 320.

[337] David Toshio Tsumura, "AXYB Pattern in Amos 17: 5 and Ps 9," *Vetus Testamentum* (1988): 234-36.

Tsumura does not comment on the fact that in Genesis 1:2 the comparison is between the earth and the "deep," while in Jeremiah 4:23 the comparison is between the earth and the "heavens." But in both cases, it is true that darkness accompanies the condition of *tohu wabohu*.

Unfortunately, Tsumura does not take the significance of this fact into consideration in his conclusions about the meaning and significance of the term. It is very significant in the ideological perspective of this book, however, since darkness, in biblical literature, is a metaphor for fearful or negative circumstances, death, ignorance, and wickedness.[338] The plague of darkness was associated with the death of the firstborn sons of the Egyptians. The psalmist reflects the ancient understanding of "darkness" when he says of those taking refuge under the shadow of the Almighty, "you will not fear the terror of night, ... nor the pestilence that stalks in the darkness" (Ps. 91:5, 6). Given the associations found with the concept of darkness throughout the Old Testament, it seems logical to attribute a similar negative connotation to the contexts in which it is in a parallel construction with *tohu wabohu*.

Earlier in this chapter we examined another example of the use of parallelism in Isaiah 45:18 to discover connotations and uses of the word *tohu*. This is an example Tsumura leans heavily upon for his own conclusions:

Isaiah 45:18
    (S) For this is what the Lord says--
        (A) he who created the heavens, he is God;
        (A) he who fashioned and made the earth, he founded
it;
        (B) he did not create it to be *tohu*
        (B) but formed it to be inhabited

---

[338] These categories of metaphors are mentioned in Gesenius' *Hebrew-Chaldee Lexicon* on the Blue Letter Bible webpage for the Strong's number (H2821), *hosek* / darkness. As a metaphor for negative, even cataclysmic circumstances, see Amos 5:18: "Woe to you who long for the day of the Lord! ... That day will be darkness, not light." As a metaphor for death, see Job 3:4, 5 where Job curses the day he was born and wishes to be dead: "That day—may it turn to darkness; may God above not care about it .... May gloom and utter darkness claim it once more." Also see Psalm 107:10 (KJV): "... such as sit in darkness and in the shadow of death." As a metaphor for ignorance see Job 37:19 (KJV): "Teach us what we shall say unto him; for we cannot order our speech by reason of darkness." As a metaphor for wickedness see Proverbs 2:13 (KJV): "Who leave the paths of uprightness, to walk in the ways of darkness." The writers of the New Testament continue to see darkness as a metaphor for wickedness. See John 3:19: "people loved darkness instead of light because their deeds were evil." And Romans 13:12: "let us put aside the deeds of darkness and put on the armor of light."

(S) he says: ...

Hebrew parallelism is often synonymous, as it is in this verse. Since the grammatical structure indicates that the two phrases labeled "B" each express the same thought, one in negative and the other in positive terms, this leads to a meaning for *tohu* of "uninhabited" (Tsumura's preference for this passage) or "empty," a broader, more inclusive term which gives more flexibility in translating the same word in other contexts. In those verses that Tsumura is willing to admit the word is used abstractly he also advocates "emptiness" as the interpretation, although he prefers the literal term "desert" as the main translation for *tohu*.[339] "Empty" can mean uninhabited or desert, in the sense of physical emptiness, but in other contexts it can also mean empty of meaning, such as worthless, purposeless, or false (as in empty words).

Based on the larger context, it would be appropriate to use "purposeless" for *tohu* in Isaiah 45:18 (God did not create the world to be purposeless). Carl Armerding, respected professor of Old Testament in several evangelical institutions, comes to this conclusion as well: "Isaiah 45:18 reaffirms this human aspect of creation when it declares, 'he did not create it a chaos (or "without purpose"), he created it to be inhabited."[340] The mission and purpose of God's people is specified a few verses later: "Turn to me and be saved, all you ends of the earth ...Before me every knee will bow; by me every tongue will swear" (Isa. 45:22, 23).

Taking uninhabited or desert as the main meaning of *tohu*, as Tsumura does, does not allow one to find a root meaning of the word that can make sense in both literal and abstract uses and contexts. Tsumura's preference for a literal meaning leads him to an unhelpful conclusion in his discussion of *tohu* in Isaiah 45:19. In fact, his presupposition leads him to ignore a main exegetical principle of interpreting according to the context. He gets too close to the immediate context of the parallelism within the verse to notice the larger context of the chapter or even the rest of the verse:

Isaiah 45:19
> I have not spoken in secret,
>   from somewhere in a land of darkness;
> I have not said to Jacob's descendants,
>   "Seek me in vain (*tohu*)."

---

[339] Tsumura, "The Earth," 316.
[340] Carl E. Armerding, "An Old Testament View of Creation," *Crux* 12 (1974): 3-4.

>   I, the Lord, speak the truth;
>   I declare what is right.

In this verse Tsumura takes *tohu* to be in parallel with "in a land of darkness." He uses circular reasoning to decide which elements of the verse correspond to each other, supporting his choice "by the fact that *tohu* basically means 'a waste land' (or 'desert')."[341] Perhaps he had in mind the pairing of darkness with *tohu wabohu* in the Jeremiah and Genesis passages in his AXYB pattern and applied that in this context. After a number of pages of complicated arguments, Tsumura arrives at the following translation of Isaiah 45:19:

>   I did not speak in secret,
>   In a land of darkness,
>   I did not say to Jacob's descendants
>   (in a land of) desolation, "Seek me!"[342]

This is almost the exact opposite of the conclusion we are reaching here, which uses a broader term for *tohu* that incorporates abstract as well as physical meanings. Tsumura is implying that God did not speak at all. (He did not say, "Seek me.") It is hard to understand why Tsumura insists on *tohu* being a physical place. And he does not account for the last phrases of the verse that say God speaks right things; the truth. Tsumura's translation is unhelpful for illuminating the context of the chapter. In fact, he completely ignores the immediate context in his discussion. His insistence on a literal desert for *tohu* is not in harmony with the text. *Tohu* in Isaiah 45:19 means "empty" in the sense of "no purpose, in vain, falsely." God is not giving false testimony. (See this obvious use of *tohu* in Isaiah 29:20, 21: "The ruthless ... ensnare the defender in court and with false testimony (*tohu*) and deprive the innocent of justice."

Tsumura has overlooked the rest of the verse in his eagerness to find support for his literal interpretation of *tohu*. The parallelism and translation should be as follows:

>   (A) I have not spoken in secret,
>   (A) from somewhere in a land of darkness;
>   (B) I have not said to Jacob's descendants, "Seek me," in vain
>   [*tohu*, falsely/to no purpose]
>   (C) I, the Lord, speak the truth;
>   (C) I declare what is right.

---

341 Tsumura, "The Earth," 362.
342 Tsumura, "The Earth," 362.

The middle phrase (B) is explained by both sets of parallelisms: God did not speak to them in secret, but openly, and he did not speak to them falsely or to no purpose, but truthfully. In describing God as speaking openly, and not in a secret, dark place, Isaiah may have had in mind the incident in Genesis 18:17, 18, when the Lord said, "Shall I hide from Abraham what I am about to do? Abraham will surely become a great and powerful nation, and all nations on earth will be blessed through him." This also fits the larger context of the Isaiah 45 in which God is inviting all the peoples of the earth to turn to him. The implication of Isaiah 45:19, is that it is through Jacob's seed that the peoples of the earth should know God and be able to seek him.

The fact that God's plea to Abraham's and Jacob's descendants was not worthless or false is supported by the use of the word *tohu* in Isaiah 29:21 to mean "falsely." In that context Isaiah reports the Lord as saying the people are displeasing him by turning things "upside down" (29:16) from what is right, and one way they are doing this is by depriving the innocent of justice with a "vain thing" or "worthless thing" (*tohu*), translated "false testimony" by the NIV. God's words are not false testimony, they are not worthless or in vain, or to no purpose. Interpreting *tohu* as "to no purpose," also applies to the usage of *tohu* in the preceding verse (Isaiah 45:18: God did not create the world to be purposeless or meaningless, but to be inhabited [by people with a purpose that is spelled out in the larger context of the chapter].)

The larger context of the chapter shows that God did not create the world to be judged (*tohu*), in which case there would have been no purpose in creating it in the first place; the world would have been *tohu*, purposeless. The context of the chapter shows that Cyrus, as God's servant, is going to rebuild what God had allowed to be destroyed. God wants all nations to be included in this rebuilding, not just Israel. The sense of Isaiah 45:19 is that what God declares (not in secret, and not to no purpose) is right and true when he says, "turn to me and be saved all you ends of the earth" (verse 22). The content of what God said to Jacob's descendants in relation to "seek me" is "turn to me and be saved"—and God intends for that to happen. He is not giving a false word of hope, and he is not saying that he never said, "seek me," as Tsumura's translation implies.

This interpretation, based on inductive studies, finds confirmation from a number of commentators. Brevard Childs, Professor of Old Testament at Yale University from 1958 until 1999 and who is considered one of the most influential biblical scholars of the 20th century, summarizes: "God did not speak in secret, or conceal himself in ambiguous oracle. ... God has always spoken the truth and declared with is right."[343] Hebrew professor Michael Rosenbaum points out that Israel had brought the charge against Yahweh that he had hidden himself from them: "Why do you say, Israel, 'My way is hidden from the Lord; my cause is disregarded by my God" (Isa. 40:27); "Truly you are a God who has been hiding himself, the God and Savior of Israel" (Isa. 45:15).

> [God's people] wondered whether it was worthwhile seeking Yahweh at all. Their claim was that it was 'vain' to seek Yahweh since he did not answer. Yahweh counters that he can be trusted to do what is right; it is not 'vain' to seek him."[344]

Yehoshua Gitay, professor of Hebrew and prophetic discourse at the University of Haifa and the University of Stellenbosch draws on the political context:

> The complaint about God's hiddenness [v. 15] sounds also like a complaint about God's apparently passive role in the current political situation [v. 19]: "I have not said to Jacob's descendants: seek me for nothing," which declares that there is a purpose and benefit in seeking God, responds in general terms to the complaint.[345]

G. W. Wade, early 20th century author of *The Book of the Prophet Isaiah*, gives additional historical background for the verse:

> The Lord's predictions were public and explicit so that men could judge of the correspondence of events with them and in this respect they differed from many heathen oracles which were often to be obtained only in out-of-the-way localities and were ambiguous and enigmatic in character. ... It was not the custom of the Lord, as it was of the heathen oracles, to invite men to consult Him and then afford them no real help.[346]

---

[343] Brevard S. Childs, "The Enemy from the North and the Chaos Tradition," *Journal of Biblical Literature* 78 (1959): 197.

[344] Michael Rosenbaum, *Word-Order Variation in Isaiah 40–55: A Functional Perspective* (Assen, the Netherlands: Van Gorcum, 1997), 116.

[345] Yehoshua Gitay, "Prophecy and Persuasion: A Study of Isaiah 40–48," *Linguistica Biblica Bonn* (1981): 195.

[346] G. W. Wade, *The Book of the Prophet Isaiah* (London: Methuen & Co, 1929), 297. John Walton seems to agree with Wade when he says about Isaiah 45:19

Wade's explanation combines both the literal and figurative aspects of what is meant by God not speaking in "*tohu.*" In light of Wade's historical-cultural contribution to this discussion, it must be admitted that Tsumura is not completely wrong in his very detailed justification for a physical location as the meaning of *tohu* in Isaiah 45:19. *Tohu* can be taken in two ways simultaneously: as a place parallel to a land of darkness (such as a wilderness) and also as not being "in vain" or "false." God did not speak from a desert area or secret, dark place, because this is true, public information, and it was not for no purpose (*tohu*) that God said to his people, "seek me."

This interpretation is confirmed by God's invitation given two verses later, "Turn to me and be saved, all you ends of the earth" (Isa. 45:22). In other words, God spoke plainly, in the light, and his righteous speaking was not in vain, purposeless, or for nothing. Some of Jacob's seed did seek him and some of his descendents did fulfill God's purposes. Israel was created as a nation to make him known to the ends of the earth.

It may be that Tsumura's overlooking of the last phrases of the verse, and as a consequence missing the meaning of the passage, is due to his specialty of technical etymological studies, which requires paying close attention to one word at a time. Through these studies Tsumura reaches the conclusion, "it is probable that Ugaritic *thw* is a cognate of Hebrew *tohu* and that both have the common meaning of 'a desert.'"[347]

An example of how Tsumura' etymological studies led him to this understanding of *tohu* is found in a Ugaritic text in which parallelism assists in discovering shades of meaning:

"The earth shakes
the earth is out of order (*thw*)."

In this line the Ugaritic term for "out of order" is equivalent to the Hebrew *tohu*, and both are equivalent, according to the parallelism, with "the earth shakes."[348]

Another example of shaking being associated with *tohu* is found in the verse following the occurrence of *tohu wabohu* in Jeremiah 4:23: "I looked at the mountains, and they were quaking; all the hills were swaying" (Jer. 4:24). In his commentary on the book of Jeremiah, Elliott Binns remarks,

---

that the Israelites were instructed not to seek God in waste places (Walton, *Lost World*, 48).

[347] Tsumura, "The Earth," 312.

[348] Tsumura, *Creation and Destruction*, 21.

> The effect of earthquakes seems to have made a deep impression on the mind of [people] in all ages. ... The trembling of the mountains represents to them the overturning of all that is stable and trustworthy. Our Lord adopts this kind of language in speaking of the "last things: (Mark 8:8, 24 ff.) and Muhammed habitually speaks of the judgement as the day when the mountains will be set in motion (Koran, lxix. 14, lxxviii.20, xcix. etc.)"[349]

This context of shaking shows that *tohu* and *tohu wabohu* refer to something that is out of order from God's purposes for creation or for people. From the Ugaritic parallelism, Tsumura concludes that "unproductive" is an appropriate translation both for the Ugaritic and the Hebrew term.[350] "Unproductive" is descriptive of Tsumura's favorite translation for *tohu*, "desert," as well as part of his final conclusion for the translation *tohu wabohu*.

In summary, in Tsumura's classification of the uses of *tohu*, he sees both literal and figurative or abstract uses, but he concludes that the word most often means "desert" or "uninhabited." As a result he gives unsatisfying explanations for the cases in which the term is used abstractly, or when it is used symbolically as a literal metaphor. In the end Tsumura does not even make a good case for *tohu* usually meaning desert, since in Genesis 1:2 everything is under water. But at least he considers the term "empty / desolate" to be an implication of his preferred interpretation, "desert-like." He recognizes that in Isaiah 24:10-12, *tohu* is synonymously parallel to the term for desolation following the destruction of a city.[351] "Desolation" is more helpful than "desert" in arriving at an explanation for the compound phrase, *tohu wabohu*. Tsumura's final conclusion at the end of a long and complex investigation is that,

> Both the biblical context and extra-biblical parallels suggest that the phrase *tohu wabohu* in Genesis 1:2 has nothing to do with "chaos" and simply means "emptiness" and refers to the earth which is an empty place, i.e., an unproductive and uninhabited place.[352]

---

[349] L. Elliott Binns, *The Book of the Prophet Jeremiah* (London: Methuen & Co, 1919), 45.

[350] Tsumura, *Creation and Destruction*, 21.

[351] Tsumura, "The Earth," 319.

[352] Tsumura, "The Earth," 338.

This conclusion does not adequately take into account the contexts of the other occurrences of the terms, *tohu* and *tohu wabohu*, which demonstrate conclusively that the terms refer to something out of order, chaotic, contrary to God's will.

JOHN H. WALTON (2009)

In his book, *The Lost World of Genesis One,* Wheaton College professor of Old Testament, John Walton, starts with the assumption that the ancient world thought about existence in functional terms rather than in material terms.[353] He sees Genesis 1 as beginning with a description of "no functions rather than with no material."[354] He explains the historical translation of *tohu wabohu* ("formless and void," the absence of material form), as coming from "the predominant material focus of the cultures that produced the translations."[355] (See especially Bernard Ramm's explanation above of *tohu wabohu* referring to a "marble block" ready to be shaped.) Instead, Walton says, Genesis 1 speaks of God ordering material that already existed (the undefined heavens and earth, darkness, and the waters of the deep) and making it function to meet the needs of humans.[356] After listing each of the occurrences of the word *tohu*, Walton concludes that this word is an adjective that can refer to:
- the pre-cosmic condition (the beginning state in Genesis)
- the functionless cosmic waters
- those places in the ordered creation on which order had not yet been imposed—the desert and the cosmic waters above and below.[357]

Walton's point that *tohu* is a (predicate) adjective implies that *tohu wabohu* is a condition, not something concrete. It describes something that is not functioning the way it is supposed to function. It is out of order, not supporting life. These insights are important, although other Hebrew scholars, such as the editors of the online *Blue Letter Bible,* and the *Theological Word Book of the Old Testament*[358] have identified *tohu* as a noun.

---

[353] Walton, *Lost World*, 47.
[354] Walton, *Lost World*, 50.
[355] Walton, *Lost World*, 49.
[356] Walton, *Lost World*, 51.
[357] Walton, *Lost World*, 50.
[358] R. Laird Harris, Gleason L. Archer, and Bruce K. Waltke, eds., *"Tohu,"* in *Theological Word Book of the Old Testament* (Chicago: Moody, 1980), 964.

Consolidated List of Commentators' Interpretations of Tohu Wabohu

The commentators we have consulted disagree about the interpretation of *tohu wabohu*, due to their ideological perspectives and theological assumptions. In the list below is the range of meanings our conversation partners have contributed to the discussion of what it meant when Moses told the ancient Israelites that the land, before God started his creative activity, was *tohu wabohu*. These interpretations are in approximate order from least to most violent:

Without form and void
Unformed mass
Unformed and unfilled
Unordered, functionless
Nothing whatever, emptiness
Non-existence
Formless waste
Waste and void
Empty and waste
Meaninglessness, shapelessness
Desolate and empty
Astonishment at emptiness and desolation
Instability and emptiness
Wreck and ruin
Desolation and disorder
Welter and waste
Wild and waste
Desert-like
Uninhabitable and wilderness
Unproductive and uninhabitable
Chaos and jumble
Chaos and confusion
Destroyed and desolate
Desolation and disorder
Not producing or supporting life
Opposite or contrary to creation

A Rationale for the Most Helpful Translation of Tohu *and* Tohu
Wabohu

We can summarize this list of interpretations by saying that something can be described as *tohu wabohu* when it is out of order or upside down from God's intended purposes, with the inevitable result of negative and chaotic conditions. *Tohu* refers to something that is out of order and needs to be set right: idols, false testimony, a trackless waste that describes the minds of leaders who have lost their ability to reason, a desert or wilderness where human life cannot survive, an empty space where there should be something life-giving. *Tohu* AND *bohu* is an emphatic and unforgettable figure of speech that says something is not only out of order, but the entity described as *tohu wabohu* has also experienced judgment, with chaos as the result. Something that was worthless, from the perspective of God's purposes, has been shaken up to make room for a new beginning—an opportunity for God's will to be done on earth as it is in heaven.

Two examples, from the contexts of Job 26:6, 7 and Isaiah 59:4, will serve to illustrate the value of this interpretation of *tohu*, as part of the understanding of *tohu wabohu*.

> *"The realm of the dead is naked before God;*
> *Destruction [Abaddon] lies uncovered.*
> *He spreads out the northern skies over empty space* [tohu];
> *he suspends the earth over nothing"* (Job 26:6, 7).

In this passage, we see God correcting something that is out of order and contrary to his will. Destruction, literally *Abbadon*, has been uncovered and defeated (as described in the context of the rest of Job chapter 26), with the result of an empty, disordered space where the Destroyer had formerly been active. This describes the view we are adopting in this book for what lies behind the scenes in Genesis 1:2. Empty space [*tohu,* out-of-order], that is a result of rebellion against God and consequent judgment, is not God's will. We know from Isaiah 45:18 that God did not intend for the world to be *tohu* / empty / out of order. So over this "nothingness" that is the aftermath of the downfall of the Destroyer (see Job 26:11, 12 for a poetic description of God's victory),[359] God spreads out the northern skies and begins to put things in order so that humans can live well in the land. God is overcoming evil with good.

Again, in Isaiah 59:4 ff, God demonstrates his ongoing plan to overcome evil with good; to overcome *tohu* with *tob*. In Isaiah 59 we see a description of a society that is radically out of order (*tohu*) and needs to be set right.

---

[359] The pillars of the heavens quake,
   aghast at his rebuke.
By his power he churned up the sea;
   by his wisdom he cut Rahab to pieces (Job 26:11, 12).

> *No one calls for justice; no one pleads a case with integrity.*
> *They rely on empty arguments* (tohu) [arguments that are not
> right], *they utter lies; they conceive trouble and give birth to*
> *evil. ... They pursue evil schemes; acts of violence mark their*
> *ways. The way of peace* (shalom) *they do not know; ... So justice*
> *is far from us, and righteousness does not reach us. We look for*
> *light, but all is darkness; for brightness, but we walk in deep*
> *shadows. ...*
>
> *The Lord looked and was displeased that there was no justice.*
> *He ... was appalled that there was no one to intervene; so his*
> *own arm achieved salvation for him, and his own righteousness*
> *sustained him. He put on righteousness as his breastplate, and*
> *the helmet of salvation on his head. ... "The Redeemer will*
> *come to Zion, to those in Jacob who repent of their sins,"*
> *declares the Lord.*

Clearly the empty arguments and behavior described in Isaiah 59 are
not God's will and need to be corrected, which is our understanding of
the meaning of *tohu*. In the next chapter we will explore what it meant
for God himself to come and take up the cause of righteousness and
justice since there was no one else to intervene. Ultimately God took the
condition of *tohu wabohu* onto himself, in the violent death of his Son,
in order to nullify the works of the devil (1 John 3:8).

The three occurrences of the term *tohu wabohu* in Scripture serve as
a metaphor for the root of personal and social problems that God and his
people must address. God's mandate to his people in Genesis 1:28 was
to subdue and steward whatever was not functioning according to God's
will. The theme of the Bible is the record of God's attempts to work
through his people to make things right and good (as Walton says,
"functioning properly"[360]). According to the ideological perspective of
this book, God's purposes for humans in history have to do with
overcoming or correcting conditions that can be described as *tohu* or
tohu wabohu, by following the example given in Genesis 1 as well as in
many other passages of Scripture such as these:

> "Do not be overcome by evil, but overcome evil with good"
> (Rom. 12:21).
>
> "The reason the Son of God appeared was to destroy the devil's
> work" (1 John 3:8).

---

[360] Walton, *Lost World*, 51.

> The Spirit of the Sovereign Lord is on me, because the Lord has anointed me to proclaim good news to the poor. He has sent me to bind up the brokenhearted, to proclaim freedom for the captives and release from darkness for the prisoners (Isa. 61:1).

Luke 4:18 shows Jesus claiming this passage from Isaiah as the purpose of his ministry: to demonstrate a correction of chaos at personal and societal levels by overcoming evil with good.

Insights and Application of Conditions Described as Tohu Wabohu

"The 'chaos and desolation' of Genesis 1:2 is not just a statement about primeval times; it is a statement about a present possibility."[361] Anderson, von Rad, and Levenson each pointed out this application of *tohu* in the ideological conversation above. These insights are part of the exegetical "quilt" we are piecing together. *Tohu wabohu* describes conditions that are violently upside down from God's will for people and creation. These visible or felt conditions are the root cause of human problems, which gives rise to the need for international development.

It is important to see no dichotomy between the visible *tohu wabohu* described in the dark terms we have seen in this chapter and an inner or spiritual *tohu wabohu*. As Levenson says, "the forces of disorder, injustice, affliction, and chaos, … are, in the Israelite worldview, one."[362] There is a continuum rather than a dichotomy ranging from disorder within a person's mind (spiritual and mental disorders), to disorder in one's body (disease), to disorder within a group of people (social problems), to disorder at the political level (nations in conflict), to disorder in the realm of nature (inappropriately labeled "acts of God"). When evil choices are made intentionally and repeatedly, the heart, body, society, or land begins to self-destruct as the Spirit of God withdraws. Ezekiel's vision of the Spirit in the wheels leaving the temple and the land (Ezekiel 10:17-22) serves as a visual metaphor of what happens when a person's mind or a society is twisted and turned to wrong purposes. Eventually it becomes purposeless and desolate (*tohu wabohu*), without the help of the Spirit of God. "As for those whose hearts are devoted to their vile images and detestable idols, I will bring down on their own heads what they have done, declares the Sovereign Lord" (Ezek. 11:21).

---

[361] von Rad, *Genesis*, 51.
[362] Levenson, *Creation*, xix.

REVIEW OF WORD ASSOCIATIONS IN *TOHU* PASSAGES

The following themes and conditions are found in the various contexts of whatever is being described as "*tohu*":

Death
Darkness
Shaking; drunken staggering
Water in negative connotations: flood or lack of it in drought
Destruction
Desert, wasteland
Vain, nothing, no purpose
Worthless (idols, foreign gods)
Lack of purpose, lack of justice
False testimony
Judgment
Uninhabited
Confusion
Desolation
Fear
Wickedness
Ruins
Insanity, deprived of reason
Fools
Skilled at doing evil

PARALLEL WORD ASSOCIATIONS WITH THE HEART

These same themes, or their opposites, are found in passages of Scripture that speak about the heart. A heart that is in opposition to God's will is described by terms similar to those used in association with the condition of *tohu* or *tohu wabohu*. On the other hand, a heart that is right with God is described in terms that are the opposite of the words used in association with the condition of *tohu* or *tohu wabohu*. It is the condition of the heart that determines a person's behavior and the natural or logical consequences of that behavior (judgment or blessing).

Representative passages are quoted here to show descriptions of both those whose hearts are not right with God and the opposite descriptions of those whose hearts *are* right with God.

Genesis 6:5 (The Flood)

The Lord saw how great the wickedness of the human race had become on the earth, and that every inclination of the thoughts of the human <u>heart</u> was only evil all the time.

Tohu themes found in the context of Noah's flood:

Death
Water in a negative context
Judgment
Confusion
Destruction
Evil

Psalm 15

Lord, who may dwell in your sanctuary? ... The one whose walk is blameless, who does what is righteous, who speaks the truth from their <u>heart</u>; ... whose tongue utters no slander, who does no wrong to a neighbor; ... who does not accept a bribe against the innocent. Whoever does these things will never be shaken.

People who fit the description of Psalm 15 demonstrate the opposite of the characteristics of something that is *tohu*:

Never shaken vs. shaken and destroyed
No slander vs. lack of justice for the innocent
Speaks the truth vs. false testimony
Blameless and righteous vs. evil

Psalm 36: 1-4, 10-12

I have a message from God in my heart concerning the sinfulness of the wicked: There is no fear of God before their eyes. ... The words of their mouths are wicked and deceitful; they fail to act wisely or do good. Even on their beds they plot evil; they commit themselves to a sinful course and do not reject what is wrong. ... Continue your love to those who know you, your righteousness to the upright in <u>heart</u>. May the foot of the proud not come against me. ... See how the evildoers lie fallen— thrown down, not able to rise!

In this Psalm we see that inner *tohu* results in physical *tohu wabohu*. The origin of disaster was that the wicked were plotting evil and choosing a course that was contrary to God's will. The result is that evildoers will be thrown down and not be able to get up again. God withholds his protection from these types of people, but those who are following God's righteous ways can claim the promise in verse 6 of this chapter: "You, Lord, preserve both people and animals." This Psalm indicates that characteristics of *tohu* are present even at the thought level as well as in outward words and deeds:

Deceitfulness (False Testimony)
Failure to act wisely (they are fools)
Plotting evil (the thought life)
Evildoers are fallen (the result of shaking and destruction)

Psalm 51:10, 17

Create in me a pure <u>heart</u>, O God. ... Do not cast me from your presence or take your Holy Spirit from me. A broken and contrite heart, you, God, will not despise.

In the context of Psalm 51 we see that a heart right with God exhibits the opposite of the characteristics of *tohu*:
Truth vs. false testimony
Presence of God's Spirit vs. desolation
Joy and gladness vs. fear
Wisdom vs. foolishness
Cleansed from sin vs. "skilled at doing evil"

Isaiah 59:12-15

Our offenses are many in your sight, and our sins testify against us. Our offenses are ever with us, and we acknowledge our iniquities: rebellion and treachery against the Lord, turning our backs on our God, inciting revolt and oppression, uttering lies our <u>hearts</u> have conceived. So justice is driven back, and righteousness stands at a distance; truth has stumbled in the streets, honesty cannot enter. Truth is nowhere to be found, and whoever shuns evil becomes a prey.

Here we see that the origin of the evidences of *tohu* (rebellion against God's will, oppression, lies, lack of justice, evil) was in the heart. These themes echo those found in association with conditions described as *tohu*:

Stumbling (shaking, staggering)
Oppression, lack of justice
Lies (false testimony)
Rebellion against God's will (wickedness)
Evil

THE PROPHETS' COMMENTARY ON *TOHU* OF THE HEART

Jeremiah

Jeremiah offers a commentary on the type of behavior attributed to the heart that is characterized by conditions associated with *tohu*: "The heart is deceitful above all things and beyond cure. Who can understand it?" (Jer. 17:9). In his next chapter Jeremiah continues, speaking for God: "I am preparing a disaster for you and devising a plan against you. So turn from your evil ways. ... They will reply, ... we will continue with our own plans; we will all follow the stubbornness of our evil hearts" (Jer. 18:11, 12).

Following this rebellious declaration is a description of *tohu wabohu*—people whose behavior is worthless, from the perspective of God's purposes, are going to be shaken up to make room for a new beginning: "My people have forgotten me; they burn incense to worthless idols, which made them stumble in their ways... Their land will be an object of horror and of lasting scorn;... I will show them my back and not my face in the day of their disaster. ... Should good be repaid with evil?" (Jer. 18:15-17, 20).

We have been calling attention to the fact that a major theme of Scripture is God's ability and intention to overcome evil with good. But here Jeremiah is saying that God's people had repaid with evil what God had done that was good. In order to demonstrate his goodness God sometimes allows disasters to fall on people and societies whose hearts are stubbornly turned away from him. Then those who are not intentionally rebellious will have opportunity to experience God's restoration and goodness.

Isaiah

This opportunity to return to God is symbolized in Isaiah's prophecy of the lifeless desert becoming fruitful when God's favor and God's Spirit rest on his people. Then the conditions of *tohu wabohu* are turned back to *tob* / good.

> The fortress will be abandoned, the noisy city deserted; ... till the Spirit is poured on us from on high, and the desert becomes a fertile field, and the fertile field seems like a forest. The Lord's justice will dwell in the desert, his righteousness live in the fertile field. The fruit of that righteousness will be peace [*shalom*]; its effect will be quietness and confidence forever (Isa. 32: 14-17).

Ezekiel

The prophet Ezekiel gives the key to achieving the reality of Isaiah's description of *shalom,* which is the exact opposite of *tohu wabohu.* Ezekiel's solution for the root of all human problems is a new heart that follows God's ways and avoids the chaos that is not God's will: "I will give them an undivided <u>heart</u> and put a new spirit in them" (Ezek. 11:19). "Rid yourselves of all the offenses you have committed, and get a new <u>heart</u> and a new spirit" (Ezek. 18:31).

Conclusions

These sample passages in which the word "heart" occurs show that a mind rebelling against God is inherently out of order from God's intended purposes. Evil choices are the evidence of a mind in opposition to God, and that mind (or society) can be described as *tohu wabohu*— out of order, chaotic, destroyed and desolate, upside down from God's intended purposes. When a person or society is upside down from God's intentions God sometimes allows something to be shaken to get peoples' attention and to rearrange what is out of order back to life-giving purposes.

The context in which the concept of *tohu wabohu* is introduced, right at the beginning of Scripture, shows God's purpose is to correct conditions that are contrary to his will. By describing the opposite of God's intentions in the context of the creation account, *tohu wabohu* points toward the goal of that creation—a place that can be inhabited by humans in purposeful fellowship with God.

This term gives the key to the entire Bible. The whole theme of Scripture is to fight back against the disorder and chaos orchestrated by the adversary who opposes God's will. At the end of Scripture, in the Book of Revelation, we see the fulfillment of God's purposes in history described in terms showing that the state of *tohu wabohu* has finally been reversed: there is no more death, crying, or pain, and darkness and night have been permanently replaced with "good" light (see Rev. 21: 3, 4; 22: 5). In between this beginning and ending of Scripture, the rest of the Bible explains how to overcome and / or avoid conditions that fit the description of *tohu* at various levels or it shows what happens when those conditions are not corrected.

Humans joining God to fight back against opposition to God's will can turn their world upside down, as some accused the disciples of doing in Acts 17:6. Or perhaps we should say, they can help turn some portion of the world right side up, restoring it in some ways to God's original intentions and bringing God glory in the process. This is the origin of international development that attempts, in God's name, to bring order out of chaos and to demonstrate God's will for people, societies, and all creation.

God's Spirit hovers over chaotic land and societies, waiting for willing people and the right time for new beginnings. In the next chapter we will look at the miraculous new beginning when God sent his Son who was willing to humble himself to take on the nature of humanity in order to change the dynamics of human history.

Chapter Eight

Jesus, the New Beginning

Images of Jesus Overcoming Opposition to God's Will

In the beginning was the Word, and the Word was with God, and the Word was God. He was with God in the beginning. Through him all things were made; without him nothing was made that has been made. In him was life, and that life was the light of all mankind. The light shines in the darkness, and the darkness has not overcome it.
(John 1:1-5)

The Word became flesh and made his dwelling among us. We have seen his glory, the glory of the one and only Son, who came from the Father, full of grace and truth.
(John 1:14)

Just as Moses lifted up the snake in the wilderness, so the Son of Man must be lifted up, that everyone who believes may have eternal life in him.
(John 3:14, 15)

Now is the time for judgment on this world; now the prince of this world will be driven out.
(John 12:31)

God anointed Jesus of Nazareth with the Holy Spirit and power, and ... he went around doing good and healing all who were under the power of the devil.
(Acts 10:38)

The reason the Son of God appeared was to destroy [nullify] the devil's work.
(1 John 3:8b)

General Overview

Tohu wabohu, chaos, destroyed and desolate, referring to both people and land; this is not God's will. In his wisdom God knew that humans, without supernatural help, would not be able to resist the evil one's influence. The people of Israel demonstrated their inability to follow God's ways over and over throughout their history. Finally, at the right time, God set about correcting distortions to his purposes by making a radical new beginning: the Word became flesh (John 1:14).

From the very first, Jesus' acts of ministry made it clear that he had come to wage war against evil. "Jesus' earthly ministry reflected the belief that the world had been seized by a hostile, sinister lord. Jesus came to take it back," says apologist and scientist Bruce McLaughlin.[363] As Greg Boyd stated in his blog on the Reknew.org website, "Each one of Jesus' many healings and deliverances were understood to diminish Satan's hold on the world and to liberate people, to whatever degree, from his stronghold." Even the evil influences on nature had to obey Jesus when he rebuked the storm (Mark 4: 39) with the same authority he used in casting out evil spirits (Mark 5:8). Jesus explicitly announced that his victory over demons was the evidence that "the Kingdom of God has come upon you" (Luke 11:20). As Satan's kingdom is diminished, the Kingdom of God advances and "the prince of this world now stands condemned" (John 16:11). Biblical scholar, Trevor Ling explains,

> This judgment and casting out of the ruler of this world follows from the simple fact that a Man has appeared who is not, like all other men, subject to the compulsive power of corporate evil, but is able to live a life of obedience to God. It is this obedience of Jesus which is, *ipso facto*, the dethronement of the devil.[364]

In his obedience to the Father's will, Jesus did what the first Adam and his descendants could not do. Jesus' sinless death was the climax of the cosmic battle[365]: "Now shall the ruler of this world be driven out" (John 12:31), Jesus said, in the context of discussing his death. In his resurrection, Jesus triumphed over the one who holds the power of death, that is the devil (Heb. 2:14), and brought his people through a new exodus: out of the kingdom of darkness into his marvelous light, the kingdom of the beloved Son (Col. 1:12, 13; 1 Pet. 2:9).

Because of the work of Jesus, his followers are able to "walk in the light as he is in the light," and to have rightly ordered relationships with each other (1 John 1:7). Jesus made it possible for his followers to serve as a showcase or display window for what God's will and God's Kingdom looks like, including joining the Son of God in defeating the

---

[363] McLaughlin "From Whence Evil?" 237.

[364] Trevor Ling, *The Significance of Satan* (London: S.P.C.K., 1961), 35.

[365] Judith Kovacs, "'Now Shall the Ruler of This World Be Driven Out': Death as Cosmic Battle in John 12: 20-36," *Journal of Biblical Literature* 114, no. 233 (1995): 227-47.

chaos of the works of the devil. While the enemy's works can be summarized as bringing death—both physical (disease and deformity, social and mental chaos) and spiritual (unbelief, hatred), the Son of God appeared to give life (1 John 4:9). The coming of the Son of God resulted in works and characteristics that are exactly the opposite of those associated with the death-dealing works of the devil, thus nullifying or destroying them (1 John 3:8).

In the next part of this chapter we will engage in detailed inner texture studies to see the perspective of the Johannine community on the cosmic battle raging between light and dark, between love and hate, between the characteristics of those who are "of God" and those who are "of the devil." After studies that support the claim that the Johannine community was well aware of this cosmic battle, we will delve into even more detailed inner texture studies to demonstrate the means by which Jesus expected himself and his followers to engage in this battle. In this we will see a variation on the familiar biblical theme of overcoming evil with good. In the Johannine worldview, Jesus and his followers overcome and nullify hatred and death with love and life.

Particular Details about Jesus and the New Beginning

The Johannine community would have been very familiar with the allusion in John 3:14 to the story of Moses lifting up the bronze snake on a pole in the wilderness. Instead of dying, all the people of God who had been bitten by snakes and looked up at it were healed (Num. 21:4-9). Moses was demonstrating that the evil one had been conquered, and the captured snake on a stake has been the symbol for the healing arts and sciences throughout history. Jesus said in John 3 that even as Moses lifted up the serpent (in demonstration of a defeat of one of the devil's works) so the Son of Man would be lifted up (also in defeat of the works of the devil—see 1 John 3:8). This was the new beginning and new exodus for God's people whom he has called to come "out of darkness into his marvelous light" (1 Pet. 2:9). Jesus declared to his disciples, as he prepared them for his death, "I have come into the world as a light, so that no one who believes in me should stay in darkness" (John 12:46). This darkness was defined by the Johannine community as the cause for stumbling and hatred, the opposite of God's will: "Whoever loves his brother abides in the light, and in him there is no cause for stumbling. But whoever hates his brother is in the darkness and walks in the darkness, and does not know where he is going, because the darkness has blinded his eyes" (1 John 2:10, 11, ESV). We will see in the detailed inner texture studies later in this chapter that love, the opposite of hatred, has a role to play in the cosmic battle to defeat the evil one's intentions.

Jesus' Demonstrations of God's Will

The appearing of the Son of God resulted in characteristics that are the opposite of those associated with the darkness and hatred of the devil, and in fact, as we will see later, Jesus' work nullifies the works of the devil. The ultimate purpose of Jesus' appearing was to glorify God by bringing life to the children of God, replacing death that is a work of the devil in the present age. Jesus demonstrated the nature of the life of God, the *shalom* spoken of by the Old Testament prophets, by overcoming evil with good in his acts of ministry.

The author of the Gospel of John selected six "signs," or miracles, that represent the ways in which Jesus demonstrated God's will for the "*kosmos*," the world:

1. Turning water into wine (John 2:1-11) demonstrated Jesus' power over nature. This miracle met a social need and revealed Jesus' glory, with the result that his disciples believed in him.

2. Healing the official's son who was dying (John 4:43-54) showed God's will for good health and life. Jesus says as result of this miraculous sign, "your son will live."

3. Healing the man at the pool who had been an invalid for 38 years (John 5:1-15) showed Jesus' concern for true righteousness when he did God's work by healing on the Sabbath and instructing the man to stop sinning. A discourse about life through the Son and the works of God follows this miracle.

4. Feeding the 5000 (John 6: 1-15) again demonstrated Jesus' power over nature and met a physical need. The bread of life discourse follows, including a definition of the work of God in verse 29, "the work of God is this: to believe in the one he has sent."

5. Healing the man born blind (John 9:1-41) illustrated God's will for physical wholeness. This miracle was accompanied by two statements about the work of God and was followed by a conversation about the spiritual blindness of those who do not believe in Jesus (9:35-41).

6. Raising Lazarus from the dead (John 11:1-43) demonstrated Jesus' power over death. Jesus claims in 11:25: "I am the resurrection and the life."

In addition to these generalizations of the six signs, statements in John's Gospel and in First John about the nature of the works of God, reflect the following principles:

> Works done through God are done in the light and can be seen by others (John 3:21; 9:4; 10:25).
> The work of God is to believe in the one he has sent (John 6:29).
> God's work can be displayed in a person's life (John 9:3; 14:12).
> Jesus did the works his Father does, demonstrating that he is from the Father (John 10:37, 38; 14:10).
> God's love is made evident through works that meet human needs (1 John 3:17, 18).

"The Works of the Devil" that Jesus Came to Nullify

The Johannine community would have recognized that the devil's works were the exact opposite of Jesus' works. In the ideological perspective of Johannine theology, the devil is an evil being who is identified with darkness and hatred, who has been sinning since the beginning of his rulership over the earth. The Son of God appeared to give life (1 John 4:9), while the devil's fundamentally sinful nature aggressively models all the characteristics that are opposite of and opposed to God's will (described in the Hebrew Bible as *tohu*). The antithetical worldview found in the Johannine literature is illustrated in the chart in an upcoming section showing how the author of the First Epistle of John contrasted the characteristics of God and the Johannine community with the opposite characteristics of those who were not part of this community and not "of God."

Following the example of the author of First John, we can take the opposite of the qualities of Jesus' works and the opposite of statements about the works of God in the Johannine writings to arrive at a list of activities characteristic of God's opponent:

1. Jesus met physical and social needs by providing drink and food.

   The opposite: the devil's work is to cause physical and social chaos (i.e., famine).

2. Jesus healed the sick, crippled, and blind.

   The opposite: the devil's work is to cause sickness, crippling, and blindness.

3. Jesus raised the dead.

   The opposite: the devil's work is to cause death, including disease, which is death at the cellular level.

4. The works of God can be seen by others to be clearly of God.

   The opposite: the devil's work is to deceive and confuse.

5. The work of God is to believe in the one he has sent.

   The opposite: the devil's work is to turn people away from truth, from belief in Jesus.

7. The Father does his work through Jesus (and by extension, through his followers).

   The opposite: the devil does his work through his own "children."

8. God's love is made evident through works that meet human needs.

   The opposite: the devil's hatred results in human neediness.

From this consolidated list we see that the devil's works can be summarized as bringing death—both physical (disease and deformity, social chaos, mental chaos) and spiritual (unbelief, hatred). Recognition of the use of antithetical language, which is found in both the Gospel and First Epistle of John, has helped us identify characteristics of the devil's work that Jesus came to destroy or nullify (1 John 3:8).

Cosmic Battle in the Johannine Literature

The use of antithetical language in the First Epistle confirms that a conflict is taking place and we will see in the upcoming detailed inner texture studies that this conflict is part of the "cosmic battle" in which Jesus came to engage with the prince of this world, the devil. These exegetical studies, and those in previous chapters, are necessary background to support the unconventional theme of this book, that the chaos in this world is not God's will, it is caused by someone or something other than God, and that God desires for his people to join him in fighting back against this opposition. Some may wish to skim over these detailed studies (the "quilt squares" we are piecing together in a fabric of discourse) or read selectively, knowing this research is available for future reference.

Examination of the antithetical statements in First John is the first of five socio-rhetorical approaches to examining the text in significant detail in order to demonstrate the understanding of the Johannine community of the cosmic battle. In a second approach to analyzing the inner texture of First John we will look at the chiastic structure of these antithetical statements, with reference to the cosmic battle as the central focus.

The third rhetorical device we will explore is a technique of transitioning from one topic to another that Baylor Professor of Religion, Bruce Longenecker, calls "chain-link interlock."[366] Through this study we will see that at the center of both the Gospel and the First Epistle of John the same complex transitional device highlights the cosmic battle between the Son of God and the evil one. This, and other transitional techniques, would have helped the audience follow and remember the main points of the author's argument when hearing the epistle read aloud in an oral / aural culture.[367] To accomplish his purpose, the author of First John uses rhetorical techniques that are discussed and illustrated in numerous ancient Graeco-Roman rhetorical handbooks, particularly in the anonymous *Rhetorica ad Herennium* and in Quintilian's *Institutio Oratoria*.[368]

After these three detailed inner texture studies, to support the claim that the Johannine community was well aware of the cosmic battle, we will delve into two even more detailed inner texture studies of repetitive-progressive texture[369] in First John, combined with inter-texture word studies, to further explore the nature of this cosmic battle and the means by which Jesus expected himself and his followers to engage in the battle. Through examining two separate charts of repetitive-progressive themes in First John we will see a variation on the familiar biblical theme of overcoming evil with good. In the Johannine worldview, Jesus and his followers will overcome and nullify hatred with love.

COSMIC BATTLE SEEN IN ANTITHETICAL LANGUAGE IN FIRST JOHN

The first of the three detailed inner texture studies is the use of antithetical language in First John. The qualities of love and hatred are included several times in the antithetical statements throughout First

---

[366] Bruce Longenecker, *Rhetoric at the Boundaries* (Waco, TX: Baylor University Press, 2005), 9.

[367] George Kennedy, a scholar of classical rhetoric, emphasizes that "the Bible in early Christian times was more often heard when read aloud to a group than read privately; very few early Christians owned copies of the Bible, and some did not know how to read. The rhetorical qualities inherent in the text were originally intended to have an impact on first hearing and to be heard by a group" (George Kennedy, *New Testament Interpretation through Rhetorical Criticism* [Chapel Hill: University of North Carolina, 1984], 5.

[368] Longenecker, *Rhetoric*, 4, 5.

[369] Robbins, *Texture*, 8. One of the ways in which Robbins advocates exploring words and meanings is through charts of repetitive and progressive texture. Words that occur more than once in a unit can be mapped out through charts, giving the interpreter insights into the overall picture of the discourse.

John. These statements showcase the difference the author sees in the behavior and beliefs of those following Jesus, who are "walking in the light as he is in the light" (1 John 1:7), and those who do not acknowledge the authority and example of Jesus in their lives. These are the ones who are characterized as walking in the dark and not knowing where they are going (1 John 2:11). For every statement characterizing the believers ("children of God") there is, in close proximity, an opposite statement about the people who are not following the group norms, labeled in 1 John 3:10 as "children of the devil."

<u>Antithetical Statements in the First Epistle of John</u>

"Children of God" (3:1)	*"Children of the Devil" (3:10)*
Walk in the light; have fellowship (1:7)	Walk in darkness; do not have fellowship (1:6)
Keep his commands (2:3b)	Do not keep his commands (2:4b)
Cleansed from sin (1:9)	Claim to have no sin (1:8, 10) Truth and word is not in him (1:8, 10)
A new command is true … in you	The truth is not in a person who is a liar (2:4)
Loves his brother (and sister) (2:10a)	Hates his brother (2:9a; 11a)
Abides in the light (2:10a)	Is in darkness (2:9b; 11a)
Does the will of God (2:17b)	Loves the world, which is not of the Father (2:15b, 16c)
You have the anointing (*chrisma*) from the Holy One (2:20)	Now many antichrists (*antichristoi*) have come … they were not of us (2:18, 19)
You know the truth (2:21a)	No lie is of the truth (2:21b)
Confesses the Son (2:23c)	Denies the Son (2:23a)
Has the Father also (2:23c)	Do not have the Father (2:23b)
In him there is no sin (3:5b)	All who practice sin also practice lawlessness (3:4a)
Those who abide in him do not sin (3:6a)	Those who sin have not seen or known him (3:6b)
Practice righteousness; are righteous (3:7)	Practice sinning; of the devil (3:8a)
Those who are born of God do not sin (3:9a)	Those who do not practice righteousness are not of God (3:10b)
Not like Cain (3:12a)	Cain was of the evil one and murdered his brother (3:12a)

His brother's deeds were righteous (3:12d)	His deeds were evil (3:12c)
Have passed out of death into life because we love the brothers (3:14a)	Whoever does not abide in love remains in death (3:14b)
Ought to lay down our lives for the brothers (3:16b)	Everyone who hates his brother is a murderer (3:15a)
Love in deed and truth (3:18)	Closes his heart against a brother in need (3:17)
We know we are of the truth (3:19)	Many false prophets have gone out into the world (4:1b)
Confess that Jesus Christ has come in the flesh (4:2b)	Does not confess Jesus (4:3a)
Are from God (4:4a)	Is not of God (4:3a) but from the world (4:5a)
Born of God and know God (4:7b)	Do not love and do not know God (4:8)
Love God and love the brother (4:21b)	Lies if he says he loves God but hates his brother (4:20)
Believes in the Son of God and has this witness in himself (5:10a)	Does not believe God or God's witness (5:10b)
Has the Son and has life (5:12a)	Does not have the Son and does not have life (5:12b)
Know that we are from God (5:19a) and we are in him who is true, in his Son Jesus Christ (5:20b)	The whole world lies in the power of the evil one; false gods and false teaching (idols) (5:19b, 21)

Through this series of antithetical labels throughout the epistle, it is clear that a conflict of some kind is involved. The author is attempting to persuade the believing community to disassociate themselves from those who are trying to deceive them. The closely paired contrasts of these lists leave the audience with only one real choice. "Keep yourselves from idols" is the summary image in the last sentence of the book, in which the ancient image of idolatry serves as a metaphor for all that is opposite to the Word of life. Psalm 115:4-9 describes the futility of following false gods and teachers: "Their idols ... are man-made. They have mouths, but cannot speak, eyes, but cannot see, ears, but cannot hear, noses, but cannot smell, hands, but cannot touch, feet, but cannot walk. ... Those who make them will end up like them, as will everyone who trusts in them." This description is similar to some of the uses of the word *tohu*, such as in Isaiah 44:9: "All who make idols are nothing [*tohu*], and the things they treasure are worthless. Those who would speak up for them are blind; they are ignorant, to their own shame." "Little children, keep yourselves from idols," urges the author of First John in 5:21, in his attempt to persuade his audience to disavow the false teachers (antichrists) and avoid ending up like them. ("The one who does not love remains in death" [1 John 3:14].)

The ultimate consequence of not keeping oneself from idols is stated in 1 John 5:12: "Whoever has the Son has life; whoever does not have the Son of God does not have life." This ultimate result of being on the wrong side of the antithetical chart, so to speak, makes it clear that more than just human dysfunctional relationships are being described in First John. The stark contrasts between the antithetical labels describe a cosmic battle. At the beginning of the Epistle the contrast is between light and darkness, and at the end the contrast is between those who have eternal life and those who do not, two ways of expressing the same spiritual realities. In the middle of the text we discover how to distinguish between the "children of God" and the "children of the devil," based on their works. At this central climax of the book we learn that the Son of God came to destroy the works of the devil (1 John 3:8).

COSMIC BATTLE SEEN THROUGH THE FOCUS OF A CHIASTIC STRUCTURE IN FIRST JOHN

The parallels between the beginning and ending of First John, with a central climax, point to an overall chiastic structure for the book. At the central climax we read that the Son of God came to destroy the works of the devil (1 John 3:8).

Chiasm, following the general form of ABCBA, was a common oral-literary device in ancient Hebrew literature[370] and was used by the author of First John as a means of organizing the antithetical statements and other material for his readers and listeners. Nils Lund, in his ground-breaking survey of the use of chiasms in the Old and New Testaments, states, "I have reached the conclusion that much of these symmetries was altogether subconscious, ... the writers had learned their forms so thoroughly that they had forgotten them as forms."[371] This structure may have been as common in biblical times as the modern academic structure of essays, taught to children beginning in grade school: "Introduction, Body, and Conclusion." Jerome Neyrey, a New Testament scholar known for applying social science insights to the study of the New Testament, adds the insight that this common form "was anticipated by audiences to aid in following the argument or

---

[370] Nils Wilhelm Lund, *Chiasmus in the New Testament: A Study in Formgeschichte* (Chapel Hill: University of North Carolina Press, 1942), 15.

[371] Lund, *Chiasmus,* ix.

narrative."[372] In a partially oral culture, chiastic structure would have helped make a text memorable.

In addition to serving as a memory aid in the 1st century Mediterranean world for those listening to a text being read or recited aloud,[373] the center of a chiasm focuses the attention of the reader or listener on the central climax of the literary work.[374] Ian Thomson comments, "The center often contains the focus of the author's thought. ... This is a particularly powerful feature with obvious implications for exegesis."[375]

Given the presence in First John of chiastic parallelism at the verse level[376] it seems reasonable to look for the possibility of chiasm in larger portions of the book. This possibility is strengthened by the obvious balanced parallels at the beginning and ending of the book (the theme of witnesses to the life in 1:1, 2 and 5:20) and the references to the antichrist at about equal distances on either side of the center of the

---

[372] Jerome Neyrey, *The Gospel of John* (Cambridge: Cambridge University Press, 2006), 38.

[373] James Bailey, a New Testament scholar with expertise in literary forms in the New Testament, comments on the thought patterns of ancient people: "Relatively unconcerned about a linear and logical flow of ideas, biblical communities relished sayings and stories that were memorable, and they thus appreciated repetition that we might consider redundant. ... Chiastic patterns ... served both pedagogical and liturgical purposes" (James L. Bailey and Lyle D. Van der Broek, *Literary Forms in the New Testament: A Handbook* [Louisville: Westminster John Knox Press, 1992], 182).

[374] Ronald Man comments, "To the biblical authors, artistry in the use of structure was not an end in itself; it was a means toward more effective communication of their messages. In the case of chiasm, this is accomplished by underlining the central emphasis or clarifying correspondences in the text" (Ronald E. Man, "The Value of Chiasm for New Testament Interpretation," *Bibliotheca Sacra* 141 [1984]: 148).

[375] Ian H. Thomson, *Chiasmus in the Pauline Letters. JSNTSupp* 111, (Sheffield: Sheffield Academic Press, 1995), 27.

[376] In the Greek text, the main words of 1 John 3:8a are arranged in chiastic order:
The one doing sin is of the devil, because from the beginning the devil sins.
　　　　　a　　　　　　b　　　　　　　　　c　　　　　b　　　　a
In 1 John 3:9 the Greek word order also demonstrates a chiastic relationship:
The one born
　　of God
　　　sin
　　　　does not do.
　　　　　His seed abides in him,
　　　he is not able
　　to sin
　　of God
he is born.

book (2:18 and 4:3b). In the list of antithetical statements shown earlier, a thought experiment of folding the list in half at the center yields a roughly chiastic chart.[377] The result of this mental matching exercise is arranged here in a "U" shape (using only the general categories), for convenience in seeing the parallelisms side by side. As in a typical chiastic chart, letters are assigned to each main section[378]:

Antithetical Statements Grouped and Arranged in Chiastic Order

A. Light and Fellowship with God vs. Dark and No Fellowship (1:5-10)

A' Have the Son and Life vs. Do Not Have the Son and Life (5:10-21)

B. Love vs. Hate (2:9-11)

B' Love vs. Hate (4:8-20)

C. The Father vs. the World (2:15-17)

C' God vs. World (4:4-6)

D. Anointing (*chrisma*) vs. Antichrists (2:18-27)

D' Truth vs. False Prophets and Antichrist (3:18-20) (4:1-3)

E. Righteousness vs. Lawlessness, Sin, Works of the Devil (3:4-15)

The chiastic center in 3:4-15 focuses attention on the cosmic battle between the Son of God and the devil. The insight we find here is the intention of the Son of God to destroy the works of the devil and to distinguish between the "children of God" and the "children of the devil." To put it in simplest terms: one of these groups is characterized by "righteousness" and the other is characterized by "sin" (3:7b, 8a, 10b).

COSMIC BATTLE SEEN THROUGH THE INTERPRETIVE LENS OF A RHETORICAL TRANSITION

We find confirmation of this central focus on the cosmic battle by looking through the interpretive lens of another literary technique used in both the Gospel and the First Epistle of John—the connection of the author's thoughts through intricate transitions. These rhetorical devices, used by Graeco-Roman rhetoricians, would have reinforced in the readers' and hearers' minds the author's main points and would have helped a first century Mediterranean audience to follow and remember the train of thought.[379]

---

[377] The lack of chiastic balance in the full text is due to intervening explanatory material that is not directly connected to the contrasting labels that display the chiastic relationships.

[378] The author's dissertation contains the full text chart in chiastic format ("A Socio-Rhetorical Analysis of the Johannine Understanding of 'the Works of the Devil' in 1 John 3: 8" [DLitt et Phil diss., University of South Africa, 2009], 52, 53).

[379] Longenecker, *Rhetoric*, 4. Also see H. van Dyke Parunak, "Transitional Techniques in the Bible," *Journal of Biblical Literature* 102 (1983): 546.

One of these transitions, which follows the pattern AbaB that Bruce Longenecker calls "chain-link interlock,"[380] demonstrates the emphasis in Johannine theology on the cosmic battle between the Son of God and the evil one. New Testament scholar Pheme Perkins affirms that "it is a fundamental conviction of Johannine theology that Jesus' coming accomplished the victory over evil which had been the object of so much apocalyptic preaching."[381] In First John, as part of an intricate chain-link interlock, reference is made to the Son of God coming to destroy the works of the devil. Longenecker's similar finding in the Gospel of John, described in his book, *Rhetoric at the Boundaries,* reinforces the value of these inter-locked passages as interpretive lenses for identifying the central purpose of each book.

Explanation of "Chain-link Interlock" Transitions

In the technique that Longenecker calls "chain-link interlock," the first of two major themes (A) is interlocked with the second theme by a short anticipatory treatment of the upcoming theme (b), followed by a short retrospective look at the previous major theme (a), ending with the next major theme (B), summarized as AbaB.[382] Parunak speculates that a reason ancient writers may have used the AbaB pattern frequently was because it was especially effective in helping the reader or listener follow the writer's shift of thought.[383] He points out that in situations where a text is read aloud, a shift directly from topic A to topic B could easily be missed by a hearer who happened to be momentarily inattentive. "On the other hand, in a transition with the pattern AbaB, the topic shifts three times: once from A to b, once from b to a, and finally from a to B. The effect is to slow down the transition and give listeners more opportunity to note that a change is taking place."[384]

Longnecker applies this technique to themes within large segments of text, including the Gospel of John.[385] He notes, "several New Testament passages that have frequently been thought to involve structural clutter and disorder are in fact text-book cases of first-class

---

[380] Longenecker, *Rhetoric,* 18. Parunak says this transitional technique was very popular in ancient Mediterranean rhetoric (Parunak, "Transitional Techniques," 546), although it is not commonly noticed by modern commentators.

[381] Pheme Perkins, *The Johannine Epistles* (Wilmington, DE: Michael Glazier, 1979), 43.

[382] Longenecker, *Rhetoric,* 18.

[383] Parunak, "Transitional Techniques," 546.

[384] Parunak, "Transitional Techniques," 546.

[385] Longenecker, *Rhetoric,* 6, 7.

style being animated by chain-link construction."[386] After looking at Longenecker's explanation of the chain-link transitional technique in the Gospel of John, we will look at an example in the First Epistle of John. Later we will "stitch" these and other examples of inner and inter-texture analysis into the larger picture of God's purpose in this world to defeat the enemy and win his people back to himself.

Chain-link Interlock in the Gospel of John: Longenecker's Findings

Longenecker sees the chain-link interlock transition as establishing "an interpretative lens" through which to view other aspects of the text.[387] In a compact outline he finds the following pattern in the Gospel of John:

> **Text unit A**: John 1:1–12:19 (Jesus' public ministry)
>
> > **Interlocked unit b** (*anticipatory*): John 12:20-36 (Jesus' advance preparation for his death, including reference in 12:31 to the ruler of this world being driven out)
> >
> > **Interlocked unit a (retrospective)**: John 12:37-50 (Jesus' public works)
>
> **Text Unit B**: John 13:1–21:25 (Jesus' private ministry, preparing his disciples for his death; the account of his death and resurrection; reference in 14:30 to "the ruler of this world is coming. He has no power over me.")

An example of Longenecker's idea of an "interpretive lens" is seen in the allusion to the cosmic battle between Jesus and "the ruler of this world" at the hinge of the Gospel of John (in unit "b"), intricately woven together with unit "B" through chain-link interlock. This finds a counterpart at the center of First John, where a chain-link interlock transition also occurs in connection with reference to the cosmic battle. ("The reason the Son of God appeared was to destroy the works of the devil." [3:8b, ESV].)

Chain-link Interlock in First John

The example of chain-link interlock in First John that includes reference to the cosmic battle is found in the text unit of 1 John 2:28–4:21. This is the pattern identified through inner-texture analysis:

---

[386] Longenecker, *Rhetoric*, 6.
[387] Longenecker, *Rhetoric*, 122.

Text unit A: 2:28–3:10 (Confidence in being children of God, or "of God," comes from doing right / being righteous, in contrast to those who are "of the devil," whose works the Son of God came to destroy)

> **Interlocked unit b** (*anticipatory*): 3:11-18 (Love: how to know what love really is and is not, namely hatred)

> **Interlocked unit a** (*retrospective*): 3:19–4:6 (Confidence to know the difference between the spirit of truth and the antichrist / deception)

Text Unit B: 4:7-21: Love: God is love, love one another in imitation of him (God sent his son to save the *kosmos*)

Significance of Chain-link Interlock for the Cosmic Battle Theme

As mentioned earlier, Longenecker describes a chain-link interlock transition between the two halves of the Gospel of John, with mention of the "ruler of this world" being cast out occurring in the transitional unit that anticipates the last major unit of the book. In First John, again as part of an intricate chain-link interlock, reference is made to the Son of God coming to destroy the works of the devil. These similarities in structure and theme at the center of each book hint that the cosmic battle between the Son of God and the evil one is of central importance to Johannine theology. These interlocked passages are lenses through which to look both backward and forward at the rest of each book, to see what works the devil, the ruler of the world, has been doing that need to be cast out and destroyed and how this was and is to be accomplished.

In the both Gospel and First Epistle of John, by looking backwards and forwards from the highlight of the cosmic conflict in each book's example of chain-link interlock, we can see that one of the things the devil and ruler of this world has been doing is to inspire hatred and murder. In the Gospel of John Jesus tells the Jewish leaders, "You are of your father the devil, … and your will is to do your father's desires. He was a murderer from the beginning" (John 8:44). Later, as he prepared for his death, Jesus discussed the results of the evil one's murderous influence with his disciples. "If the world hates you, know that it has hated me before it hated you" (John 15:18. Also see John 15:19, 23, 24, 25; 17:14). In First John the community is warned that anyone who hates his fellow-believer is in darkness (1 John 2:11), and they should not be surprised if the world hates them (1 John 3:13). Anyone who hates his brother is murderer like Cain, who was of the evil one (1 John 3:12, 15). No one can hate his "brother" and love God at the same time (1 John 4:20).

Hatred is clearly a work of the devil that Jesus came to correct. But in the antithetical worldview of the Johannine community, it might have been tempting for them to think they should love believers but hate those who were not part of their community. In fact, this was the teaching of the Qumran community at that time.[388] Repaying hatred for hatred may have seemed reasonable given the stark contrasts and accusations of sin and unrighteousness against the "children of the devil." Since the author of First John stresses love for the "brothers" and for "one another" so often, some commentators have wondered whether members of the Johannine community expected to demonstrate love to anyone at all outside their own fellowship. Dirk Van der Merwe quotes an extreme critic of the Johannine group's ingrown concern for fellow believers as saying that a Johannine Christian, "on seeing a wounded traveler would ask: 'Are you saved, brother?' instead of giving aid."[389] Judith Lieu[390] and J. G. van der Watt[391] each conclude that the group's love involved only internal relationships. Van der Watt stresses the familial metaphors of First John and simply dismisses the question of whether the believer has any responsibility to those outside the family of God. He claims that this question, which is not addressed in the letter, "is raised in an extraneous theological perspective."[392] However, the chain-link transitional structure gives a new perspective showing that First John does, in fact, have something to say about the believer's responsibility to those outside the family of God. This should be a welcome interpretation to those throughout time and in various cultures who have wondered about this "extraneous theological" question.

To arrive at this new perspective, a brief review of the chain-link interlock involving 2:28–4:21 is necessary. Verse 3:17, in which the author calls for demonstrating love to a "brother in need," is part of

---

[388] See 1*QS* (*Qumran Manual of Discipline*) I, 1-5: "He shall admit into the Covenant of Grace all those who have freely devoted themselves to the observance of God's precepts, ... that they may love all the sons of light,... and hate all the sons of darkness."

[389] Dirk G. van der Merwe, "A Matter of Having Fellowship: Ethics in the Johannine Epistles," in *Identity, Ethics, and Ethos in the New Testament*, ed. Jan G. van der Watt (Berlin: Walter de Gruyter, 2006), 535.

[390] Judith M. Lieu, *The Theology of the Johannine Epistles* (Cambridge: Cambridge University Press, 1991), 53.

[391] J. G. van der Watt "Ethics in First John: A Literary and Socioscientific Perspective," *Catholic Biblical Quarterly* 61 (1999): 510.

[392] Van der Watt, "Ethics," 510.

transitional unit "b" in the chain link diagram reviewed below, anticipating the major unit "B," both of which have love as the main focus. The question needing an answer is, "who is included in the term 'brother'?"

> **Text unit A**: 2:28–3:10 (Confidence in being children of God, or "of God," comes from doing right/being righteous, in contrast to those who are "of the devil" whose works the Son of God came to destroy)
>
>> **Interlocked unit b** (*anticipatory*): 3:11-18 (Love: how to know what love really is and is not, namely hatred; "If anyone has the world's goods and sees his brother in need, yet closes his heart against him, how does God's love abide in him?" [3:17, ESV])
>>
>> **Interlocked unit a** (*retrospective*): 3:19–4:6 (Confidence to **know** the difference between the spirit of truth and antichrist/deception)
>
> **Text Unit B**: 4:7-21: Love: God is love, love one another in imitation of him ("We have seen and testify that the Father has sent his Son to be the Savior of the world / *kosmos*" [4:14, ESV])

This complex inter-locking transition pulls God's concern for the "*kosmos*" shown in unit B in 4:14, into the discussion of whom the believer should love in 3:17. The section that 3:17 falls in is anticipatory of the full treatment in 4:7ff of what it means to love "one another" (1 John 3:11). The *kosmos* in 4:14c defines who should be included in "one another" in 1 John 3:11 and the "brother in need" in verse 17. God sacrificed his Son for the whole world, not just for the Johannine community.[393]

Considering the world as an object of God's love, and therefore also an object of the believers' love, who are to love just as God did,[394] solves the theological problem some have had in thinking that the

---

[393] In a consultation at William Carey International University on March 1, 2014, Native American theologian Terry LeBlanc stated his perspective that all of creation, not just humans, is included in the *kosmos* that Jesus came to rescue and set right. Gregory Boyd agrees that "all creation is corrupted and needs saving" (Gregory Boyd, "A War-Torn Creation," in *Evangelical and Frontier Mission Perspectives On the Global Progress of the Gospel*, ed. Beth Snodderly and A. Scott Moreau [Oxford, UK: Regnum, 2011], 286-93).

[394] "If God so loved us, we also ought to love one another" (1 John 4:11, ESV); "Just as Jesus is, so also are we in this world" ((1 John 4:17).

emphasis in First John is on loving the fellow believer to the neglect of the rest of the world. This argument reinforces the view being developed in this book that international development is a means by which believers demonstrate God's will and God's love. We will see in the next section that this radical love is a means by which the devil's works, that are holding many of the world's people in bondage, are to be destroyed.

COSMIC BATTLE SEEN IN REPETITIVE AND PROGRESSIVE TEXTURE STUDIES

Love and the "children of God" have a role to play in working with the unique Son of God to destroy or "nullify" the works of the devil. To reach this conclusion, we will look at two original charts of repetitive and progressive texture that explore key themes in First John. This is a method that Vernon Robbins advocates for mapping out words that occur more than once in a unit, giving the interpreter insights into the overall picture of the discourse, which will then lead to closer investigation of the details of the text.[395] Two charts represent the results of an investigation of repeated themes and repeated key words:

CHART 1: Cosmic Battle Themes in First John

CHART 2: Key Terms from the Center of the Epistle, 1 John 3:8-10

With each chart, the themes to be charted will be listed first, with each occurrence in the order of its appearance in the book of First John. For the first chart, due to the complexity of the clusters of themes, a number is assigned to each theme-cluster. In the second chart, each of the key terms is listed across the top. Divisions of First John, chosen according to insights gained from the analysis of a variety of rhetorical transitions,[396] are listed on the left side of the chart. An "x" identifies each occurrence of the theme-cluster or key term within each division of the book.

Chart 1: Cosmic Battle Themes in First John

This chart portrays a rhetorical word picture in which opposing forces are engaged in a cosmic battle. These clusters of themes have been chosen based on participants in the battle, what they can be seen doing, and how they can be characterized in terms of beliefs and behavior. First we will look at how each theme cluster is described

---

[395] Robbins, *Texture*, 8.
[396] See Snodderly, "A Socio-Rhetorical Analysis," 229.

within the Epistle, then we will chart the occurrence of each theme in the section divisions of First John:

1. Participants on the devil's side
2. What the opponents are doing
3. Characteristics of the opposition
4. Participants on God's side
5. What God, the Son, and Jesus are doing
6. What believers are doing
7. Characteristics of God and his children

1. Participants on the devil's side
Liars, false prophets: 1:6; 1:10; 2:4; 2:21; 2:22; 2:27; 4:1; 4:20; 5:10
Those who deceive: 1:8; 2:26; 3:7; 4:6
Those who are of the world: 2:2; 2:15 (3x); 2:16 (2x); 2:17; 3:1; 3:13; 3:17; 4:1; 4:3; 4:4; 4:5 (3x); 4:9; 4:14; 4:17; 5:4 (2x); 5:5; 5:19
Those who are of the evil one: 2:13; 2:14; 3:12 (2x); 5:18; 5:19
Antichrists: 2:18 (2x); 2:22; 4:3
The devil: 3:8 (3x)
Children of the devil: 3:10
Cain: 3:12
Murderer: 3:15 (2x)
Spirit that does not confess Jesus, or spirit of deception: 4:3, 4:6

2. What the opponents are doing
Walking in darkness: 1:6; 2:8; 2:9; 2:11 (3x)
Lying: 1:6; 1:10; 2:4; 2:21; 2:22; 2:27; 4:1; 4:20; 5:10
Sinning: 1:7; 1:8; 1:9 (2x); 1:10; 2:1 (2x); 2:2; 2:12; 3:4 (2x); 3:5 (2x); 3:6 (2x); 3:8 (2x); 3:9 (2x); 4:10; 5;16 (4x); 5:17 (2x); 5:18
Deceiving: 1:8; 2:26; 3:7; 4:6
Hating: 2:9; 2:11; 3:13; 3:15; 4:20
Being blinded: 2:11
Slaughtering: 3:12 (2x)
Behaving unlawfully: 3:4 (2x)

3. Characteristics of the opposition
Passing away: 2:8; 2:17
Lustful: 2:16 (2x); 2:17
Of the flesh: 2:16
Arrogance, pride: 2:16
Death: 3:14; 3:14; 5:16 (3x); 5:17
Attempting to control the whole world: 5:19

4. Participants on God's side
The Father: 1:2; 1:3; 2:1; 2:15; 2:16; 2:22; 2:23 (3x); 2:24; 3:1; 4:14
Son (of God): 1:3; 1:7; 2:22; 2:23 (2x); 2:24; 3:8; 3:23; 4:9; 4:10; 4:14; 4:15; 5:5; 5:9; 5:10; 5:11; 5:12 (2x); 5:13; 5:20 (2x)

Jesus / Jesus Christ): 1:3; 1:7; 2:1; 2:22; 3:23; 4:2; 4:3; 4:15; 5:1; 5:5; 5:6; 5:20
God: 1:5b; 2:5; 2:14; 2:17; 3:1; 3:2; 3:8; 3:9 (2x); 3:10 (2x); 3:17; 3:20; 3:21;
    4:1; 4:2 (2x); 4:3; 4:4; 4:6 (2x)s; 4:7 (3x); 4:8 (2x); 4:9 (2x); 4:10; 4:11;
    4:12 (2x); 4:15 (3x); 4:16 (3x); 4;16; 4:20 (2x); 4:21; 5:1; 5:2 (2x); 5:3; 5:4;
    5:5; 5:9 (2x); 5:10; 5:10 (2x); 5:11; 5:13; 5:18 (2x); 5:19; 5:20 (2x)
Little children: 2:1; 2:12; 2:28; 3:7; 3:18; 4:4; 5:21
Children: 3:1; 3:2; 5:2
That one: 2:6; 3:3; 3:5; 3:7; 3:16; 4:17; 5:16
Fathers: 2:13, 14
Young men: 2:13; 2:14
Those born of God: 2:29; 3:9 (2x); 4:7; 5;1 (3x); 5:4; 5:18
Children of God: 3:10
Spirit (of truth): 3:24; 4:2 (2x); 4:6; 4:13; 5:6 (2x)
One and only: 4:9
Savior: 4:14

5. What God, the Son, and Jesus are doing
Being manifested, appearing: 1:2 (2x); 2:19; 2:28; 3:2 (2x); 3:5; 3:8; 3:10; 4:9
Forgiving: 1:9; 2:12
Serving as propitiation (atoning sacrifice, oil on troubled waters, substitute):
    2:2; 4:10
Loving: 2:5; 3:1; 3:16; 3:17; 4:7; 4:8; 4:9; 4:10 (2x); 4:11; 4:12; 4:16 (2x); 4:19
Abiding: 2:14; 2:24; 2:27; 3:17; 3:24; 4:12; 4:13; 4:15; 4:16
Doing righteousness: 2:1; 2:29 (2x); 3:7 (3x); 3:10; 3:12; 5:17
Taking away sins: 3:5
Destroying works of devil 3:8
Laying down life: 3:16 (2x)
Keeping those born of God from the evil one: 5:18

6. What believers are doing
Walking in the light: 1:7 (2x); 2:8; 2:9; 2:10
Having fellowship: 1:3 (2x); 1:6; 1:7
Obeying commands: 2:3; 2:8; 3:22; 3:23 (2x); 3:24; 4:21; 5:2; 5:3 (2x)
Keeping, obeying: 2:3; 2:5; 3:22; 3:24; 5:3; 5:18
Loving: 2:7; 2:10; 3:2; 3:10; 3:11; 3:14 (2x); 3:18; 3:21; 3:23; 4:1; 4:7 (3x);
    4:8; 4:10; 4:11 (2x); 4:12; 4:16; 4:17; 4:18 (3x); 4:19; 4:20 (3x); 4:21 (2x);
    5:1 (2x); 5:2 (2x); 5:3
Remaining, abiding: 2:6; 2:10; 2:17; 2:24 (2x); 2:27; 2:28; 3:6; 3:9; 3:24 4:13;
    4:15; 4:16 (2x)
Overcoming, having victory over: 2:13; 2:14; 4:4; 5:4 (3x); 5:5
Being strong: 2:14
Being righteous: 2:1; 2:29 92x); 3:7 (3x); 3:10; 3:12; 5:17
Laying down life: 3:16 (2x)
Being faithful, believing: 3:23; 4:16; 5:4; 5:5; 5:10; 5:10; 5:10; 5:13
Being kept from being touched by the evil one: 5:18

7. Characteristics of God and His Children

Life: 1:1; 1:2 (2x); 2:25; 3:14; 3:15; 4:9; 5:11 (2x); 5:13; 5:16; 5:20

Light: 1:5b; 1:7 (2x); 2:8; 2:9; 2:10

Love: 2:5; 2:7; 2:10; 3:1; 3:2; 3:10; 3:11; 3:14 (2x); 3:16; 3:17; 3:18; 3:21;
    3:23; 4:1; 4:7 (4x); 4:8 (2x); 4:9; 4:10 (3x); 4:11 (3x); 4:12 2x); 4:16 (3x);
    4:17; 4:18 (3x); 4:19 (2x); 4:20 (3x); 4:21 (2x); 5:1 (2x); 5:2 (2x); 5:3

Remain, abide: 2:6; 2:10; 2:14; 2:17; 2:19; 2:24 (3x); 2:27 (2x); 2:28; 3:6; 3:9;
    3:14; 3:15; 3:17; 3:24 (2x); 4:12; 4:13; 4:15; 4:16 (3x)

Faithful, believe: 1:9; 3:23; 4:16; 5:4; 5:5; 5:10 (3x); 5:13

Righteous: 1:9 (2x); 2:1; 2:29 (2x); 3:7 (3x); 3:10; 3:12; 5:17

Truth, truly, true) 1:6; 1:8; 2:4; 2:5; 2:8 (2x); 2:21 (2x); 2:27; 3:18; 3:19; 4:6;
    5:6; 5:20 (3x)

CHART 1   Cosmic Battle Themes

1. Participants on the Devil's side
2. What the opponents are doing
3. Characteristics of the opposition
4. Participants on God's side
5. What God, the Son, and Jesus are doing
6. What believers are doing
7. Characteristics of God and his children

Sections of 1 Jn	1	2	3	4	5	6	7
1:1-5a				xxxxx x	xx		xxx
1:5b-2:2	xxxx	xxxxx xxxxx x		xxxx	xxx	xxxxx x	xxxxx xxxx
2:3-11	x	xxxxx xxxx	x	xx	x	xxxxx xxxx	xxxxx xxxxx xx
2:12-14	xx	x		xxxx	xx	xxx	x
2:15-17a	xxxxx x		xxxxx x	xxx			x
2:17b-28	xxxxx xxx	xxxx		xxxxx xx	xxx		xxxxx xxxxx xx
2:28-3:10	xxxxx	xxxxx xxxxx xxx		xxxxx xxxxx xxxxx xxxx	xxxxx xxxxx xxxx	xxxxx xxxxx	xxxxx xxxxx

	1	2	3	4	5	6	7
3:11-18	XXXXX X	XXXX	XX	XXX	XXXXX X	XXXXX XX	XXXXX XXXXX XX
3:19-24				XXXXX	X	XXXXX XXX	XXXXX
4:1-6	XXXXX XXXX	XX		XXXXX XXXXX XXX		X	XX
4:7-21	XXXX	XXX		XXXXX XXXXX XXXXX XXXXX XXXXX XXXXX XX	XXXXX XXXXX XXXXX X	XXXXX XXXXX XXXXX XXXXX XXXXX	XXXXX XXXXX XXXXX XXXXX XXXXX XXXXX XXXXX XX
5:1-5	XXX			XXXXX XXXXX XXXX		XXXXX XXXXX XXXX	XXXXX XX
5:6-12	X	X		XXXXX XXXXX XXXX		XXXX	XXXXX
5:13-21	XXX	XXXXX XX	XXXXX	XXXXX XXXXX XXX	XX	XXX	XXXXX XXX

Insights from Chart 1: Cosmic Battle Themes in First John

This chart groups the activities and characteristics of the two types of people, those on God's side and those on the side of the devil or evil one. Theme 4, participants on God's side, has an increased number of occurrences in the central section, 2:28–3:10 (highlighted above). This corresponds with the first mention of the devil and it is also where the children of God are first mentioned, joining in the cosmic battle that is part of the ideological perspective of the author of First John.

Theme 5, what God, the Son, and Jesus are doing, is also particularly concentrated in the central section of the Epistle, where the cosmic battle is highlighted, as well as in 4:7-21, where the full treatment of the theme of love occurs. The fact that demonstrating love is one of the key things God and the Son can be seen doing seems to indicate that love has a role to play in the cosmic battle in the Johannine worldview.

Theme 6, what believers are doing, shows even more activity charted than for what God, the Son, and Jesus are doing in the second half of the book, after the "entrance" of the devil, so to speak. This indicates an important role for God's children in the battle, including joining the Son of God in some sense to destroy the works of the devil. Again, love is an important aspect of what believers are seen doing, further evidence of the role of love in overcoming evil in the cosmic battle.

CHART 2: Key Terms from the Center of the Epistle, 1 John 3:8-10

Key terms from the central section of First John are listed here in the order in which the words first occur in the full Epistle:

From the beginning: 1:1; 2:7; 2:13; 2:14; 2:24 (2x); 3:8; 3:11
Appeared: 1:2 (2x); 2:19; 2:28; 3:2 (2x); 3:5; 3:8; 3:10; 4:9
Sin: 1:7; 1:8; 1:9 (2x); 1:10; 2:1 (2x); 2:2; 2:12; 3:4 (2x); 3:5 (2x); 3:6 (2x); 3:8 (2x); 3:9 (2x); 4:10; 5:16 (4x); 5:17 (2x); 5:18
Righteousness: 1:9 (2x); 2:1; 2:29 (2x); 3:7 (3x); 3:10; 3:12; 5:17
Love: 2:5; 2:7; 2:10; 2:15 (3x); 3:1; 3:2; 3:10; 3:11; 3:14 (2x); 3:16; 3:17; 3:18; 3:21; 3:23; 4:1; 4:7 (4x); 4:8 (2x); 4:9; 4:10 (3x); 4:11 (3x); 4:12 (2x); 4:16 (3x); 4:17; 4:18 (3x); 4:19 (2x); 4:20 (3x); 4:21 (2x); 5:1 (2x); 5:2 (2x); 5:3
Evil one/Devil: 2:13; 2:14; 3:8 (3x); 3:10; 3:12 (2x); 5:18; 5:19
Children of God; Born of God: 2:29; 3:1; 3:2; 3:9 (2x); 3:10; 4:7; 5:1 (2x); 5:2; 5:4; 5:18 (2x)

Sections of 1 John	From the Beginning	Appeared	Sin	Righteousness	Love	Children/ Born of God	Evil one Devil
1:1-5a	x	xx					
1:5b-2:2			xxxxx xxx	xxx			
2:3-11	x				xxx		
2:12-14	xx		x				xx
2:15-17a					xxx		
2:17b-28	xx	x					
2:28-3:10	x	xxxxx x	xxxxx xxxxx	xxxxx x	xxx	xxx xxx	xxxx
3:11-18	x			x	xxxxx x		
3:19-24					xx		
4:1-6					x		
4:7-21		x	x		xxxxx xxxxx xxxxx xxxxx xxxxx xxxx	x	
5:1-5					xxxxx	xxxx	
5:6-12		x					
5:13-21			xxxxx xx	x		xx	

Insights and Further Studies from Chart 2: Key Terms Related to 1 John 3:8-10

<u>The Theme of "From the Beginning"</u>

The title of this chapter, "Jesus, the New Beginning," is supported by a key theme in First John of what has been "from the beginning." If we temporarily set aside the first occurrence of this phrase in 1 John 1:1, we will find the author has made typical use of chiasm to arrange the remaining statements about what has been "from the beginning." This chiastic arrangement gives helpful insights for the ideological perspective of the cosmic battle that we are developing in these in-depth exegetical / socio-rhetorical studies.[397]

A 2:7: It is not a new command, but an old command you have had <u>from the beginning</u>

    B 2:13, 14: Fathers ... have known "<u>the [one] from the beginning</u>"

        C 2:24, 25: Let what you have heard <u>from the beginning</u> remain in you; ... eternal life promised (also see 1:1: the Word of Life)

    B' 3:8: The devil has been sinning <u>from the beginning</u>

A' 3:11: This is the message you have heard <u>from the beginning</u>, that we should love one another.

"Life" is the highlight of the centerpiece of this chiastic diagram of the phrases related to the theme of what was "from the beginning." In the battle between life and death, between the Son of the God and the devil, between the children of God and the children of the devil, eternal life is what is at stake. The Johannine community has known about this life "from the beginning" (1 John 1:1).

Sections A and A' discuss the command or message the recipients have had "from the beginning." The specific content of that command is stated in the last phrase of the diagram above: "love one another." These verses are an inter-textual echo of John 13:34: "A new command I give you: love one another." The content of the command is reaffirmed in 1 John 3:23: And this is his command: ... to love one another as he

---

[397] We are admittedly creating a very large number of quilt pieces, as mentioned in chapter 2, in the process of constructing a "fabric of discourse" about the biblical theme of cosmic battle as the origin of the need for international development.

commanded us."[398] Obeying the command given by Jesus is an aspect of knowing Jesus.

Sections B and B' mention a person the recipients know who has been "from the beginning." Both Jesus (the Word of life) and the devil's sinning are referred to as being "from the beginning." "That which was from the beginning, ... the word of life" (1 John 1:1 ESV) echoes "in the beginning was the Word" in John 1:1 (ESV) and contrasts with 1 John 3:8a: "the devil has been sinning from the beginning." Because it is stated twice in 1 John 2:13, 14 that the fathers have known, literally, "the from the beginning," we can consider the possibility that this could refer both to the fact that the fathers have known about Jesus "from the beginning," and that they have also known about the evil one who has been "sinning from the beginning."

The audience's knowledge of the evil one is clear in 2:13, 14 which is addressed not only to the fathers who have known what is "from the beginning," but also to the young men who have "overcome the evil one," who is the devil who has been "sinning from the beginning" (1 John 3:8a). This phrase would no doubt have brought to the audience's mind a similar phrase in John 8:44: "your father, the devil ... was a murderer from the beginning." We have already seen through several exegetical approaches that the "works of the devil" (1 John 3:8b) are associated with sin and death. Doing away with those works, then, should result in the qualities being revealed that are opposite to those of the devil, namely life, righteousness, and love.

The devil, who has been sinning "from the beginning," does not acknowledge the authority of God and demonstrates hatred instead of the love Jesus commanded (John 13:34). The devil's followers are just like him. Cain, who murdered his brother, is an archetypal example of the devil's "children." The fact that the devil's followers are like him demonstrates his rulership over them, which is explicitly stated in John 12:31 ("now the ruler / *archōn* of this world will be cast out"). Jesus came to "destroy the works of the devil" (1 John 3:8b) that are causing chaos and opposition to God's good will for people and all creation.

---

[398] Also see 2 John 5, 6 which gives another chiastic arrangement of the same themes:

A And now, dear lady, I am not writing you a new command
  B but one we have had from the beginning.
    C I ask that we love one another.
    C And this is love: that we walk in obedience to his commands.
  B As you have heard from the beginning,
A his command is that you walk in love.

Not only do we see the devil being cast out / destroyed in both John 12:31 and 1 John 3:8, but the same root word for primacy of rulership or of temporal beginning (*archōn* / ruler; *archē* / beginning) is used in these climactic verses in the chain-link interlock in each passage that we looked at earlier. It is possible that the phrase, "the devil has been sinning from the beginning," may be a play on words, with the author having two meanings of the root word for *archē* in mind:[399] the devil has been sinning from the temporal beginning (*archē*) of his rulership (*archōn*) of earth.

Themes of "Appeared" and "Destroy"

Jesus came to "destroy [*lusē*] the works of the devil" (1 John 3:8b) that are causing chaos and opposition to God's good will for people and all creation. "We know that … the whole world lies in the power of the evil one" (1 John 5:19 ESV). This is the primary problem that Jesus appeared in this world to solve. In connection with examining insights into the theme of Jesus' appearing, we will also examine the word for "destroy" that occurs only once in First John.

Of the ten references in First John to the theme of "appeared / *phaneroō*," six of these occur in the central (highlighted) section in which the purpose of the appearing of the Son of God is announced, to destroy the works of the devil: 1:2; 1:2; 2:19; 2:28; 3:2; 3:2; 3:5; 3:8; 3:10; 4:9. In the first occurrence of this term in the Epistle (1:2), the life of God is made evident by the appearance of the Son in this world. In the last occurrence of the term, we see that God shares his life with believers as a manifestation of his love by sending "his one and only Son into the world that we might live through him" (1 John 4:9). Life and love are bound up together in the appearing of the Son of God.

God's will is characterized by life, love, and righteousness according to major themes included in Chart 2. In Johannine theology, these qualities are summed up by saying that "God is light; in him there is no darkness at all" (1 John 1:5), and as Jesus' said of himself, "I am the light of the world" (John 9:5). When the light shines in the darkness, the darkness is not able to overcome it (John 1:5). Instead, when the light appears, it causes the works of the devil to dis-appear, or to be nullified, destroyed / *lusē*.

An examination of the word *lusē* in the New Testament reveals two basic uses of the term. This becomes clear in a comparison of seven

---

[399] Trevor Ling agrees with the possibility that "from the beginning" can mean two things at once. In his case he is thinking of the devil's sin "in the beginning of history and at the root of the universe" (Ling, *Significance of Satan*, 31).

word pictures in which this term is used, which we can group into two sets:

Group 1:
    1. Untying the colt (Luke 19:33)
    2. Untying sandals (John 1:27)
    3. Unbinding Lazarus from his grave clothes (John 11:44)

Group 2:
    4. "Destroy this temple and in three days I will raise it up" (John 2:19)
    5. The back part of the ship was being broken up (Acts 27:41)
    6. Breaking down the dividing wall between Jews and Gentiles (Eph. 2:14)
    7. The elements will be set ablaze and dissolved (2 Pet. 3:10-12)

In the first group of usages, *lusē* is used in the sense of undoing something that had previously been attached.[400] In the second group the word pictures depict violence and destruction.[401] The question we have to decide, then, is in which group of word pictures the use of *lusē* in 1 John 3:8 belongs. Some commentators avoid this decision by claiming both uses of the term.[402] Robert Kysar uses his own theology to decide that *lusē* means "to destroy: 'to loose.' It means to free humans from the power of evil. Here the author [of First John] invokes a slightly different concept of atonement which centers in the objective forces of opposition to God."[403] Although Kysar is on the right track in referring to "the objective forces of opposition to God," his explanation betrays an anthropocentric viewpoint, as if the works of the devil were only about humans. We have seen that the devil's work has been directed "from the beginning" against God and only secondarily against humans, according to the interpretation of Genesis 1:2 discussed earlier. In that exegesis of Genesis 1, before humans were created the earth was already in a

---

[400] Johannes P. Louw and Eugene A. Nida, eds., *Greek-English Lexicon of the New Testament Based on Semantic Domains* (New York: United Bible Societies, 1988), 221. This is under the semantic domain of "attachment" according to Louw and Nida.

[401] Louw and Nida, *Lexicon*, 230. This usage is reminiscent of the Hebrew phrase, studied earlier, in Genesis 1:2, *tohu wabohu*, which describes the condition of the land after it had been destroyed.

[402] See for example Alfred Plummer who does not distinguish between the two usages: "Loosening or dissolving is appropriate. ... The works of the devil are the sins which he causes men to commit. Christ came to undo these sins" (Alfred Plummer, *The Epistles of St. John* [1886; repr., Grand Rapids: Baker, 1980], 79).

[403] Robert Kysar, *I, II, III John, Augsburg Commentary on the New Testament* (Minneapolis: Augsburg Publishing House, 1986), 81.

condition of chaos as a result of a destruction of the evil one's work of rebellion against God's purposes. It would seem reasonable that the "objective forces of opposition" would require more than just a rescue of the victims of the opposition's work. In a war, such as the cosmic war of the Johannine worldview, the source of the opposition has to be destroyed and eliminated.

These definitions that attempt to use both senses of the meaning of *lusē* are inadequate, given the reality of the seriousness and nature of the works of the devil as outlined earlier in this chapter. Those works were seen to be much more than just tempting humans to sin, therefore "destroying the works of the devil" must be more than just loosing people from the power of sin. The devil has been sinning from the beginning and his works are characterized by intentional opposition to God's will, including disease, deceit, lying, injustice, hatred, bloodshed, and turning people away from belief in Jesus.

The definition in Bauer's *Greek-English Lexicon of the New Testament and Other Early Christian Literature* is more helpful for understanding the force behind the word *lusē* as it is used in 1 John 3:8: the Son of God came to "destroy, bring to an end, abolish, do away with" [404] the works of the devil. Respected Johannine commentator Raymond Brown summarizes his preferred definition: "to destroy, dissolve, nullify"[405] the works of the devil. These works are opposed to God. In Johannine theology the appearing of the Son of God brings the light and the glory of God, in the face of which the works of the devil are nullified and done away with.

The Early Church father, Ignatius, gives an example of the destruction of the works of the devil as a result of the appearance of God through his Son:

> Consequently all magic and every kind of spell were dissolved, the ignorance so characteristic of wickedness vanished, and the ancient kingdom was abolished when God appeared in human form to bring the newness of eternal life, and what had been

---

[404] W. A. A. Bauer, *Greek-English Lexicon of the New Testament and Other Early Christian Literature*, 2nd ed., trans. W. F. Arndt and F. W. Gingrich (Chicago: University of Chicago Press, 1979), 483. Haas, DeJonge, and Swellengrebel give a similar definition for the context of 1 John 3:8, saying that "to destroy is sometimes rendered 'to undo, to do away with, to cause to be lost for sure, to put/make an end to, to wipe out'" (M. Haas, C. DeJonge, and J. L. Swellengrebel, *A Translator's Handbook on The Letters of John*. Helps for Translators Series [London: United Bible Societies, 1972], 84).

[405] Raymond E. Brown, *The Epistles of John (The Anchor Bible, Vol. 30)* (Garden City, NY: Anchor Bible, 1982), 406.

prepared by God began to take effect (*Ignatius to the Ephesians* 19:3).

This inter-textual example affirms the understanding that the appearing of the Son overturns the kingdom of darkness that had set itself in opposition to God's kingdom "before the beginning" of the world as we know it. The appearing of the Son of God does away with wickedness, brings right knowledge, and the end result of his appearing is eternal life (1 John 4:9), lived according to God's ways. This is a good description of turning *tohu wabohu* upside down, making things right.

The Theme of "Sin"

"He appeared in order to take away sins" (1 John 3:5).

The NIV mis-translates this verse as "to take away *our* sins," even though the word for "our" is not in the original Greek. This again betrays a common anthropocentric view of the nature of sin. In the cosmic battle, the devil's rebellion against God's will, from before the beginning, has to be taken into account in interpreting the climactic verses at the heart of First John and what is included in the term "sin."

A striking feature related to the key themes found in the central section of First John is visibly evident from this short version of Chart 2, "Key Themes." The theme of sin is concentrated in the chiastic center of First John, with similar numbers of occurrences of the term at approximately equal distances from the center section:

Sin: 1:7; 1:8; 1:9; 1:9; 1:10; 2:1; 2:1; 2:2; 2:12
         3:4; 3:4; 3:5; 3:5; 3:6; 3:6; 3:8; 3:8; 3:9; 3:9
         4:10; 5;16; 5:16; 5:16; 5;16; 5:17; 5:17; 5:18

The fact that "sin" is positioned in and around the chiastic center, as well as the fact that it is in this central section that the destruction of the works of the devil is mentioned, indicates that sin is closely related to the works of the devil that Jesus came to destroy. This mini chart also confirms that the verses at the hinge of the chiastic structure (3:8-12) can be viewed as a central lens through which to look both backwards and forwards at the rest of the book.

The definition of sin is enhanced by the findings of the chiastic structure discussed earlier in this chapter, in which verses 3:4 and 3:15 are found to be aligned:

Everyone who makes a practice of sinning also practices lawlessness [*anomia*]; sin is lawlessness [*anomia*] (1 John 3:4 ESV).

> Everyone who hates his brother is a murderer, and you know that no
> murderer has eternal life abiding in him (1 John 3:15 ESV).

If we accept the validity of the chiastic parallels between these verses
we find that sin and lawlessness / *anomia*, are associated with both
physical death (murder) and spiritual death (lack of eternal life). In this
context when we hear, "he appeared in order to take away sins" (1 John
3:5) and we compare this with the similar sentence construction 3
verses later, "[he] appeared ... to destroy the works of the devil" (who
has himself been "sinning from the beginning, 1 John 3:8), we can see
that Jesus appeared to destroy the devil's sins, lawlessness, and
opposition to God. This opposition includes causing humans to sin, but
it also includes the devil's own murderous character, which extends
beyond humans to affect all of creation.

A brief inter-textual word study demonstrates the nature of the
lawlessness / *anomia* of the devil and those influenced by him. The
prefix "*a*" before "*nomia*" indicates "not," the law (*nomos*). Without the
law, people are ignorant of what God's will is. One way to view the law
that God gave to Moses is to realize that God was trying to educate and
protect his children; to train them up in the way they should go (Prov.
22:6); to illustrate that it is not God's will that any should perish (2 Pet.
3:9). For example, by following the instructions in the laws God gave to
Moses, the people could avoid the types of diseases and disasters that
God brought on the Egyptians at the time of the Exodus (Exod. 15:26).

By not following God's law, the people would bring down on
themselves the consequences of doing what is not right, of making
choices that go against God's will. This lawless behavior is most often
translated in English as "iniquities," "wickedness," or sometimes
"transgressions" or "sins" from the Greek New Testament and from the
Greek version of the Old Testament (the Septuagint). In a few cases a
stronger word is used in the English translation where the context
indicates extreme consequences for going against God's will

> For I know that after my death you are sure to become utterly
> corrupt [*anomia*] and to turn from the way I have commanded
> you. In days to come, disaster will fall on you because you will
> do evil in the sight of the Lord and arouse his anger by what
> your hands have made (Deut. 31:29).

> Then [the lepers outside the city gate] said to each other, "What
> we're doing is not right. This is a day of good news and we are
> keeping it to ourselves. If we wait until daylight, punishment

[*anomia*] will overtake us. Let's go at once and report this to the royal palace (2 Kings 7:9).

The Lord said to me: "Son of man, will you judge Oholah and Oholibah? Then confront them with their detestable [*anomia*] practices" (Ezek. 23:36).

When God cleanses his people from their sins he promises to reverse the consequences for lawlessness: "Thus says the Lord God: On the day that I cleanse you from all your iniquities [*anomia*], I will cause the cities to be inhabited, and the waste places shall be rebuilt" (Ezek. 36:33 ESV). Jesus came to take away sins and to reverse the consequences of opposition to God's will that we saw described as "*tohu*" in an earlier chapter.

The Theme of "Righteousness" in 2:28–3:10

The opposite of lawlessness and sin is "righteousness." A brief intertextual comparison gives background for appreciating the significance of this term. Isaiah described the Messiah's Kingdom of Righteousness which is in stark contrast to the consequences God's people had experienced for purposely following evil schemes and engaging in the type of lewd behavior God condemned in Oholah and Oholibah (Ezek. 23:36).

> … The fortress will be abandoned, the noisy city deserted;
> citadel and watchtower will become a wasteland …
> Till the Spirit is poured on us from on high,
>   and the desert becomes a fertile field,
>   and the fertile field seems like a forest.
> The Lord's justice will dwell in the desert,
>   his righteousness live in the fertile field.
> The fruit of that righteousness will be peace;
>   its effect will be quietness and confidence forever (Isa. 32:14-17).

The theme of "righteousness" is concentrated in 1 John 2:28–3:10 with emphasis on the reality that God's children are righteous like he is. The opposite is also shown to be true in this section—the devil's children are like him in failing to do what is right (3:10). This contrast emphasizes the clash of two types of people and their spiritual leaders. Doing works righteousness in 2:28–3:10 is the antithesis of the works of the devil that the Son of God appeared to do away with and destroy.

The Theme of "Love"

One work of righteousness in particular is emphasized in First John. The chart on the key terms found 1 John 3:8-10 shows that the theme of "love" is concentrated in two places in 1 John: in 3:11-18, which we found earlier to be anticipatory of the second section, and in 4:7-21, where the theme of love is concentrated more fully. The fact that the theme of "love" visually dominates the chart once the defeat of the devil is announced in 2:28–3:10, leads to the same conclusion we reached in Chart 1, "Cosmic Battle Themes in First John," namely that love has an important role to play in the cosmic battle, perhaps as a means of defeating the devil by nullifying his works of hatred and murder.

SUMMARY OF LITERARY FINDINGS RELATED TO THE COSMIC BATTLE
   AND JESUS' NEW BEGINNING

What has this detailed exploration of the literary textures of First John contributed to our understanding of the cosmic battle in which Jesus' appearing constituted a new beginning? What "fabrics of discourse" do we need to stitch together to see the bigger picture? The rhetorical and literary means by which the author of First John has organized his arguments each point to an important aspect of the author's ideological perspective that a cosmic battle is raging, that the Son of God came in person to make a new beginning in this battle, and that the battle involves God's people ("children") in making choices that work toward nullifying or destroying the works of the devil.

In summary we will review the fabric of this discourse by briefly re-stating what we have learned from each of the rhetorical-literary "quilt squares" we have constructed in this chapter in relation to (a) Jesus as the new beginning in the cosmic battle and (b) the role of God's children in joining the Son of God to nullify the works of the devil.

Antithetical Language

Through the stark contrasts in First John between who is of God and who is not, we see that Jesus initiated a new beginning in the cosmic battle that makes life possible for those who believe in him and keep his commands. Midway through the list of antithetical statements, the author shows how to distinguish between the "children of God" and the "children of the devil" based on their works: righteousness vs. lawlessness; love vs. hate. The author of First John urges his audience to choose not to associate with those teaching and practicing lawlessness in order to avoid ending up like them.

Chiastic Structure

The chiastic center in 1 John 3:4-15 focuses attention on the cosmic battle between the Son of God and the devil. The insight we find here is the intention of the Son of God to destroy the works of the devil. The work of Jesus made a new beginning possible for God's people—a fresh start at turning away from the sin and lawlessness that had plagued them throughout their history. Other parallels in the chiastic chart show that those who have the Son have life, they have fellowship with him, and they walk in the light. Each of these realities cancels out a corresponding work of the devil that leads to death.

Chain-link Interlock Rhetorical Transition

The use of this rhetorical transitional technique in both the Gospel and First Epistle of John focuses attention once again on the cosmic battle that Jesus' appearing served to re-set with new possibilities and even new rules of engagement. Because Jesus was laying down his life voluntarily he could say in the interlocking section of the Gospel of John that the prince of this world was being driven out. It was the beginning of an era in which the ruler of this world would not have as much control over humanity. The First Epistle of John confirms this by highlighting the purpose of Jesus' appearing: to destroy the works of the devil (1 John 3:8b). In the Epistle, the interlocking sections lead to a major theme about God's love and the responsibility of God's children to love one another. The full treatment of "love" includes the love of God for the whole world (1 John 4:14), which makes the "whole world" also the object of the believers' love. This love for the world is in stark contrast to the hatred and death the current ruler of this world has in mind for his subjects.

Repetitive and Progressive Texture Charts

In the first chart showing clusters of themes, we see that one of the characteristics of the opposition in the cosmic battle is that it attempts to control the "whole world" (1 John 5:19)—the world that Jesus loves, that he appeared in order to rescue and give a chance at life (1 John 4:9). This chart shows an increase in the number of references to participants on God's side in the central section, 2:28–3:10. This corresponds with the first mention of the devil and it is also where the children of God are first mentioned, joining in the cosmic battle through their acts of righteousness and love. In fact, after the "entrance" of the devil in 1 John 3:8, there are more references to what believers are doing than to what God and the Son are doing. This is in the major section about "love," indicating the important role of believers in demonstrating love as a means of overcoming evil in the cosmic battle.

In the second chart, the theme of "love" visually dominates the chart once the defeat of the devil is announced in the central section, 2:28–3:10. This leads to the same conclusion we reached with Chart 1, that the love shown by God's children has an important role to play in the cosmic battle. In the inter-textual word studies that accompanied the key terms of this chart we saw that in the new beginning made possible by Jesus, God's children are becoming more aware of what they have known "from the beginning." The light Jesus brings makes it clear that believers must follow Jesus' command, that they have known about "from the beginning," to love one another. In addition, they can now clearly see that the devil has been sinning and opposing God "from the beginning." The theme of "appearing" announces the primary problem that Jesus' new beginning would solve. He came to "destroy the works of the devil" (1 John 3:8b) that are causing chaos and opposition to God's good will. This opposition is called "sin" (*hamartia*) and "lawlessness" (*anomia*).

Contributions to the Fabric of Discourse about God's Will to Overturn Chaos

Jesus' appearance on earth was a new beginning in which he came to take away sins and to make it possible for people (and societies) to experience the reverse of the consequences of opposition to God's will that we saw described as "*tohu*" in the Old Testament. Instead of the disastrous consequences of detestable and corrupt practices, God's people can thrive in righteousness and confidence. In contrast to the hatred and murder typical of the devil and his children, love is the characteristic of God and his children.

Winter's article in the *Perspectives Reader*, "The Kingdom Strikes Back," describes the history of the battle against the evil intelligence that is distorting our world.

> The Bible shows the gradual but irresistible power of God reconquering and redeeming His fallen creation; giving His own Son at the center of the 4000 year period beginning with 2000 BC. ..."The Son of God appeared for this purpose, that He might destroy the works of the devil" (1 John 3:8).[406]

---

[406] Ralph D. Winter, "The Kingdom Strikes Back," in *Perspectives on the World Christian Movement: Reader*, 3rd ed., ed. Ralph D. Winter and Stephen C. Hawthorne (Pasadena, CA: William Carey Library, 1999), 196.

In short, these studies have led to the conclusion that the devil is an evil being who has been sinning since the beginning of his rulership over the earth. The evil one's inherently lawless nature demonstrates opposition to God's will. While the devil's works can be summarized as bringing death—both physical (disease and deformity, social chaos, mental chaos) and spiritual (unbelief, hatred)—the Son of God appeared, in a new beginning, to give life (1 John 4:9). The appearing of the Son of God results in works and characteristics in the children of God that are the opposite of those associated with the sin of the devil, thus nullifying or destroying them.

We have now made a case in our exegetical / socio-rhetorical investigations for three of four foundational premises:

1. God is the Lord of history, but we are locked in a cosmic struggle.

2. God reveals himself, but an intelligent evil power distorts both general and special revelation and all of God's handiwork. God did not create or intend evil, but he created spirit and human beings with free will who chose to use their free will to rebel against him.

3. On the basis of Jesus' life, death, and resurrection, God defeats evil and redeems and restores humanity and creation.

In the next chapter we will explore the fourth premise:

4. God desires humans to work with him as agents in history for his purposes in defeating evil. Practical and loving works are a major mechanism through which individual members of the body of Christ participate in the conquest of evil.

Chapter Nine

God's Children Join the Cosmic Battle

Images of God's Children

When Israel was a child, I loved him,
and out of Egypt I called my son.
But the more they were called,
the more they went away from me.
(Hosea 11:1)

He came to his own and his own people did not receive him. But to all
who did receive him, who believed in his name, he gave the right to
become children of God.
(John 1:11, 12 ESV)

My children, I will be with you only a little longer. ... A new command I
give you: Love one another. As I have loved you, so you must love one
another. By this everyone will know that you are my disciples, if you
love one another.
(John 13:33-35)

I write to you, young men,
because you are strong,
and the word of God lives in you,
and you have overcome the evil one.
(1 John 2:14b)

Dear children, let us not love with words or speech but with actions and
in truth.
(1 John 3:18)

General Overview

The Son of God came in person to make a new beginning in the cosmic battle that has been raging in this world since before the beginning, and he wants God's children to join him in this battle. In the previous chapter we saw through analysis of the "signs" in the Gospel of John, that Jesus overturned the works of the devil by meeting social needs, providing the basic necessities of food and drink, showing God's will for good health and life, and reflecting God's concern for true righteousness and belief in the truth.

The following chart summarizes the way Jesus' works and words demonstrated God's will for the world:

God's Will Revealed *by*	*Jesus' "Work" or Statement*
Cares about social needs	Turning water into wine (John 2:1-11)
Provides food and drink	Turning water into wine (John 2:1-11) Feeding the 5000 (John 6:1-15)
Desires health & life	Healing official's dying son (John 4:43-54) Healing invalid at pool who had been crippled for 38 years (John 5:1-15) Healing man born blind (John 9:1-41) Raising Lazarus from the dead (John 11:1-43)
Concerned for true righteousness and belief	Healing on the Sabbath; telling the man to stop sinning (John 5:1-15) Conversation about spiritual blindness (John 9:1-14) "The work of God is to believe in the one he has sent" (John 6:29)

We see these same concerns in the Gospel of Luke when Jesus announced his purpose on earth by quoting from Isaiah 61:1, 2:

> The Spirit of the Lord is on me, because he has anointed me to proclaim good news to the poor. He has sent me to proclaim freedom for the prisoners and recovery of sight for the blind, to set the oppressed free, to proclaim the year of the Lord's favor (Luke 4:18, 19).

Not only did Jesus accomplish what he set out to do while he was on earth, he promised in John 14:12 that his followers would continue doing what he had been doing and even greater works. In the book of Acts, the works done by the apostles began to fulfill this promise.

Deeds of Jesus' Followers in the Book of Acts

Acts 3:1-10: Peter heals the crippled beggar

Acts 4:32-37: believers share their possessions so there are no needy people among them

Acts 5:12-16: the Apostles heal many sick and those tormented by evil spirits

Acts 6:1-6: seven men are chosen to care for the physical needs of the widows

Acts 8:4: the disciples are scattered and preach the word wherever they go

Acts 8:5-8: Philip does miraculous signs: evil spirits come out of many, cripples are healed

Acts 9:7-19: Ananias prays for Saul's eyesight to be restored

Acts 9:36: Dorcas "was always doing good and helping the poor"

Acts 9:37-42: Dorcas is raised from the dead

Acts 10 and throughout the rest of the book: followers of Jesus preach the good news in the wider Mediterranean area

God's character and love is made evident to the world through the works done in his name. As we saw in the previous chapter, the children of God join in the cosmic battle through their acts of love and righteousness. In fact, after the "entrance" of the devil in 1 John 3:8, there are more references in First John to what believers are doing in the cosmic battle than to what God and the Son are doing. In Matthew's Gospel Jesus gave specific examples of how God's children can display God's will through acts of love:

> Come, you who are blessed by my Father; ... for I was hungry and you gave me something to eat, I was thirsty and you gave me something to drink, I was a stranger and you invited me in, I needed clothes and you clothed me, I was sick and you looked after me, I was in prison and you came to visit me" (Matt. 25:34-36).

Since the appearing of Jesus, his Spirit empowers God's people to make choices like these that work toward nullifying or destroying the works of the devil. In contrast to the hatred characteristic of the devil and his children, Jesus gave his followers the ultimate example of love by laying down his life for us.

This is how we know what love is: Jesus Christ laid down his life for us. And we ought to lay down our lives for our brothers and sisters. If anyone has material possessions and sees a brother or sister in need but has no pity on them, how can the love of God be in that person? Dear children, let us not love with words or speech but with actions and in truth (1 John 3:16-18).

The importance of believers' works being aligned with Jesus' example and God's truth is also seen in 2 John 8 in which the elder reminds the community to watch out for deceivers, the enemies of the truth, "that you do not lose what you have worked for," implying that "truth" is the goal of the works of believers. That this goal is worked toward collectively is shown in 3 John 8: "we ought ... to show hospitality to such people [who are going out for the sake of the Name] so that we may work together for the truth." The important conclusions to note about the works done by Jesus and his followers are 1) that these works are done through God and his Spirit, and 2) that these are always directed toward demonstrating God's true and good will, or toward correcting, or overcoming, what is not true to God's will (such as sickness or destructive behavior).

In summary: God's love was made evident through Jesus' works that meet human needs. In contrast, the devil's hatred results in human neediness. The work of God's children, then, is to align themselves with God's character and Jesus' works, and demonstrate the opposite of the devil's works. In other words, the work of God's children is to obey Jesus' command to "love one another" as he loved them, and we saw in the previous chapter that Jesus' love includes the whole world (John 3:16; 1 John 4:9).

In the Johannine worldview, the following syllogism is in effect until Jesus returns to earth to conclude the cosmic battle:

> Major premise: God's work on earth is to defeat the devil's work, which is opposing God's will, or law, for the earth.
>
> Minor premise: Jesus' followers are meant to join him in doing God's works.
>
> Conclusion: Therefore, Jesus' followers are meant to participate in defeating or destroying the works of the devil in order to demonstrate God's will on earth.

Pastor-theologian Gregory Boyd summarizes the responsibility of God's children in this war-torn world this way:

> Followers of Jesus are called and empowered to individually and corporately manifest the beautiful reign of God, just as Jesus did, and to therefore live as social-spiritual revolutionaries, just as Jesus did. Our lifestyle is to manifest God's reign and revolt against greed and poverty, social oppression, sexism, racism, classism, nationalism, violence, and every other aspect of society that conflicts with God's loving reign. And in living this way, we are to understand that we are engaging in spiritual warfare.[407]

Believers need to ready for serious opposition in the spiritual battle for the rulership of this world. Jesus came and "made peace" by his death on the cross. Believers should expect no less opposition than he faced when they join him in making (waging) peace in a broken, war-torn world. "Blessed are the peacemakers, for they will be called children of God" (Matthew 5:9).

Particular Details: God's Children Participate in Destroying the Works of the Devil

Destroying the works of the devil is what the Son of God appeared on earth to do, and he passed this responsibility on to the children of God. In the detailed explorations of this chapter we will see that love is the motivating factor in the works of Jesus and he expected love to be the motivation for God's children as well. When God's children do works that are aligned with Jesus' works, their works and motivations are opposite to the devil's works, thereby cancelling and nullifying them, overcoming evil with good, so that *tohu* becomes *tob* / good. We will see that God's character is revealed through the good works of God's children, including the fact that chaos, hatred, and desolation are not God's will. The socio-rhetorical and exegetical approaches in this chapter contribute additional "quilt squares" to the fabric of discourse we are constructing to show the origin (and nature) of international development from the perspective of the Kingdom of God.

---

[407] Gregory Boyd, "A Different Kind of Kingdom," in *Servant God: The Cosmic Conflict Over God's Trustworthiness*, ed. Dorothee Cole (Loma Linda, CA: Loma Linda University Press, 2013), 370.

*Expectation that God's Children Participate in Nullifying
the Works of the Devil*

Earlier we looked at a syllogism that concludes that the children of
God participate along with the Son of God in defeating the works of the
devil until Jesus returns to earth to usher in his new Kingdom of
Righteousness:

> Major premise: God's work on earth is to defeat the devil's
> work, which is opposing God's will, or law, for the earth.
>
> Minor premise: Jesus' followers are meant to join him in doing
> God's works.
>
> Conclusion: Therefore, Jesus' followers are meant to participate
> in defeating or destroying the works of the devil in order to
> demonstrate God's will on earth.

SCRIBAL INTER-TEXTURE EXAMPLES OF GOD'S CHILDREN
OVERCOMING THE EVIL ONE

We can see the expectation in extra-biblical as well as in biblical
literature, that God's children need to participate in overcoming the
opposition to God's will. The influential Early Church father, Ignatius,
wrote that when believers "meet together frequently, the powers of
Satan are overthrown and his destructiveness is nullified by the
unanimity of your faith" (*Ignatius to the Ephesians* 13.1).[408] The Greek
word Ignatius used for "nullified" is the same rare word used in 1 John
3:8: the Son of God came to *lusē* / destroy / nullify the works of the
devil. Ignatius' letter shows that early believers considered that
collectively they had the ability to do what 1 John 3:8 says the Son of
God came to do: to destroy (overthrow) the works (powers) of the devil
(Satan). This passage in Ignatius might be thought of as a paraphrase of
1 John 3:8, applied to the followers of Jesus as they continue his work.
Ignatius contributes a further insight to this discourse in his letter to the
Trallians, where he explains that in his personal life he needs gentleness
or meekness "by which the ruler of this age is destroyed" [again, a form
of the rare verb, *lusē* / destroy] (*Ignatius to the Trallians* 4.2).[409] Once
again we see the expectation that the behavior of God's children can
have a destructive and nullifying effect on the intentions and works of
the devil, the ruler of this world.

---

[408] Michael W. Holmes, *The Apostolic Fathers in English*, 3rd ed. (Grand
Rapids: Baker Academic, 2006), 100.

[409] Holmes, *Apostolic Fathers*, 109.

The author of First John writes to the "young men" in 1 John 2:13, 14 that they are strong and have victory over the evil one. This statement would almost inevitably have reminded anyone living in Ephesus at the time the Johannine writings were circulating, of the statue of the strong young Heracles in that city, put up over the spot where a "plague demon" was supposed to have been killed.[410] In the myths of Heracles, he was considered to have great strength, he demonstrated victory over evil entities, and he was viewed as a defender against disease and death. For Jewish Christian believers in Ephesus, the verbal picture of strong young men overcoming the evil one would likely have brought to mind Heracles' examples of defeating evil. Believers in Ephesus might also have been familiar with a relevant passage from the *Testament of Naphtali* 8:2-4:

> If ye work that which is good, my children, ...
> The devil shall flee from you,
> And the wild beasts shall fear you,
> And the Lord shall love you,
> And the angels shall cleave to you.

This passage, in turn, sounds similar to the account in Mark 1:13 of Jesus being among the wild animals in the desert without harm, while angels attended to his needs (Mark 1:13). Shortly after this experience, according to Mark's account, Jesus began demonstrating his authority over demons (Mark 1:23ff) and healing many who were sick with various diseases caused by demons (Mark 1:34). In this context Mark introduces the account of Jesus and Beelzebul, and the necessity to bind the strong man (Mark 3:20-27). Luke's version adds that a stronger one, meaning Jesus, overcomes the strong man, referring to Satan. This is another scribal inter-textual echo that would likely have been noticed by the Johannine community when they heard that the strong young men have overcome the evil one. They would have recognized the role of Jesus, the unique Son of God, as the one who overcomes Satan, the evil one, and defeats him (1 John 3:8). But they would also realize that the strong young men, and other children of God, have a role in working with the unique and strong Son of God to overcome and destroy the works of the devil.

In fact, the whole of God's creation is waiting "in eager expectation for the sons of God to be revealed. ... We know that the whole creation

---

[410] J. Edgar Bruns, "A Note on John 16:33 and 1 John 2:13, 14," *Journal of Biblical Literature* 86 (1967): 453. Also see F. C. Conybeare, trans., "Apollonius of Tyana by Flavius Philostratus," accessed May 25, 2008, http://www.chrestos.com/.

has been groaning as in the pains of childbirth right up to the present time (Rom. 8:20, 22)." Under a burden of evil that God did not intend for it, creation groans as it waits for the body of Christ to fulfill its purpose to work with God to defeat evil and its resulting distortions. David Neff once commented in *Christianity Today*, "as Christians we cannot be honest about reality without seeing the world as a struggle between good and evil."[411] The free will of humankind aligning itself with God's will is a means of overcoming the evil results of choices made by both human and spirit free beings. Gregory Boyd states in his book, *God at War*, "Humans are made in the image of God and placed on earth so that they might gradually vanquish this chaos."[412]

WAR AGAINST AN INTELLIGENT ENEMY

God's children are in a war against an intelligent enemy. It would be appropriate to view the mandate of Genesis 1:28 ("fill the earth and subdue it. Rule over … every living creature") as being, from the start, part of an inclusive wartime mandate since evil had already been at work on this planet before humans were created and told to "subdue it" (Gen. 1:28). Humans were created to join a war that was already taking place. Boyd summarizes this perspective: "We are co-rulers with God over the earth and co-warriors with God against the forces of chaos."[413]

This interpretation of Genesis 1, which we explored in earlier chapters, implies that God's plan to strike back at the enemy is to overcome the free choices of evil agents with the free choices of good agents. Perhaps in God's free will universe he needs more creatures, clothed in his righteousness, to choose his way, to ask him to take action to annihilate evil, to make themselves available to participate in freely chosen acts of love and self-sacrifice that will nullify specific examples of evil. Is God waiting for the time when he has enough of the free choices of humans and spirit beings on his side to win the battle at the end of the age, as described in the last book of the Bible? As Boyd says, "the church as the body of Christ has been called to be a decisive means by which this final overthrow is to be carried out."[414]

AN OBSTACLE TO OPPOSING EVIL

Unfortunately a major obstacle preventing God's children from opposing evil is that believers often mistakenly attribute evidences of

---

[411] David Neff, "Naming the Horror," *Christianity Today* (April, 2005): 76.

[412] Boyd, *God at War*, 107.

[413] Boyd, *God at War*, 106.

[414] Boyd, *God at War*, 19.

evil to God's will. Ralph Winter stated in an email to a friend, "If believers have all kinds of misunderstandings that prevent them from 'destroying the works of the devil' I want desperately to help remove those misunderstandings."[415] A major source of these misunderstandings comes from the early theologian, Augustine of Hippo (around 400 CE), whose writings continue to influence the thinking of evangelical believers today. He assumed God's omnipotence meant God was in direct control of everything and had his purposes in permitting evil. Greg Boyd notes,

> It is curious that the evil one to whom the Bible directly or indirectly attributes all evil has played a rather insignificant role in the theodicy of the church after Augustine. This, I contend, is directly connected to the fact that the church generally accepted the blueprint worldview that Augustine espoused.[416]

In *City of God*, Augustine argued that God permits evil so we will desire the future "blessed life."

> Even baptized infants, who are certainly unsurpassed in innocence, are sometimes so tormented, that God, who permits it, teaches us hereby to bewail the calamities of this life, and to desire the felicity of the life to come (*City of God* 22.22).

The concept of fighting back against atrocities, such as the torment experienced by innocent babies, is missing in Augustine's theology. A logical consequence of his "blueprint" worldview, as Boyd calls it, is passivity. If God has pre-ordained all evil for some mysterious purpose, why pray, why act? Why not sadly and passively wait until one is able to enter the happier life to come? Boyd reflects on how contrary this thinking is to the example Jesus set for his followers.

> In contrast with any view that would suggest that disease and demonization somehow serve a divine purpose, Jesus never treated such phenomenon as anything other than the work of the enemy. He consistently treated diseased and demonized people as casualties of war. Furthermore, rather than accepting their circumstances as mysteriously fitting into God's sovereign plan,

---

[415] Ralph D. Winter, "Disease / Evil Explanations" (email to snoke@pitt.edu, July 8, 2004).

[416] Boyd, *Satan*, 36.

Jesus revolted against them as something that God did not will and something that ought to be vanquished by God's power.[417]

The authors of the New Testament, and the Early Church fathers prior to Augustine, expected evil and were prepared to fight it. They had no problem with the concept that a good God had allowed freedom of choice and was bound by his own decision to fight a real war against evil that Christ's followers must join.[418]

THE KINGDOM STRIKES BACK

The biblical record, which we have been exploring, sets the direction for believers to follow in the fight against evil. Jesus passed his mission on to his followers, teaching them to pray that God's will would be done "on earth as it is in heaven" (Matt. 6:10) and telling them the gates of hell would not prevail against the Church's proactive works to counteract evil (Matt. 16:18). Jesus did what he saw the Father doing (John 5:19) and he told his followers they would do even greater things than he had been doing (John 14:12).

God intends for his Kingdom to continue advancing in Jesus' absence on earth. Through his Spirit, God now works through the body of Christ to expand Jesus' ministry of pushing back the powers of darkness. In the brief theologies of the body of Christ in Romans 12 and 1 Corinthians 12, each shows that when Christ's body, the Church, is functioning as it should, it demonstrates the character and will of God and what he is concerned about: his righteousness, justice, mercy, and his power over evil. Since the Son of God appeared to destroy the devil's work (1 John 3:8), this is also the mission of Christ's body. In the article, "The Kingdom Strikes Back," Ralph Winter describes five epochs of church history in which, almost in spite of the negative behavior of many representatives of the Church, the Kingdom has gradually advanced around the world.[419] This advance is occurring even in the context of two conflicting kingdoms existing side by side, as in Jesus' parable of the weeds and the good seed growing side by side (Matt. 13:24-30). Real changes occur when some of God's people act on God's behalf.

---

[417] Boyd, *Satan*, 36.
[418] Boyd, *Satan*, 24, 49.
[419] Winter, "Kingdom," 195.

MOSES AS AN EXAMPLE OF A CHANGE AGENT

Moses is an example of one who acted faithfully on God's behalf—a free agent who chose to work with God to accomplish God's purposes, even in the face of severe difficulty. "When he can no longer bear the burden of his quarrelsome people, ... Moses mocks himself as a 'nursing father,'"[420] says Aaron Wildovsky in a book that examines Moses' leadership style. God speaks of Moses as his faithful servant (*therapon*) in all God's house (Num. 11:7; Heb. 3:5).

The term *therapon,* that occurs only once in the New Testament and only a few times in the Greek version of the Old Testament, the Septuagint, refers to people who work on behalf of someone else to bring about change. In the Greek Old Testament, in Genesis 24:43, 44, God refers to Isaac as his servant (*therapon*), while instructing Abraham's servant (using a different Greek term) in how to find a wife for Isaac. Isaac was in a line of change agents working on God's behalf and is routinely included in the phrase identifying the God of the Hebrew people as "the God of Abraham, Isaac, and Jacob" (Exod. 3:6; Acts 3:13, etc.). In Genesis 50:15-20, Joseph's brothers call themselves the servants / *therapon* of the God of Jacob. They were instruments of major change even though their motives were wrong. Joseph tells them, "you meant evil against me, but God meant it for good (Gen. 50:20, ESV). Pharaoh also had servants / *theraponton* (Exod. 5:21 ESV) working on his behalf who had the power and authority to make changes. When they required the people of Israel to produce more bricks while also gathering their own straw, the people railed against Moses, foreshadowing the way they would treat him throughout their journey in the wilderness. Another group of Pharaoh's servants (*therapon*) imitated some of the miracles God told Moses and Aaron to perform as signs that God wanted Pharaoh to let God's people go. These servants / *therapon* appear to be magicians, which is related to the concept of changing things (such as water into blood; a staff into a snake and back again into a staff). Moses was greater than the servants / *therapon* of Pharaoh. God used Moses, God's *therapon,* to make more changes than what the magicians or servants / *therapon* of Pharaoh were able to do.

It is likely that the miracles Moses announced in advance that God was planning to do, were the reason the children of Israel were willing to let Moses be their leader. They saw the mighty things the Lord did to the Egyptians through Moses and as a result put their trust in the Lord and in Moses, God's servant / *therapon* (Exod. 14:31). A major change

---

[420] Wildavsky, *Nursing Father*, 216.

in the identity of the children of Israel occurred because of the willingness of Moses to be God's servant / *therapon*, God's change agent. During their wanderings in the desert, when the children of Israel got tired of eating only manna and wanted meat to eat, Moses asked God why he had afflicted him, God's servant / *theraponta*, with these complaining people (Num. 11:13). After a delay, God provided the meat, but Moses was the spokesperson to announce this change. Finally, God punished Miriam and Aaron for speaking against Moses, God's servant / *therapon*, who God described as, "faithful in all my house" (Num. 12:7).

The following characteristics of Moses, the *therapon* / servant can apply to God's children working with God throughout history:

- He was an agent, not just a slave who is told what to do (Num. 11:11).
- He was a nurturing leader, a "nursing father" (Num. 11:12).
- He was burdened for the people beyond what he could bear (Num. 11:18).
- He had to endure jealousy and people speaking against him (Num. 12).
- He was meek (Num. 12:3).
- He was faithful (Num. 12:7).
- He spoke with God face to face (Num. 12:8).

God needs servants who can make a difference and change the way things are in this world that "lies in the power of the evil one" (1 John 5:19). Lesslie Newbigin explained, "the one who wishes to love and serve the Lord will want to be where he is. And where he is, is on that frontier which runs between the kingdom of God and the usurped power of the evil one"[421] The problems Moses had with the people he was serving, to the point he wished he could die rather than face his own ruin (Num. 11:15), show how necessary it is to have love as the motivation behind fighting the works of the devil in order not to "become weary in doing good" (Gal. 6:9).

Love as the Means of Nullifying the Devil's Works

Moses' faithfulness was an advance illustration of Jesus' declaration to his disciples, "greater love has no one than this: to lay down one's life for one's friends" (John 15:13). Like Moses, Jesus suffered in trying to serve his people, leaving the people of God "an example, that you

---

[421] Lesslie Newbigin, *The Gospel in a Pluralist Society* (Grand Rapids: Eerdmans, 1989), 127.

should follow in his steps" (1 Pet. 2:21). In the context of his example of washing the disciples feet, Jesus gave them a new command, "As I have loved you, so you must love one another" (John 13:15, 34).

Love is a major theme of the Gospel and First Epistle of John. Each of these books has nearly twice as many occurrences of the noun and verb forms of the Greek word for "love" (*agape / agapao*) as in the New Testament book with the next highest number of occurrences of the term (Ephesians). Although there is an emphasis on love in the Gospel and First Epistle of John, the specific ways of demonstrating love for others is found in only a few verses. This is true in the rest of the New Testament as well. Even in the famous "Love Chapter" (1 Corinthians 13), love is either not defined, or it refers to attitudes (patient, kind, not boastful, etc.) rather than to specific actions. In those passages that do state specific ways to demonstrate love, the theme they have in common is to imitate Jesus' example in one of two ways: acts of humble service and / or in laying down one's life for others, as seen in these representative examples:

> Now that I, your Lord and Teacher, have washed your feet, you also should wash one another's feet. I have set you an example that you should do as I have done for you. Very truly I tell you, no servant (*doulos*) is greater than his master, nor is a messenger greater than the one who sent him. Now that you know these things, you will be blessed if you do them. ... A new command I give you: Love one another. *As I have loved you, so you must love one another* (John 13:14-17, 34).

> Greater love has no one than this: to *lay down one's life for one's friends* (John 15:13).

> From [Christ] the whole body, joined and held together by every supporting ligament, grows and builds itself up in love, *as each part does its work* (Eph. 4:15, 16).

> Walk in the way of love, *just as Christ loved us and gave himself up for us* as a fragrant offering and sacrifice to God (Eph. 5:2).

> God is not unjust; he will not forget *your work and the love you have shown him as you have* helped *his people and continue to help them* (Heb. 6:10).

> And let us consider how to stir up one another to *love and good works* (Heb. 10:24).

This is how we know what love is: *Jesus Christ laid down his life for us. And we ought to lay down our lives for our brothers and sisters.* If anyone has material possessions and sees a brother or sister in need but has no pity on them, how can the love of God be in that person? Dear children, *let us not love with words or speech but with actions and in truth* (1 John 3:16-18).

As we noticed in the previous chapter, in a chart of the occurrences of major themes in First John, the theme of "love" visually dominates the chart once the defeat of the devil is announced in section 2:28–3:10. This reinforces the proposal that "love" may be a means of defeating the devil or a result of the defeat of the devil, or both. The fact that demonstrating love is one of the key things God and the Son can be seen doing in First John also seems to indicate that love has a role to play in the cosmic battle. "The weapons we fight with are not the weapons of the world. On the contrary, they have divine power to demolish strongholds" (2 Cor. 10:4). Gregory Boyd states succinctly, "there's nothing that should ever compete with love as our highest priority."[422]

Examples of the Works of God's Children

Loving service is the way in which God's children serve as change agents in the cosmic battle. As mentioned earlier, the work of God's children is to align themselves with God's character and Jesus' works, and to demonstrate the opposite of the devil's hatred that results in human neediness. In other words, the work of God's children is to obey Jesus' command to "love one another" as he loved them. Practical demonstrations of love follow Jesus' example of meeting physical and social needs. If the devil's work is to cause physical and social chaos, sickness, crippling, blindness, disease, and death, then God's children have their work laid out for them to reverse these works of the devil in social and physical spheres.

What is the responsibility, then, of the body of Christ to those in harm's way? In a 2008 address to a group of educators and NGO workers, Paul Pierson said, "we are called to call people to become followers of Jesus as authentic disciples of Jesus in their culture and to show something to the world of what the Kingdom of God means, and what are its values." Pierson asked, "What does God want human life to look like?" and answered with a good description of *shalom*, which is

---

[422] Boyd, "Living in, and Looking Like, Christ," 410.

also a good description of the goals of international development: grace, health, education, safety, well-being for all people. Pierson then asked, "What passion has God given you? If he gives you a passion he'll give you the gifts to go with it."[423] The body of Christ contains people with the gifts to "do" or "make" *shalom* in many different areas: justice, peace-keeping, skill-building for economic independence, health, fighting and eradicating disease, etc.

All of these peace-making activities can potentially demonstrate the values of God's Kingdom and bring *shalom* into the lives of troubled people and societies. A comparison of maps of high incidences of disease, child mortality, and violence with the areas of the world where the gospel has had the least influence[424] shows that these are the places where there is the most suffering, disease, war, and poverty. This is not a coincidence. An adversary is a work, instigating and taking advantage of unjust social structures, ignorance, greed, disease, and more. A medical missionary to India from 1939–1969 wrote in his journal, "This kingdom of disease, death, ignorance, prejudice, fear, malnutrition, and abject poverty is most surely a kingdom which ought to be overthrown by the Kingdom of our God."[425] "Overcome evil with good," the apostle Paul urged the body of Christ in Romans 12:20.

Colossians 3 gives examples of overcoming evil with good. At first one might think this chapter is encouraging people to forget about developing good societies on earth and just concentrate on the future reality of heaven: "Set your minds on things above, not on earthly things" (vs. 2); "when Christ, who is your life, appears, then you also will appear with him in glory" (vs. 4). But actually this chapter is full of principles for living well in a thriving, developed society. First it describes negative moral characteristics that belong to the "earthly nature": immorality, greed, anger, lying (vs. 5-10). When people relate to each other in these ways, they cannot trust each other, cannot work well together, cannot agree on goals and ways to accomplish those goals, etc. A society dominated by these characteristics is also a society that is likely to be underdeveloped in terms of meeting peoples' basic needs.

Next Colossians 3 gives a list of the positive characteristics of the kind of people needed in order for a society to thrive: "compassion,

---

[423] Quoted by Beth Snodderly in "Shalom: The Goal of the Kingdom and of International Development," in *The Goal of International Development: God's Will on Earth as It Is in Heaven* (Pasadena: WCIU Press, 2009), 161.

[424] Bryant Myers, *The New Context of World Missions* (Monrovia: MARC).

[425] Rees, *Vehicles*.

kindness, humility, gentleness, patience, forgiving one another, love"
(vs. 12-14). When people demonstrate Jesus' love in these ways, the
result is peace and thankfulness (vs. 15). These positive demonstrations
of love in the way God's people go about their daily lives counteract the
negative qualities instigated by the evil one. A society with a tipping
point of enough people demonstrating the principles of Colossians 3
through their businesses, their politics, through social entrepreneurship,
agriculture, community development, and health initiatives will be an
example to the world of overcoming evil with good, of international
development that turns physical and social chaos into *shalom*. A society
without a sufficient number of God's children demonstrating theses
positive qualities, motivated by God's love, will remain underdeveloped, chaotic, and even dangerous.

Displaying God's Character and Rescuing God's Reputation

All societies have to answer the question, How shall we bring order
out of chaos? People trying to be submitted to God in any culture need
to find their own particular implications for how to live in right
relationship with God within that culture, including overcoming *tohu
wabohu* / chaos and evil, with good (Rom. 12:13). God's children
allowing God's Spirit to work through them to defeat the adversary in
this way can turn their world upside down, as was said of the disciples
in the book of Acts. Or perhaps we should say, they can help turn the
world right side up, restoring it in substantial ways to God's original
intentions and bringing him glory in the process.

As God's children intentionally demonstrate God's will through their
interactions with each other and in their societies, God's character will
be better known among the peoples of the earth and many will be
attracted to follow that kind of God. The enemy is defeated and some
part of his work is nullified when believers intentionally join God in
overcoming evil with good.

To take the sphere of health care as an example, believers may
demonstrate God's loving character through healing the sick in Jesus'
name. Or believers may restore *shalom* relationships by discovering the
origins of an infectious disease and working toward its elimination.
Inevitably there will be casualties in this war with the adversary.
Psychologists, nurses, and other health workers can bring *shalom* to the
dying, as they reflect God's lovingkindness and mercy, pointing them at
the end of their battle in this life to the perfect Kingdom. When Jesus'
followers demonstrate God's character in these ways, they serve as a
"display window" for what God's Kingdom will some day look like. As

broken relationships are healed, a measure of *shalom* is restored and God receives the credit and glory as people recognize God's character through the actions of God's children. As Richard Stearns, President of World Vision, said in his book, *The Hole in Our Gospel*, about believers joining God together to combat massive world problems,

> [It] would be on the lips of every citizen in the world and in the pages of every newspaper—in a good way. The world would see the whole gospel—the good news of the kingdom of God— not just spoken but demonstrated, by people whose faith is not devoid of deeds but defined by love and backed up with action. His kingdom come, His will be done, on earth, as it is in heaven. This was the whole gospel that Jesus proclaimed in Luke 4, and if we would embrace it, it would literally change everything.[426]

Shalom is the description of God's will for the earth and everything living in it. *Shalom* is the goal of international development because this is the goal of God's Kingdom: "Our Father in heaven ... your kingdom come, your will be done on earth as it is in heaven" (Matthew 6:10).

---

[426] Richard Stearns, *The Hole in Our Gospel* (Nashville: Thomas Nelson, 2009), 219.

Epilogue

And Finally—He Will Reign Forever and Ever

*"He will swallow up death forever. The Sovereign Lord will wipe away
the tears from all faces"* (Isa. 25:8).

"I will give them an undivided heart and put a new spirit in them"
(Ezek. 11:19).

Through demonstrations of God's will on earth, that there should be
no sickness, no death, no hatred, injustice, or pain, believers' actions
"vote" for God's Kingdom to come, and hold evil back from engulfing
the earth. But the final victory comes in an unexpected way. "The way
the Messiah won his victory is explained by the image of the Lamb,
while the significance of the image of the Lamb is now seen to lie in the
fact that his sacrificial death was a victory over evil."[427] "The one who is
strong enough to bear the weight of the cosmic conflict, to break the
seals, is the Lamb that was slaughtered."[428]

*Then I saw a Lamb, looking as if it had been slain, standing at the
center of the throne, encircled by the four living creatures and the
elders. ... And they sang a new song, saying:*
"You are worthy to take the scroll
and to open its seals,
because you were slain,
and with your blood you purchased for God
persons from every tribe and language and people and nation.
You have made them to be a kingdom and priests to serve our God,
and they will reign on the earth."

At the end of Scripture, in the Book of Revelation, we see the
fulfillment of God's purposes in history described in terms showing that

---

[427] Richard Bauckham, *The Theology of the Book of Revelation* (Cambridge:
Cambridge University Press, 1993), 74.

[428] Sigve Tonstad, "Revelation, Vision of Healing, Video Lecture 17," May 2013,
accessed August 17, 2013, http://www.youtube.com/watch?v=SfcggURm9YI.

the state of *tohu wabohu* has finally been fully reversed. Chaos is not God's will! As Boyd says,

> The malevolent forces that have corrupted nature from time immemorial will cease. Nature will no longer be "red in tooth and claw." ... The whole of creation will reflect the benevolent character of the gentle lamb, instead of the vicious carnage of a roaring lion.[429]

Isaiah foresaw that the *shalom* at the end of history included salvation from feared enemies in the realm of nature (which can also represent disease micro-organisms that were unknown at that time): "The wolf will live with the lamb, the leopard will lie down with the goat, ... and a little child will lead them. They will neither harm nor destroy on all my holy mountain, for the earth will be full of the knowledge of the Lord as the [good] waters (*mayim*) cover the [feared] sea (*yam*)" (Isa. 11:6, 9). God will dry even the smallest amounts of salty water, the tears spoken of in Revelation 21:4, representative of the troubles and chaos the ancient Hebrew people traditionally associated with the sea. There will be no more death, crying, or pain. Darkness and night will be permanently replaced with "good" light (Rev. 21: 3, 4; 22: 5). In this vision of the future, relationships are healed: with creation, with one's self (a hew heart), with other humans, and, most importantly, with God. The river of life in the heavenly city waters the tree of life on each side of the river, "and the leaves of the tree are for the healing of the nations" (Rev. 22:2).

Then I heard every creature in heaven and on earth and under the earth
and on the sea, and all that is in them, saying:
"To him who sits on the throne and to the Lamb
be praise and honor and glory and power,
for ever and ever!" (Rev. 5:6, 9-13).

"The kingdom of the world has become the kingdom of our Lord and of
his Messiah, and he will reign for ever and ever." (Rev. 11:15).

---

[429] Boyd, "Evolution as Cosmic Warfare," 145.

Bibliography

Alter, Robert. *The Art of Biblical Narrative*. New York: Basic Books, 1981.

Anderson, Bernhard. *From Creation to New Creation: Old Testament Perspectives*. Minneapolis: Fortress, 1994.

Armerding, Carl E. "An Old Testament View of Creation." *Crux* 12 (1974): 3-4.

Averbeck, Richard. "A Literary Day, Inter-Textual, and Contextual Reading of Genesis 1–2." In *Reading Genesis 1–2: An Evangelical Conversation*, edited by J. Daryl Charles, 7-34. Peabody, MA: Hendrickson, 2013.

Bailey, James L. and Lyle D. Vander Broek. *Literary Forms in the New Testament: A Handbook*. Louisville: Westminster John Knox Press, 1992.s

Barnhouse, Donald G. *The Invisible War*. Grand Rapids: Zondervan, 1965.

Barth, Karl. *Church Dogmatics Study Edition 13: The Doctrine of Creation*. 1945. Translated by G. W. Bromiley and et al. Vol. 3. London: T & T Clark, 2010.

Bauckham, Richard. *The Theology of the Book of Revelation*. Cambridge: Cambridge University Press, 1993.

Bauer, W. A. A. *Greek-English Lexicon of the New Testament and Other Early Christian Literature*. 2nd ed. Translated and edited by W. F. Arndt and F. W. Gingrich. Chicago: University of Chicago Press, 1979.

Binns, L. Elliott. *The Book of the Prophet Jeremiah*. London: Methuen & Co, 1919.

Blocher, Henri. *In the Beginning: The Opening Chapters of Genesis*. Downers Grove: InterVarsity, 1984.

Bloomquist, L. Gregory, Duane F. Watson, and David B. Gowler, eds. *Fabrics of Discourse: Essays in Honor of Vernon K. Robbins*. Harrisburg, PA: Bloomsbury T&T Clark, 2003.

Boyd, Gregory A. "A Different Kind of Kingdom." In *Servant God: The Cosmic Conflict over God's Trustworthiness*, edited by Dorothee Cole, 367-80. Loma Linda: Loma Linda University Press, 2013.

_____. "Evolution as Cosmic Warfare A Biblical Perspective on Satan and 'Natural' Evil." In *Creation Made Free: Open Theology Engaging Science,* edited by Thomas Jay Oord, 125-47. Eugene, OR: Pickwick Publications, 2009.

_____. *God at War: The Bible and Spirtiual Conflict*. Downer's Grove: InterVarsity Press, 1997.

_____. "Living in, and Looking Like, Christ." In *Servant God: The Cosmic Conflict over God's Trustworthiness*, edited by Dorothee Cole, 405-15. Loma Linda: Loma Linda University Press, 2013.

_____. *Satan and the Problem of Evil: Constructing a Trinitarian Warfare Theodicy*. Downer's Grove: InterVarsity Press, 2001.

_____. "A Wartorn Creation." In *Evangelical and Frontier Mission Perspectives On the Global Progress of the Gospel*, edited by Beth Snodderly and A. Scott Moreau, 286-93. Oxford, UK: Regnum, 2011.

Brown, Raymond E. *The Epistles of John (The Anchor Bible, Vol 30)*. Garden City, NY: Anchor Bible, 1982.

Bullinger, E.W. Figures of Speech Used in the Bible, Explained and Illustrated. Longdon: Eyre & Spottiswoode, 1898.

Cassuto, Umberto. *A Commentary On the Book of Genesis. Part One: From Adam to Noah*. Jerusalem: The Magnes Press, 1945.

Calvin, John. *Genesis*. 1554. Edited by Alister McGrath and J. I. Packer. Wheaton: Crossway Books, 2001.

Campolo, Tony. *How to Rescue the Earth Without Worshiping Nature: A Christian's Call to Save Creation*. Nashville: Thomas Nelson, 1992.

Charles, J. Daryl, ed. *Reading Genesis 1–2: An Evangelical Conversation*. Peabody, MA: Hendrickson, 2013.

Childs, Brevard S. "The Enemy from the North and the Chaos Tradition." *Journal of Biblical Literature* 78 (1959): 187-98.

Clifford, J. S.J. "The Hebrew Scriptures and the Theology of Creation." *Theological Studies* 46 (1985): 507-23.

Conybeare, F. C. "Apollonius of Tyana by Flavius Philostratus." Accessed May 25, 2008. http://www.chrestos.com/.

Cullmann, Oscar. *The Johannine Circle*. Philadelphia: Westminster Press, 1975

deSilva, David A. *An Introduction to the New Testament: Contexts, Methods and Ministry Formation*. Downers Grove: InterVarsity, 2004.

Elwell, Walter A., ed. *Baker's Evangelical Dictionary of Biblical Theology*. Grand Rapids: Baker, 1996.

Fee, Gordon, and Douglas Stuart. *How to Read the Bible for All Its Worth*. 2nd ed. Grand Rapids: Zondervan, 1993.

Feinberg, Charles L. *Jeremiah: A Commentary*. Grand Rapids: Zondervan Regency Reference Library, 1982.

Finegan, Jack. *In the Beginning: A Journey through Genesis*. New York: Harper & Brothers, 1962.

Fishbane, Michael. "Jeremiah IV 23-26 and Job III 3-13: A Recovered Use of the Creation Pattern." *Vetus Testamentum* 21 (1971): 151-63.

Fokkelman, J. P. *Narrative Art in Genesis: Specimens of Stylistic and Structural Analysis*. Amsterdam: Van Gorcum, Assen, 1975.

Fortey, Richard A. *Life: A Natural History of the First Four Billion Years of Life on Earth*. New York: Alfred A. Knopf, 1998.

Fox, Everett, trans. *In the Beginning: A New English Rendition of the Book of Genesis, Translated with Commentary and Notes*. New York: Schocken Books, 1983.

Fretheim, Terrence E. *Creation, Fall, and Flood: Studies in Genesis 1–11*. Minneapolis: Augsburg, 1969.

_____. *God and World in the Old Testament: a Relational Theology of Creation* (New York: Abingdon, 2005), 27.

Gibson, John C. *Daily Study Bible Series: Genesis*. Vol. 1. Louisville, KY: Westminster, John Knox Press, 1981.

Gitay, Yehoshua. "Prophecy and Persuasion: A Study of Isaiah 40–48." *Linguistica Biblica Bonn* (1981): 195-204.

Haas, C., M. DeJonge, and J. L. Swellengrebel. *A Translator's Handbook on the Letters of John*. London: United Bible Societies, 1972.

Harner, P. B. "Creation Faith in Deutero-Isaiah." *Vetus Testamentum* 17 (1967): 298-306.

Harris, R. Laird, Gleason L. Archer, and Bruce K. Waltke, eds. "Tohu." In *Theological Word Book of the Old Testament*, 964. Chicago: Moody, 1980.

Heidel, Alexander. *The Babylonian Genesis*. 2nd ed. Chicago: University of Chicago Press, 1951.

Hengel, Martin. *The Johannine Question*. London: SCM Press, 1989.

Hobbs, Herschel. *The Epistles of John*. Nashville: Thomas Nelson, 1983.

Holmes, Michael W. *The Apostolic Fathers in English*. 3d ed. Grand Rapids: Baker Academic, 2006.

Jaki, Stanley. *Science and Creation: From Eternal Cycles to an Oscillating Universe*. New York: Science History Publications, 1974.

_____. *Genesis 1 through the Ages*. London: Thomas More, 1998

Jeal, Roy R. "Blending Two Arts: Rhetorical Words, Rhetorical Pictures, and Social Formation in the Letter to Philemon." *Sino-Christian Studies* 5 (June 2008): 9.

Jenkins, Philip. *The New Faces of Christianity: Believing the Bible in the Global South*. New York: Oxford University Press, USA, 2008.

Kaiser, Walter C. "The Literary Form of Genesis 1–11." In *New Perspectives in the Old Testament*, edited by J. B. Payne, 48-65. Waco, TX: Word, 1970.

Kass, Leon R. *The Beginning of Wisdom: Reading Genesis*. New York: Free Press, 2003.

Kemp, Karl T. "Verse-by-verse Study of Genesis Chapters 1–3." Master's thesis, Sermon Notes, 2003.

Kennedy, George A. *New Testament Interpretation through Rhetorical Criticism*. Chapel Hill: University of North Carolina, 1984.

Kidner, Derek. *Genesis: An Introduction and Commentary*. Downers Grove: InterVarsity, 1967.

Kovacs, Judith. "Now Shall the Ruler of This World Be Driven Out': Death as Cosmic Battle in John 12: 20-36." *Journal of Biblical Literature* 114, no. 233 (1995): 227-47.

Kselman, J. S. "The Recovery of Poetic Fragments from the Pentateuchal Priestly Source." *Journal of Biblical Literature* 97 (1978): 161-73.

Kysar, Robert. *I, II, III John. Augsburg Commentary on the New Testament.* Minneapolis: Augsburg Publishing House, 1986.

Levenson, Jon. *Creation and the Persistence of Evil: The Jewish Drama of Divine Omnipotence.* San Francisco: Harper & Row, 1988.

Lewis, C.S. *The Problem of Pain.* New York: HarperCollins, 1940.

Lewis, Edwin. *The Creator and the Adversary.* New York: Abingdon-Cokesbury, 1948.

Lewis, Tayler. *The Six Days of Creation; or the Scriptural Cosmology, with the Ancient Idea of Time-World in Distinction from Worlds in Space.* Schenectady: G.V. Van Debogert, 1855.

Lieu, Judith M. *The Theology of the Johannine Epistles.* Cambridge: Cambridge University Press, 1991.

Ling, Trevor. *The Significance of Satan.* London: S.P.C.K., 1961.

Longenecker, Bruce W. *Rhetoric at the Boundaries.* Waco, TX: Baylor University Press, 2005.

Longman, Tremper III. "What Genesis 1–2 Teaches (and What It Doesn't)." In *Reading Genesis 1–2: An Evangelical Conversation,* edited by J. Daryl Charles, 103-28. Peabody, MA: Hendrickson, 2013.

Louw, Johannes P., and Eugene A. Nida, eds. *Greek-English Lexicon of the New Testament Based on Semantic Domains.* New York: United Bible Societies, 1988.

Lund, Nils Wilhelm. *Chiasmus in the New Testament: A Study in Formgeschichte.* Chapel Hill: University of North Carolina Press, 1942.

Luther, Martin. Luther Still Speaking: The Creation; A Commentary on the First Five Chapters of the Book of Genesis: 1544. Translated by Henry Cole, Edinburgh: T &T Clark. 1858.

Man, Ronald E. "The Value of Chiasm for New Testament Interpretation." *Bibliotheca Sacra* 141 (1984): 146-57.

Mascall, Eric Lionel. *Christian Theology and Natural Science: Some Questions on Their Relations.* Longmans: Green, 1956.

McLaughlin, Bruce. "From Whence Evil?" *Perspectives on Science and the Christian Faith* 56, no. 3 (2004): 237.

Moeller, Charles "Introduction." In *Satan,* edited by Bruno de Jesus-Marie O.C.D., xv. New York: Sheed and Ward, 1952.

Moreau, A. Scott, Tokunboh Adeyemo, David G. Burnett, Bryant L. Myers, and Hwa Yung. *Deliver Us from Evil: An Uneasy Frontier in Christian Mission*. World Vision International, 2002.

Myers, Bryant. 1996. *The New Context of World Missions*. Monrovia: MARC.

Neff, David. "Naming the Horror." *Christianity Today* (April, 2005): 74-76.

Newbigin, Lesslie. *The Gospel in a Pluralist Society*. Grand Rapids: Eerdmans, 1989

Neyrey, Jerome H. *The Gospel of John*. Cambridge: Cambridge University Press, 2006.

Och, Bernard. "Creation and Redemption: Towards a Theology of Creation." *Judaism* 44 (Spring, 1995): 226-43.

Osborne, Grant. *The Hermeneutical Spiral: A Comprehensive Introduction to Biblical Interpretation*. Downers Grove: InterVarsity, 2006.

Parker, Andrew. *In the Blink of an Eye*. Cambridge, MA: Perseus Publications, 2003.

Parunak, H. van Dyke. "Transitional Techniques in the Bible." *Journal of Biblical Literature* 102 (1983): 525-48.

Perkins, Pheme. *The Johannine Epistles*. Wilmington, DL.: Michael Glazier, 1979.

Plantinga, Alvin "Supralapsarianism, or 'O Felix Culpa'." In *Christian Faith and the Problem of Evil*, edited by Peter Van Inwagen, 1-25. Grand Rapids: Eerdmans, 2004.

Plummer, Alfred. *The Epistles of St. John*. 1886. Reprint, Grand Rapids: Baker, 1980.

Ramm, Bernard. *The Christian View of Science and Scripture*. Grand Rapids: Eerdmans, 1954.

Rees, D. Ben. *Vehicles of Grace and Hope: Welsh Missionaries in India 1800–1970*. Pasadena: William Carey Library, 2003.

Renckens, Henricus S.J. *Israel's Concept of the Beginning: The Theology of Genesis 1–3*. New York: Herder and Herder, 1964.

Robbins, Vernon K. *Exploring the Texture of Texts: A Guide to Socio-Rhetorical Interpretation*. Valley Forge: PA: Trinity Press International, 1996.

_____. "Picking up the Fragments: From Crossan's Analysis to Rhetorical Analysis." *Foundations and Facets Forum* 1 (1986): 32.

_____. *The Tapestry of Early Christian Discourse: Rhetoric, Society and Ideology.* London: Routledge, 1996.

Rosenbaum, Michael. *Word-Order Variation in Isaiah 40-55: A Functional Perspective.* Assen, the Netherlands: Van Gorcum, 1997.

Rosenbaum, Morris, and Abraham M. Silbermann, trans. *Pentateuch with Targum Onkelos, Haphtaroth and Prayers for Sabbath and Rashi's Commentary.* Vol. 1. London: Shapiro, Vallentine and Co., 1929.

Ross, Allen P. *Creation and Blessing: A Guide to the Study and Exposition of Genesis.* Grand Rapids: Baker Academic, 1996.

_____. "Genesis." In *Bible Knowledge Commentary: Old Testament*, edited by John F. Walvoord and Roy B. Zuck, 11ff. Colorado Springs: David C. Cook, 1983.

Sailhamer, J. H. *Genesis Unbound: A Provocative New Look at the Creation Account.* Sisters, OR: Multnomah, 1996.

Sarna, Nahum M. *Understanding Genesis.* New York: Schocken Books, 1966.

Sauer, Erich. The King of the Earth. Grand Rapids: Eerdmans, 1962.

Schaeffer, Francis. *Genesis in Space and Time.* Glendale: Regal Books, 1972.

Schnackenburg, Rudolf. *The Johannine Epistles: Introduction and Commentary.* Translated by Reginald Fuller and Ilse Fuller. New York: Crossroad, 1992.

Schulte, Peter. "The Chicxulub Asteroid Impact and Mass Extinction at the Cretaceous-Paleogene Boundary." Science 327 (5 March 2010): 1214-18.

Seitz, Christopher R. *Isaiah 1-39. Interpretation: A Bible Commentary for Teaching and Preaching.* Louisville: John Knox Press, 1993.

Smith, John Pye. *The Relation between the Holy Scriptures and Some Parts of Geological Science.* London: Henry G. Bohn, 1854.

Snodderly, Beth. "A Socio-Rhetorical Analysis of the Johannine Understanding of 'the Works of the Devil' in 1 John 3: 8." DLitt et Phil diss., University of South Africa, 2009.

_____. "Shalom: The Goal of the Kingdom and of International Development." In *The Goal of International Development: God's Will*

   on Earth as It Is in Heaven, edited by Beth Snodderly, 157-67.
   Pasadena: WCIU Press, 2009.

Stacey, David. *Isaiah: Chapters 1–39*. London: Epworth Press, 1993.

Stearns, Richard. *The Hole in Our Gospel*. Nashville: Thomas Nelson, 2009.

Stetzer, Ed. *Subversive Kingdom: Living as Agents of Gospel Transformation*.
   Nashville: B&H., 2012.

Thomson, Ian H. *Chiasmus in the Pauline Letters*. Journal for the Study of
   the New Testament Supplement Series 111. Sheffield: Sheffield
   Academic Press, 1995.

Tolkien, J.R.R. *The Silmarillion*. New York: Ballantine Books, 1977.

Tonstad, Sigve. *Saving God's Reputation: The Theological Function of* Pistis
   Iesou *in the Cosmic Narratives of Revelation* (Library of New
   Testament Studies). London: T&T Clark, 2006.

_____. "Revelation, Vision of Healing, Video Lecture 8." April 19, 2013.
   http://www.youtube.com/watch?v=Ez7ccbmJZ4A

_____. "Revelation, Vision of Healing, Video Lecture 16," May 19, 2013,
   http://www.youtube.com/watch?v=o2JoSh7OGvg.

_____. "Revelation, Vision of Healing, Video Lecture 17." May 20, 2013.
   http://www.youtube.com/watch?v=SfcggURm9YI.

_____. "What the Early Christians Believed: The Reality of the Cosmic
   Conflict." In *Servant God: The Cosmic Conflict Over God's
   Trustworthiness*, 71-88. Loma Linda: Loma Linda University Press,
   2013.

Tsumura, David Toshio. "AXYB Pattern in Amos 17: 5 and Ps 9." *Vetus
   Testamentum* (1988): 234-36.

_____. *Creation and Destruction: A Reappraisal of the Chaoskampf Theory
   in the Old Testament*. Winona Lake, IN: Eisenbrauns, 2005.

_____. "The Earth in Genesis 1." In *"I Studied Inscriptions from Before the
   Flood": Ancient Near Eastern, Literary, and Linguistic Approaches to
   Genesis 1–11*, edited by Richard S. Hess and David Toshio Tsumura,
   310-28. Winona Lake, IN: Eisenbrauns, 1994.

_____. "Tohu in Isa 45: 19." *Vetus Testamentum* 38 (1988): 361-64.

Unger, Merrill F. "Rethinking the Genesis Account of Creation." *Bibliotheca
   Sacra* 115 (January-March 1958): 27-35.

_____. *Unger's Commentary on the Old Testament.* Vol. 1. Chicago: Moody, 1981.

van der Merwe, Dirk G. "A Matter of Having Fellowship: Ethics in the Johannine Epistles."." In *Identity, Ethics, and Ethos in the New Testament*, edited by Jan G. van der Watt, 535-63. Berlin: Walter de Gruyter, 2006.

van der Watt J. G. "Ethics in First John: A Literary and Socioscientific Perspective." *Catholic Biblical Quarterly* 61 (1999): 491-511.

von Rad, Gerhard. *Genesis: A Commentary.* Translated by John H. Marks. Philadelphia: Westminster, 1973.

Wade, G. W. *The Book of the Prophet Isaiah.* London: Methuen & Co, 1929.

Waltke, Bruce K. "The Creation Account in Genesis 1: Part 1, Introduction to Biblical Cosmology." *Bibliotheca Sacra* 132 (1975): 25-36.

_____. "The Creation Account in Genesis 1: Part 2, The Restitution Theory." *Bibliotheca Sacra* 132 (1975): 136-44.

_____. "The Creation Account in Genesis 1: Part 3, The Initial Chaos Theory and the Precreation Chaos Theory." *Bibliotheca Sacra* 132 (1975): 216-28.

_____. "The Creation Account in Genesis 1: Part 4, The Theology of Genesis 1." *Bibliotheca Sacra* 132 (1975): 327-42.

_____. "The Creation Account in Genesis 1: Part 5, The Theology of Genesis 1, Cont." *Bibliotheca Sacra* 133 (1975): 28-41.

_____. "The Literary Genre of Genesis 1." *Crux* 27 (Dec., 1991): 2-10.

Waltke, Bruce K., with Cathi J. Fredricks. *Genesis: A Commentary.* Grand Rapids: Zondervan, 2001.

Walton, John. *The Lost World of Genesis One: Ancient Cosmology and the Origins Debate.* Downers Grove: InterVarsity Academic, 2009.

Webb, Dom Bruno. *Why Does God Permit Evil?* London: Burns, Oates, and Washbourne Ltd., 1941.

Webb, Stephen. *The Dome of Eden: A New Solution to the Problem of Creation and Evolution.* Eugene, OR: Wipf and Stock, 2010.

Wenham, Gordon J. *Word Biblical Commentary: Genesis 1-15.* Waco, TX: Word Books, 1987.

Wildavsky, Aaron. *The Nursing Father: Moses as a Political Leader.* Tuscaloosa, AL: University of Alabama Press, 1984.

Winter, Ralph D. *Frontiers in Mission: Discovering and Surmounting Barriers to the* Missio Dei. 4th ed. Pasadena: WCIU Press, 2008.

_____. "Disease / Evil Explanations." Email to snoke@pitt.edu, July 8, 2004.

_____. "The Kingdom Strikes Back." In *Perspectives On the World Christian Movement: Reader.* 3rd ed, edited by Ralph D. Winter and Stephen C. Hawthorne, 195-213. Pasadena, CA: William Carey Library, 1999.

Wright, J. Stafford. "The Place of Myth in the Interpretation of the Bible." *Journal of the Transactions of the Victorian Institute* 88 (1956): 18-30.

Index